For-Profit Universities

Tressie McMillan Cottom • William A. Darity, Jr.
Editors

For-Profit Universities

The Shifting Landscape of Marketized Higher Education

palgrave
macmillan

Editors
Tressie McMillan Cottom
Virginia Commonwealth University
Department of Sociology
Richmond, Virginia, USA

William A. Darity, Jr.
Duke University
Durham, North Carolina, USA

ISBN 978-3-319-47186-0 ISBN 978-3-319-47187-7 (eBook)
DOI 10.1007/978-3-319-47187-7

Library of Congress Control Number: 2016962319

Printed on acid-free paper

This Palgrave Macmillan imprint is published by Springer Nature
The registered company is Springer International Publishing AG
The registered company address is: Gewerbestrasse 11, 6330 Cham, Switzerland

The papers in this volume were made possible with a Conference Grant from the American Educational Research Association in 2012.

Contents

Author Biographies

Victor M.H. Borden is Professor of Education in the Department of Leadership Studies and Policy at Indiana University. He also directs the Carnegie Classification of Institutions of Higher Education as well as the Project on Academic Success, both within the IU Center for Postsecondary Research, in addition to serving as Senior Advisor for the Executive Vice President for University of Academic Affairs

Tressie McMillan Cottom is an assistant professor of sociology at Virginia Commonwealth University and faculty association with Harvard University's Berkman Klein Center for Internet & Society. Her book, "Lower Ed: The Troubling Rise of For-Profit Colleges in the New Economy" will be released on The New Press Winter 2016. She has published on race/class/gender, credentialing, work and technology in the new economy.

William A. Darity, Jr. is the Samuel DuBois Cook Professor of Public Policy, African and African American Studies and Economics and Director of the Samuel DuBois Cook Center on Social Equity at Duke University. His primary area of research is Stratification Economics, and he edits a series for the Cambridge University Press under the same title.

Bonnie K. Fox Garrity is the Director of Operations at Accord Integrated Academic and Financial Information. She has done extensive comparative research on patterns of enrollment at public, not-for-profit, and for profit institutions of higher education.

David J. Harding is Associate Professor of Sociology at the University of California at Berkeley. Harding's research interests lie in inequality, poverty, urban studies, race, and qualitative and quantitative methodology. He was one of the earliest researchers to engage in systematic data-driven investigations of for-profit institutions of higher education.

Thomas A. Mays is Assistant Professor of Business Technology at Miami University (Ohio). He is an expert on the application of microelectronic technologies in both the business and higher education arenas.

Jane Rochmes is a Postdoctoral Fellow with the Center for Education Policy Analysis at Stanford University. Jane's research integrates interests in social context, stratification, and education. She is especially interested in how aspects of schooling perpetuate or ameliorate racial and socioeconomic inequality.

Rhonda Vonshay Sharpe currently serves as a Visiting Associate Professor of Economics at Bucknell University and is the Founder and President of the Women's Institute for Science, Equity and Race. Dr. Sharpe has three primary areas of research interest: the demography of higher Education, the demography of the STEM workforce, and racial, ethnic and gender inequality.

David Diego Torres is a Postdoctoral Fellow with the Houston Education Research Consortium at Rice University. He has a particular interest in child cognitive development, social class and ethnicity, and academic outcomes.

Gaye Tuchman is Professor Emeritus of Sociology at the University of Connecticut. Over the course of her career, she has engaged both in ethnographic inquiry and studies in historical methods. Her primary areas of research interest are sociologies of culture, gender, and higher education.

Jonathan White is the Bargaining Policy and Negotiations Official for the University and College Union in the UK. He led the union's campaign against government plans to allow for-profit higher education providers greater access to taxpayers' money in the form of student loans.

List of Figures

List of Tables

Introduction

Tressie McMillan Cottom

In 2011, my colleague William "Sandy" Darity, Jr. and I convened an academic conference on for-profit higher education in the U.S. at Duke University's Terry Sanford School of Public Policy. The conference was supported by the American Educational Research Association's Conference Grant and the then named Research Network on Racial and Ethnic Inequality at Duke. The conference was a response to multiple intersecting trends in work, education and racial inequality. For-profit colleges were undergoing a renaissance of sorts. Education historian Kevin Kinser has said in his institutional history of for-profit colleges that researchers "rediscover" these institutions every few years despite the fact that they have existed, in some form, for since the 19th century (Kinser 2006). This era of rediscovery did have a different flavor, if you will. Whereas for-profit college cycles had generally coincided with eras of expansion, this era was characterized by massive financial investment. As for-profit colleges became financialized they adopted shareholder logics of growth, acquisition, and expansion. These logics effectively accelerated all of the characteristics of previous eras of growth, creating something

T.M. Cottom (✉)
Department of Sociology, Virginia Commonwealth University,
Richmond, VA, USA
e-mail: tmcottom@vcu.edu

T. McMillan Cottom, W.A. Darity, Jr. (eds.), *For-Profit Universities*,
DOI 10.1007/978-3-319-47187-7_1

that felt new in scale and texture. For-profit colleges were not just a subsector or complementary sector of U.S. higher education. By some estimates, for-profit college expansion accounted for 30 percent of all U.S. higher education expansion in the 21st century (Deming et al. 2013). And, that growth was not among the sector's regional or privately owned schools but was instead occurring in massive financialized corporate entities like Corinthian, Strayer and The University of Phoenix. The financialized nature of for-profit colleges required rapid growth, quarter over quarter. To meet that growth, some argued that for-profit colleges over enrolled (or aggressively converted) "low information" students who have few traditional college choices. In our given race, gender and class hierarchy that looks like disproportionately enrolling women (especially mothers), African Americans, and working class and poor students. One way to understand this growth of for-profit higher education as we saw it at the time of our conference is thusly: massive financialization of credentials were generating significant private profit by extracting tuition revenue from status groups most vulnerable in higher education and labor markets. That is, for-profit college expansion was in its Wall Street Era of expansion and financialization intricately bound up in social inequality.

That was a funadementally different perspective than prevailing literatures on for-profit colleges, which has mostly developed in three theoretical traditions. The functional rational-choice tradition is the most dominant. This is popular in education research and economics where most of the empirical work on for-profit colleges has occured. In that tradition, for-profit colleges expanded as a response to increased consumer demand, rapid technological upskilling of the labor market, and a constrained traditional higher education market. In this literature, students' self-selection into for-profit colleges is observed through understanding their constraints and rational choices. The neo-institutional tradition also unfolds in higher education research but is also the primary mode of inquiry for the comparably scant sociological research on for-profits. Neo-institutionalism is closely related to the rational-choice tradition in that it mostly focuses on the field of higher education as rational organizations. The level of analysis is different. In neo-institutional literature, the organization is the unit of analysis and student behavior is generally observed in the aggregate as revenues, enrollments, and credential offerings. Here the consensus is that for-profit college expansion is an iteration of institutional change, the character of which is primarly defined as a response to the dominant institutional actor. In this case, the dominant institutional actor is traditional not-for-profit colleges. The third tradition is credentialing theory. Most popular in sociological research of stratification (and, to a lesser degree, older economics of education research), credentialing theory is the least utilized approach to understanding for-profit higher education. The literature mostly treats for-profits as a case of horizontal and vertical stratifaction in higher education but rarely treats for-profits fully. This is likely due to the lack of coherence in credentialing research as well as the theory's focus on the cultural and moral value of credentials as well as their functional economic value. Despite this, credentialing theories of educational expansion – of which for-profit colleges are an excellent contemporary case – best theorize the relationship between states, economies, histories, institutions and individuals. For these reasons, the conference and the resulting volume deliberately focuses on the broadest definition of credentials.

As the grant-writer and co-organizer of the conference, I thought the connections between social inequality and for-profit college expansion went without saying. There was the trend data on student demographics, which Victor Borden revisits for us in this volume. Drawing on data from the "flawed but authoritative" IPEDS data, Borden shows that women are especially concentrated in the for-profit college sector's "less than two year institutions". Further, "For-Profit institutions at all levels enroll a "majority-minority" student population, with one-half or more of the aggregate population representing students of color." Other researchers have put a finer point on these data. Given the rich literature on structural inequalities associated with race, gender, class, and parental status it isn't a surprise that for-profit students are not just "more likely to be poor but quite poor": 16 percent of for-profit students are participating in a means-tested welfare program as compared with 2.6 percent in traditional colleges (Guryan and Thompson 2010). When considered through the lens of intersecting inequality regimes, multiple vulnerabilities among for-profit students emerge. Despite being the smallest sector of higher education, "more low-income black and Hispanic women were enrolled in for-profit colleges than in four-year public and private colleges combined" in 2008 (Blumenstyk 2014, p. 32). Despite these patterns in enrollment, the literature on inequality and for-profit college expansion – especially as it related to race, class and gender – was scant. Anna Chung's paper is an exception. Using a creative data set, Chung explores the antecedents of for-profit college choice. Chung argues that "students sort themselves into 4-year schools, community colleges, and for-profit schools in descending order with respect to students' cognitive skills" (Chung 2008). The logical conclusion, according to Chung, is that black students are overenrolled in for-profit colleges because "the quality of these schools is commensurate with the corresponding students' cognitive skills". A smaller literature from education research extends Chung's rational choice framework to explain the disproportionate enrollment of minority students in the for-profit college sector (Iloh and Tierney 2013). These literatures overemphasized the individual choice frameworks of poor and minority students' college choices and de-emphasized the social construction of choice and college demand. The consequences of doing this were, for me, potentially disastrous. If for-profit colleges could be said to be the "natural" institutional fit for cognitively inferior minorities or the result of a rational cost-benefit analysis disconnected from institutional inequality, then there was little reason to critically engage how and why for-profit colleges had expanded so rapidly and to what ends. Therefore, one serious aim of the conference was to complicate the rational choice understandings of student demand and to think more critically about higher education expansion and inequality.

The conference participants responded valiantly to our call for critical, disciplined interrogation of for-profit higher education. The papers in this volume represent a part of the robust conversation that happened over two days in Durham, NC. Participants were from traditional and for-profit colleges; elite universities and less selective institutions; the ranks of tenured professors to independent researchers and graduate students. I personally extended invitations to every for-profit college contact I had acquired through my doctoral dissertation research process. I hoped that for-profit colleges and traditional researchers could learn from one another. The response was encouraging. Representatives from five of the largest for-profit colleges were in attendance, as were education sector investment analysts, think tank members (e.g. American Enterprise Institute) and higher education media. Conference debate and discussion broadly coalesced around three themes: education as a public good, higher education regulation, and the future of higher education expansion. These themes are reflected in this volume.

Bonnie K. Fox Garrity and Gaye Tuchman each approached the idea of higher education as a good other than purely economic. This is a claim that becomes harder to make as education is broadly constructed as a personal, private good. This is especially true of higher education because of the U.S. system of student aid. Our system of loans and grants have effectively voucherized individual students. Or, as Garrity puts it in her chapter:

> *Creation of the disadvantaged student market is a result of how student aid has been structured by federal policy, based upon the following aspects of the Higher Education Act: awarding of federal aid to individuals and not institutions, making aid "portable"; awarding aid to individuals on the basis of their economic means; and equalizing the status of for-profit institutions under Title IV by making students at for-profit institutions eligible to receive Federal student aid. Without the policy creation of the disadvantaged student market for-profit institutions would not have access to public funding.*

This structure of financing can obscure the role of education as democratizing, much less a public good. Garrity argues further that higher education is a "mixed-form market", comprised of various institutions with different and sometimes competing goals. The mixed form of the U.S. higher education market is one the system's strengths. It is true, as neo-institutionalists have argued, that this structure allows more responsiveness to changes in student demand. But, Garrity points out that this complexity also makes it difficult to understand the system in didactic framings like "public good" versus "private good". As a growing literature on academic capitalism has argued convincingly, all of our higher education institutions are now public-private hybrids, enmeshed in markets to various degrees in ways that shape how we enroll, matriculate and graduate students (Berman 2012; Cottom and Tuchman 2015; Neem et al. 2012; Slaughter 2004). But does this enmeshment in mixed markets mean that higher education cannot or should not be understood as a public good at all? Tuchman offers important historicizing of this debate. In her chapter on the changing ideology of higher education, Tuchman reminds us that ideologies are political constructions. And, that those political constructions have always been bound in stratified status groups like race, class and gender. If for-profit colleges are just natural extensions of market based higher education activities, Tuchman argues that these extensions are constructed as natural precisely because of who for-profit colleges serve. This work resonates nicely with invitations to explore how "timing and history generally matter" (Brown and Bills 2011, p. 134) to the economic, social and cultural meaning of new credentials.Tuchman makes the historical analogy with the creation of black colleges as a separate tier of higher education in the U.S. during the 19th century. The expansion of higher education in the U.S. has been bound up in the idea that "different sorts of people were to receive different sorts of education". Tuchman asks us to consider critically if we can argue that for-profit college expansion in the 21st century is an historical anomaly or a contemporary interaction of stratification by institutional differentiation.

This historicizing of educational expansion touches on the themes of public good and how higher education regulation interact with our construction of who gets what kind of education. Historically, we sociologists and education researchers have studied this process through the lens of social and cultural capital. The literature on for-profit colleges has ventured into these waters rarely (notable exception: Deil-Amen and Rosenbaum 2003). In this volume, Mays contributes exploratory research on a social capital model for understanding something critical to educational mobility but rarely examined in for-profit college literatures.. Mays builds on a robust literature about the importance of how students are socialized in educational contexts. This work is usually in the tradition of Bourdieu although it is also clear in more structural analyses by scholars like Randall Collins and even economists like Bowles and Gintis. Sharpe, Stokes and Darity's chapter on who attends for-profit institutions focuses even more sharply on status group differences in access, externalities and mobility. Black women, for instance, have demonstrated a "pragmatic" approach to educational attainment that may be more valued at for-profit colleges. Although, I would caution that what I call "utility accounts" (Cottom 2015) of education need not preclude black women from traditional higher education. Black colleges and community colleges, for example, have long offered pragmatic educations that value utility. Future research could consider why black colleges have or have not adapted to shifting attitudes about pragmatic educations among black students given these institutions' historical missions. One possibility is that the mixed market of higher education has simultaneously become more hostile to black institutions while legitimizing market based solutions that extract value from poor black students. Finally, Jonathan White reminds us that higher education's mixed market is a global phenomenon. While the conference focused heavily on the U.S. – as does this volume – it is true that higher education financialization is part of a global context of austerity. U.S. based for-profit education companies like Laureate and Pearson have marked "developing" nations for expansion, in many cases off-setting U.S. declining revenues by shifting to these more favorable regulatory environments. In the U.K, these institutions faced a formidable roadblock: organized faculty. White represents U.K. faculty interests and presents a case for how financialization and privatization adapt to political contexts. Like Tracy and Kleinman's chapter, White provides an important comparative context for how macro changes in privatized higher education expansion operate in the real world where politics and inequality define who gets what kind of education.

This volume is a starting point of a conversation on for-profit higher education expansion. It is a complement to the research in this area that has overwhelmingly focused on the institutional regulatory context of expansion and human capital (or rational choice) models of educational choice. The authors in this volume introduce classic concepts of status competition, inequality and philosophies of education to the contemporary conditions of for-profit college financialization, expansion, and globalization. As editor, my hope is that researchers will build on empirical models, extend theories of stratification and connect for-profit college research to social science traditions in inequality.

References

Berman, E. P. (2012). *Creating the market university: How academic science became an economic engine*. Princeton: Princeton University Press.

Blumenstyk, G. (2014). *American higher education in crisis?: What everyone needs to know*. Oxford: Oxford University Press.

Brown, D. K., & Bills, D. B. (2011). An overture for the sociology of credentialing: Empirical, theoretical, and moral considerations. *Research in Social Stratification and Mobility, 29*(1), 133–138.

Chung, A. (2008). *The Choice of for-profit college*. Retrieved August 12, 2012. http://mpra.ub.uni-muenchen.de/18971/

Cottom, T. M. (2015). *Becoming real colleges in the financialized era of US higher education: The expansion and legitimation of for-profit colleges*. Retrieved https://etd.library.emory.edu/view/record/pid/emory:phb1w

Cottom, T. M., & Tuchman, G. (2015). Rationalization of Higher Education. *Emerging trends in the social and behavioral sciences: An interdisciplinary, searchable, and linkable resource*. Retrieved May 25, 2015. http://onlinelibrary.wiley.com/doi/10.1002/9781118900772.etrds0274/full

Deil-Amen, R., & Rosenbaum, J. E. (2003). The social prerequisites of success: Can college structure reduce the need for social know-how? *The Annals of the American Academy of Political and Social Science, 586*(1), 120–143.

Deming, D., Goldin, C., & Katz, L. (2013). For-profit colleges. *The Future of Children, 23*(1), 137–163.

Guryan, J., & Thompson, M. (2010). Report on gainful employment. *Charles river associates, April* 2. Retrieved April 3, 2015. http://m.whitehouse.gov/sites/default/files/omb/assets/oira_1840/1840_04232010-h.pdf

Iloh, C. I., & Tierney, W. G. (2013). Understanding for-profit and community college choice through rational choice. *Teachers College Record*.

Kinser, K. (2006). Table of contents – 2006 – ASHE higher education report – Wiley online library. *Special Issue: From Main Street to Wall Street: The Transformation of For-Profit Education, 31*(5), 1–155.
Neem, J. N., et al. (2012). The education assembly line. *Contexts, 11*(4), 14–21.
Slaughter, S. (2004). *Academic capitalism and the new economy: Markets, state, and higher education*. Baltimore: Johns Hopkins University Press.

What Is the Difference? Public Funding of For-Profit, Not-For-Profit, and Public Institutions

Bonnie K. Fox Garrity

Postsecondary education in the United States is provided by a mix of for-profit, not-for-profit, and public institutions. Not-for-profit and public institutions dominate enrollments at the baccalaureate and post baccalaureate levels; however, recent growth in for-profit enrollments at 4-year-and-above-and-above institutions to 14.8% of the 12-month unduplicated headcount (Ginder and Kelly-Reid 2013) raises important questions about the differences among all types of institutions, particularly in light of the public funding provided to each type of institution. Most notably, public funding in the form of means-tested financial aid including Pell Grants and subsidized student loans (Title IV student aid) is available to all three types of institutions.

This raises a question: Why should one care if an institution that receives public funding is for-profit, not-for-profit, or public? In response, this paper will address the separate legal and financial restrictions and incentives that fundamentally shape the operations at each type of institution and how those differences may affect educational opportunities for students, particularly low-income students and students from underrepresented racial and ethnic groups. Trust markets will be discussed, as will the use of

B.K. Fox Garrity, EdD (✉)
D'Youville College, Buffalo, NY, USA
e-mail: garrityb@dyc.edu

T. McMillan Cottom, W.A. Darity, Jr. (eds.), *For-Profit Universities*,
DOI 10.1007/978-3-319-47187-7_2

accountability measures as an important step in increasing the acceptance of for-profit provision of postsecondary education. Connections are drawn to the enrollment patterns of different types of students and the different risks associated with noncontractible quality factors as we shift further from public provision of education toward public funding of private provision of postsecondary education and the rendering of education as a private good. Possible future developments are analyzed in light of the predictions in the mixed-form market literature. The paper concludes with a discussion of the implications of public funding of for-profit postsecondary institutions in light of the arguments presented.

Mixed-Form Markets

The term "mixed-form market" is used to describe a situation where a good or service is provided by a mix of for-profit, not-for-profit, and public providers. The use of this term is not meant to imply that postsecondary education should operate as a true market; instead, it is used to describe the mix of institutions that currently provide postsecondary education in the United States. The literature indicates that there generally is competition between different types of providers in a mixed-form market and that they may be considered to be adversaries (Bagnoli and Watts 2003; Becchetti and Huybrechts 2008; Marwell and McInerney 2005; Steinberg 1987). Mixed-form markets evolve over time in response to various internal and external factors. This evolution occurs in generally predictable patterns.

Mixed-form markets emerge after public and not-for-profit providers establish that a social need exists and begin to provide a service. These providers then grow. Eventually their costs begin to rise as a result of growth. These increasing costs drive an increase in the price charged for the services provided. At this higher price, for-profit providers will often begin to provide a subset of the services focusing on those that are most profitable (Marwell and McInerney 2005). The mixed-form market of postsecondary education has evolved to this stage with for-profit providers entering the realm of baccalaureate and post baccalaureate education rapidly during the past two decades.

However, each type of institution in this mixed-form market must conform with different legal and financial constraints and opportunities, which fundamentally alter the operations of each institution.

Legal Differences Among Institutional Types

The legal differences among institutions arise from registration with a state. A state defines the legal obligations of each type of institution regarding service of a public purpose or good.

State Registration

From a legal perspective, the different institutional types are distinguished at the time of state registration and incorporation. Public institutions are created by the state or local government in order to fulfill a public need or purpose. Most often, public institutions receive a portion of their funding from the state and/or local government in order to help fulfill the identified public need. In addition, the state or local government generally retains a level of ongoing oversight or control over the institution, which is meant to ensure that public needs are addressed, however, the level of control is often minimal as this arrangement historically has been predicated upon trust in the institution (Trow 1996).

Not-for-profit institutions register with the state in which they operate and apply for not-for-profit status. Institutions must meet requirements related to ownership, control, and purpose to gain this status. Generally, the purposes that a state may designate as qualified for not-for-profit status include civic, patriotic, political, charitable, educational, religious, and cultural in order to achieve a public or quasi-public objective.

For-profit institutions also register with the state, but the purpose of these organizations is not limited in the same way that it is at a not-for-profit. For-profit organizations are not required to serve a public or quasi-public objective, nor to have a particular purpose such as civic or patriotic.

Not-for-profit and public institutions are required by law to serve public purposes; for-profit institutions are not. This raises questions of what these public purposes are and whether or not there is a market-based imperative for for-profit institutions to provide for these same public purposes.

The Public Good

Public purposes include creation of public goods or services, which are those that provide a benefit to society in general or to a group beyond the individual enrolled student. Public purposes and goods that not-for-profit and public institutions are expected to provide are often subdivided under many labels including public goods, the public good, and the public sphere (Marginson 2011). Others use terms such as social and economic public goods (Pusser and Doane 2001). No matter the names used, the public expectations of an institution include providing space for disruptive public discourse, basic research, and community service. The public good is generally associated with "democratic forms, openness, transparency, popular sovereignty and grass-roots agency" (Marginson 2011, p. 418).

Public benefits of postsecondary education are to include creation of universal knowledge and information, creation of leaders from diverse communities, increased charitable giving, greater civic engagement, and higher voting rates (Marginson 2011; Pusser and Doane 2001).

Samuelson (1954) was the first to describe public goods as nonrivalrous (consumption by one person does not exclude consumption by another) and nonexcludable (individuals cannot be excluded from gaining benefit from these goods). The inability to exclude a person from gaining access to the benefits leads to a problem of free-riding, where an individual who does not pay cannot be excluded from accessing the benefits, meaning that payment arrangements cannot be enforced. In addition, asking one individual to pay for a public good that will be available to all is problematic. Therefore, generating a profit from production of public goods is generally unworkable. Goods that provide a benefit to society at large may be undersupplied in a market built solely on for-profit providers (Hansmann 1981) and for-profit providers focus on the production of private goods.

Public provision of public goods represents a workable solution to the free-rider problem. Governmental bodies collect funds in the form of taxes, which are then used to provide for the public good. Alternatively, not-for-profit organizations with their legally required public purposes can provide for public goods through donated resources and subsidies from the government. However, in the absence of direct government subsidies and donated resources, for-profit institutions focus on the provision of private goods.

While some may claim that the increased productivity achieved when a more educated worker enters the workforce is a public economic benefit (Pusser and Doane 2001) others consider this to be an individual good with certain positive externalities or spillover to others (Marginson 2011). Some might ask, isn't provision of access for students from underrepresented groups a public good? Similar to the issue of increased productivity of a more educated worker, mere access to education designed solely to increase employability and income is a private good for the individual student. This private good, if realized, may result in positive externalities such as increased tax revenue, but it is, in fact, imperative to successful recruitment of students at for-profit institutions that education be rendered as a private good. Since there is no direct government funding nor donated resources to subsidize the student's tuition at for-profit institutions, education must be perceived as a private good to avoid the perception that the student is being asked to fund a public good.

However, this refocusing of postsecondary education on private goods at for-profit institutions will influence not-for-profit and public institutions as they compete with for-profit institutions to enroll students. More fundamentally, this refocusing on the private goods may lead to questions about the public funding of postsecondary education in general.

The legal distinctions among the purpose of different types of institutions dictate whether an institution must serve the public good or not. Not-for-profit and public institutions are required by law to serve public purposes, for-profit institutions are not. In addition, there is no market-based imperative on for-profit institutions to provide for the public good. This raises questions about the financial distinctions and the public funding that is available to each type of institution.

Financial Differences Among Institutional Types

The financial differences among the three types of institutions relate to both sources of revenue and the distribution of excess revenue generated.

Sources of Revenue

Public institutions receive revenue from many different sources including direct public funding, tax-exempt donations, and tuition. Not-for-profit institutions receive revenue from tax-exempt donations and tuition. For-profit institutions receive a majority of their revenue from tuition. Tuition and fees account for a vastly different percentage of total revenue at for-profit institutions when compared to not-for-profit and public institutions. On average, tuition and fees account for 19% of total revenue at public institutions, 29% at not-for-profit institutions, and 90% at for-profit institutions (Knapp et al. 2012).

Each form of revenue may be publicly funded, either partially or fully. Subsidies may be in the form of direct funding or a reduction of the tax burden on the institutions. Donated resources are encouraged by favorable tax treatment for those who donate to not-for-profit organizations. The forgone tax revenue on donations and tax-exempt status is potential public money that the government agrees not to collect. However, for-profit organizations are not eligible to receive these donations. For-profit institutions generally do not receive direct subsidies from the government, nor tax-favored status or donations. However, for-profit postsecondary institutions may receive public funding in the form of Pell Grants and subsidized student loans that partially or fully fund the tuition from eligible students. These portable student grants and loans provide the greatest amount of funding to institutions that enroll students at the lowest income levels.

The policy of providing portable federal aid to students based upon economic means leads to a situation where access to these forms of public funds by institutions is contingent upon attracting students who are eligible for this aid (i.e. – low income students). This arrangement along with the traditional underrepresentation of African American, Hispanic, and Native American students at not-for-profit and public institutions has led to the creation of a "disadvantaged student market" which includes both students with low income levels and those from underrepresented racial and ethnic groups (Fox Garrity et al. 2010, p. 205).

For-profits enroll a relatively greater percentage of students who are from underrepresented racial and ethnic groups (Deming et al. 2012). Recent statistics from the National Center for Education Statistics show that while for-profits enroll 11% of all postsecondary students, they enroll 19% of all Black or African American students, 19% of all Native Hawaiian or other Pacific Islander students, and 12% of all Hispanic or Latino students. For-profits enroll just 8% of White students and 6% of Asian students (Knapp et al. 2012).

For-profits also enroll a greater percentage of the low-income students (using Pell eligibility as a proxy for income level) which provides the institutions with access to public funds (Deming et al. 2012). Access to these public funds can be highly valuable. In 2008–2009 for-profit institutions received 24% of the Pell Grants but enrolled 12% of students (Deming et al. 2012). In 2009–2010, for-profit institutions received 25% of the United States Department of Education student aid funds amounting to a total of $32 billion that included $7.5 billion in Pell Grants (Committee on Health 2012). Overall spending on Title IV components of Pell Grants and Stafford Loans was $35 billion and $86 billion respectively in 2010–2011 (Deming et al. 2013).

The renewal of the Higher Education Act in 2008, provides the framework for federal student financial aid while also delimiting the definition of an institution of higher education. This definition currently includes for-profit institutions, making them eligible to participate in the Title IV student aid programs. Creation of the disadvantaged student market is a result of how student aid has been structured by federal policy, based upon the following aspects of the Higher Education Act: awarding of federal aid to individuals and not institutions, making aid "portable"; awarding aid to individuals on the basis of their economic means; and equalizing the status of for-profit institutions under Title IV by making students at for-profit institutions eligible to receive Federal student aid. Without the policy creation of the disadvantaged student market for-profit institutions would not have access to public funding.

The flow of publicly funded Title IV aid to for-profit institutions lead to restrictions being added in the 1992 amendments to the Higher Education Act of 1965 (Kinser 2006). The 90–10 rule currently limits the percent of revenue a for-profit institution may receive from Title IV funding to 90% of total revenue. Turner (2006) notes that Title IV revenue as a percent of total revenue ranged from 55% to 82% at the largest for-profit institutions. In 2009–2010, 75% of revenue at for-profit institutions came from Title IV aid with several institutions near or above 90% (Deming et al. 2013). However, some forms of public funding are included in the 10% portion of the formula including military educational benefits such as GI Bill funds. For-profit institutions received 37% of the Post 9/11 G.I. Bill funds and 50% of the Department of Defense Tuition Assistance benefits (Committee on Health 2012). Therefore, with the right combination of students and student aid revenue, a for-profit institution theoretically could receive 100% of its revenue from public funding.

This shift toward enrollment of students who are eligible for publicly funded student aid and who are from underrepresented racial and ethnic groups at for-profit institutions is not solely the result of recruitment activities by for-profits. Public funding in the form of direct subsidies to public institutions have been reduced during the last decade. Reductions in public funding of community colleges has resulted in capped enrollments and a lack of courses available to many students (Rhoades 2012). This has resulted in an estimated 1% decrease in community college enrollment while more middle and upper income students are enrolling at Community colleges, which may be squeezing out lower income students (Rhoades 2012). Community colleges also enroll nearly one-half of the African American, Hispanic, and Native American postsecondary students in the United States (Rhoades 2012). Any public funding reduction that limits access at Community colleges will disproportionately affect these groups of students. This troubling trend of limited access to publicly provided education for underrepresented and low income students has created an environment which has provided an environment ripe for for-profit providers to increase recruitment of and enrollment of these same groups of students.

Since the 90–10 rule does not apply to not-for-profit and public institutions, it is also true that these institutions could receive 100% of their revenue from public funding; however, with the legal imperative to serve the public good this possibility may seem less troubling. In addition, not-for-profit and public institutions are restricted by additional limitations on the use of excess revenue to ensure that all revenue generated is spent on the goods and services the organization was formed to provide. This is called the nondistribution constraint.

Trust Markets and the Nondistribution Constraint

Historically postsecondary education in the United States has operated in a trust market or contract failure environment (Hansmann 1981; Winston 1999). These terms describe the risks associated with the asymmetry of information available between students (or perspective students) and the institutions in which they enroll. When these conditions exist, trust in the party with more information is critical. It is incumbent upon that party to not violate the trust placed in them. Systematic creation of conditions that do not encourage parties to violate the trust is helpful in establishing and maintaining that trust. Not-for-profit provision is generally preferred in these circumstances due to the existence of the nondistribution constraint.

The nondistribution constraint is a legal limitation on the use of revenue that is generated beyond expenses. To ensure long-term viability, all institutions must generate enough revenue to pay the expenses incurred, however, not-for-profit and for-profit institutions have different options when excess revenue beyond expenses is generated. For-profit organizations refer to excess revenue as profit and may choose to reinvest the profit in the organization or distribute the excess revenue to those who control the institution including owners, shareholders, directors, and managers. Not-for-profit organizations do not have these same options due to the nondistribution constraint. Not-for-profit institutions are required to reinvest excess revenue in the goods or services the organization was established to provide and cannot distribute excess revenue to those who control the organization.

The existence of the nondistribution constraint at not-for-profit organizations removes one incentive to violate the trust inherent in a trust market. If those who control the institution cannot be granted shares of excess revenue, this removes a personal incentive to violate the trust. While this does not guarantee that trust will not be violated, it does provide one form of reassurance that the structure of the system has been arranged to encourage trustworthy behavior. Therefore, not-for-profit provision is preferred in a trust market or contract failure environment (Hansmann 1981).

Trust is critical not just between the potential student and the institution, trust has also traditionally been an important element of the relationship between society and postsecondary institutions. Trow (1996) argued that the link between postsecondary institutions and society is based upon a shifting balance between trust, accountability, and the market. Trust is characterized by private and public funding of institutions without a detailed requirement that specific goods or services be provided and without a requirement to account for the specific use of those funds. Accountability is an alternative to trust that requires an explanation or justification of how resources were spent. The market is evident when funding is provided in return for immediate provision of a good or service. Direct public subsidies are provided in a balance between trust and accountability arrangements with an increasing focus on accountability at the expense of trust. Institutions are being asked to report outcomes measures and "consumer" information implying that potential students need more information as they can no longer trust institutions. The shift of students to consumers who need information in decisions related to which institution will receive their portable student aid brings the market to the fore in the relationship between the public that is providing the funding and the institutions that receive the funds through Pell Grants or student loan programs. These forms of student aid are provided in exchange for educational opportunities for a particular student.

Eligibility to participate in Title IV student aid programs is based upon an institution maintaining Regional or National accreditation. However, accreditation requirements do not specify each component nor do they provide detailed guidance on the specific quality level of the education that is to be provided to the student. It is difficult in funding arrangements such as this for the government to provide a contract that details the requirements for every facet of the operation of an institution. Those factors that are not detailed in the contract are left to the discretion of the provider. When public funding is provided for private provision of a good or service, the unspecified components and the difficult-to-observe quality markers are referred to as "noncontractible quality" (Hart et al. 1997).

Providing convenience and other readily observable amenities such as modern facilities, food services, and equipment has been observed in other fields where public, not-for-profit, and for-profit providers compete to provide services including hospitals and prisons (Hart et al. 1997; Picone et al. 2002). These may serve as markers of perceived quality to potential students or clients. To maximize revenues, providers may increase perceived quality by investing in these readily observable amenities while cutting less-observable inputs affecting the quality of the services provided such as employee compensation levels, minimum hiring standards, and training. Those factors that are noncontractible are left to the discretion of the provider. This phenomenon may be enhanced by portable student aid, which necessitates that students choose which institutions will receive the public funding. Attraction of students becomes primary and concerns about noncontractible quality become secondary.

In fact, expense levels at for-profit institutions are lower on average per FTE student than at not-for-profit institutions (Fox Garrity et al. 2010). Considering instructional expenses as a percentage of total expenses highlights the concerns of noncontractible quality and spending on perceived quality. Instructional expenses as a percentage of total expenses at 4-year-and-above and above institutions was 35% at not-for-profit and 28% at for-profit institutions in 2004 although the average dollar amount of instructional expenditures at not-for-profit institutions was more than double than those at for-profit institutions (Fox Garrity et al. 2010). One cannot conclude that all instructional expenses positively affect the quality of education, neither can one conclude that all non-instructional expenses are focused on perceived quality markers; however, the vastly different amounts being spent on instruction for each student encourage more detailed study of the relationships between noncontractible quality, perceived quality expenditures, and the nondistribution constraint in this trust market. The differing levels of expenditure at not-for-profit and for-profit institutions suggest that federal policy as currently written is supporting the expenditure of fewer resources on the education of students who have limited income and students who are members of underrepresented racial and ethnic groups in the United States.

As providers have the opportunity to reduce noncontractible quality and increase markers of perceived quality meant to attract students, other providers may be pressured to compete to attract and retain students. This pressure to compete may lead to all institutions implementing many of the same practices. Perceived quality factors become critical when the relationship between society and institutions is market based. The necessity to attract students who decide which institution will receive the federal aid raises the importance of perceived quality factors. This heightens concerns that the noncontractible quality factors may be compromised. Traditionally a trust-based relationship existed between not-for-profit institutions, public institutions, and society. Concerns about noncontractible quality factors being compromised to enhance perceived quality factors were less prevalent given the existence of the nondistribution constraint and the legal requirement to serve the public good. However, the growth of for-profit provision raises new questions.

The shift away from trust and toward accountability and market-based relationships between society and institutions, albeit in an environment where many components of education are considered to be noncontractible, are a result of the evolution of the mixed-form market of postsecondary education. Not-for-profit and public provision are preferred in trust markets due to the nondistribution constraint, which allows for increased trust that the noncontractible portions of quality will be provided to the best of the institution's ability. The shifts observed in accountability measures and enhancement of market-based forces have reduced the trust that was inherently part of the relationship between institutions, individual students, and society as the mixed-form market has evolved.

The financial differences between institutional types including access to different revenue sources and the nondistribution constraint fundamentally shape the operations of each institution and the educational opportunities for the students at that institution. These differences will also influence the future evolution of the mixed-form market of postsecondary education.

The Future of the Mixed–Form Market of Postsecondary Education

Marwell and McInerney (2005) have identified three potential pathways for mixed-form markets which have reached the stage where for-profit providers have entered and are growing: stratified, displaced, or defended. These three theorized arrangements will be explained and then compared to the current state of the mixed-form market of postsecondary education.

Typically, in the first possibility, a stratified market, not-for-profits and publics serve low-income clients with the cost of provision subsidized by donors (public funds or private donations), and for-profits serve higher-income clients who pay the full price for the provision of the service. However, in the mixed-form market of postsecondary education the arrangement is somewhat different than that predicted in the literature. There does appear to be a stratification of students by income level, but the lower-income students are attending for-profit institutions at disproportionate rates and the higher income students are attending the public and not-for-profit institutions at higher rates. Higher income students receive price subsidies through direct public funding and private donations by attending public or not-for-profit institutions. Lower-income students can receive these same subsidies at not-for-profit and public institutions and in addition, the low-income student can receive a subsidy in the form of Pell Grants or other Title IV student aid. However, low-income students are attending for-profit institutions in disproportionate numbers, where the only publicly funded subsidy typically provided is Title IV student aid. Clearly the general mixed-form market literature did not take into account portable public funding in its predictions.

The mixed-form market of postsecondary education presents an unusual arrangement, which raises important questions about the mission of each type of institution and its role in providing access to education for various groups of students. Public state university systems were developed in part to meet the goal of expanding access to higher education for working-class families and families from underrepresented racial and ethnic groups. However, there is a shift from publicly provided access to privately provided, publicly subsidized access. For-profit institutions are enrolling disproportionate percentages of the disadvantaged student market and gaining access to public funding through these students. Traditionally, the non-profit sector was considered to be best suited to address social needs requiring "extensive trust" and "commitment to individuals" and the public sector was best suited to ensuring "equity and stability" of service and a focus on the public interest, where public higher education facilitated democratic participation and debate. The for-profit sector was best suited to "adapting to rapid change" and performing "technical tasks" (Tierney and Hentschke 2007, pp. 26–27) (see also Pusser 2006; Starr 1989; Winston 1999). The fact that for-profit institutions are providing publicly funded access for many disadvantaged students challenges the traditional role of each type of institution.

The second possibility presented in the literature is a displaced market where not-for-profits are supplanted by the for-profits who have entered later (Marwell and McInerney 2005). This is often a result of a lack of sufficient donations to cover increasing costs at the not-for-profits. Displaced markets also may occur when there is rapid expansion of the pool of consumers or clients willing and able to purchase the service.

Reductions in public funding, especially for public institutions including Community colleges, has decreased the access provided by these institutions as they have turned away students. This has happened concurrently with a national economic downturn that negatively affected the endowment balances and private donation levels of many not-for-profit and public institutions.

In addition, the economic downturn resulted in higher than typical unemployment rates, increasing the number of nontraditional age students considering college enrollment. At the same time, the President of the United States called for an increased number of college graduates. Additionally, the creation of a disadvantaged student market has increased the focus on a group of students who may not have been traditionally recruited by colleges, thus increasing the number of potential students available. The total number of students enrolled in postsecondary education has increased, but the growth has been largest at for-profit institutions (Fox Garrity et al. 2010).

So, the reduced funding and increased demand predicted in the mixed-form market literature has occurred simultaneously, which may lead to not-for-profits and publics being displaced by for-profit competitors. While it seems quite unlikely that all public and not-for-profit postsecondary institutions will be displaced by for-profit institutions, for-profit provision of postsecondary education has a strengthened position in this mixed-form market due in part to the decreased public funding for publicly provided education. In addition there have been instances of not-for-profit and public colleges ceasing operations or losing their accreditation due to dire financial situations; however, there is currently insufficient evidence available to claim direct causation by the growth of for-profit enrollments. Further research on this question is suggested.

The third possibility presented in the literature is a defended market, where not-for-profit institutions use fundraising, regulation, or legitimacy as arguments to defend against the entry and growth of for-profit providers (Marwell and McInerney 2005). When used in this circumstance, legitimacy is more specifically defined as moral legitimacy. Moral legitimacy is judged by whether an institution's activities effectively promote societal well-being as defined by a socially-constructed value system (Suchman 1995). Moral legitimacy can be further subdivided into three forms based upon the basis of evaluation. These three bases are consequences and outputs, techniques and procedures, and categories and structures (Suchman 1995). Traditionally, the third basis of moral legitimacy was the most important in postsecondary education with institutions that were structured as not-for-profit or public deemed as legitimate. However, with calls for increased measuring and reporting of outcomes, accountability, or consumer information, the basis of legitimacy appears to be shifting toward consequences and outputs. This allows for increased perceptions of legitimacy of for-profit providers. The prediction of a defended market appears to be accurate as we observe defensive behaviors and challenges to the bases of legitimacy.

Of the three predictions for a mixed-form market at this stage, postsecondary education exhibits components of all three possibilities. Stratified markets exist, even though stratified in an unusual way; displaced markets exist to a limited extent due to reduced funding and increased demand; and defended markets exist but are being challenged on the grounds of the bases of moral legitimacy with a shift toward outputs and consequences. For those with a vested interest in the future of higher education in the United States, careful attention to the developments at this stage of the mixed-form market is encouraged.

Macro level policy and funding decisions can be analyzed in light of the predicted developments to determine potential effects and outcomes. It is imperative to consider the fundamental differences among the types of institutions when analyzing these developments, particularly the public funding of for-profit institutions.

Public Funding of For-Profit Institutions

Postsecondary education in the United States can be characterized as a mixed-form market with education provided by a shifting balance of for-profit, not-for-profit, and public institutions. Each form of institution has separate legal and financial restrictions and incentives, which fundamentally shape their operations.

For-profit institutions provide an increasing proportion of the postsecondary education in the United States, particularly at the baccalaureate and above levels. Since for-profit institutions do not face a legal requirement or a market-based imperative to serve the public good, and generation of a profit through provision of public goods is unworkable, education must be defined as a private good in order to encourage students to enroll at for-profit institutions. Up to 90% of the revenue produced from the offering of this private good can be funded by Title IV portable student aid with additional percentages available from other public funding sources. This public funding to deliver a private good is provided even though many aspects of operation are noncontractible and are not dictated in contracts for access to that public funding. In addition, regardless of calls to increase accountability measures or publication of "consumer" information, there is an asymmetry of information available to students, the public, and institutions, which characterizes a trust market environment. However, for-profit institutions operate in this trust market without a nondistribution constraint. Without a nondistribution constraint, public funding can be distributed legally as profits to those who control the institution. This encourages efficiency or a minimization of the resources spent on the education of for-profit students, many of whom are low-income or otherwise disadvantaged students. The educational opportunities of a large share of the disadvantaged student market are being shaped by the unique structure and operations of for-profit institutions and federal policies for student funding and this influence may continue and strengthen as the mixed-form market of postsecondary education evolves.

References

Bagnoli, M., & Watts, S. G. (2003). Selling to socially responsible consumers: Competition and the private provision of public goods. *Journal of Economics & Management Strategy, 12*(3), 419–445.

Becchetti, L., & Huybrechts, B. (2008). The dynamics of fair trade as a mixed-form market. *Journal of Business Ethics, 81*(4), 733–750.

Committee on Health, Education, Labor, and Pensions United States Senate. (2012). *For profit higher education: The failure to safeguard the federal investment and ensure student success* (Vol 1–4). Washington, DC: Government Printing Office.

Deming, D., Goldin, C., & Katz, L. (2012). The for-profit postsecondary school sector: Nimble critters or agile predators? *Journal of Economic Perspectives, 26*(1), 139–164.

Deming, D., Goldin, C., & Katz, L. (2013). For-profit colleges. In S. McLanahan, J. Currie, R. Haskins, C. Rouse, & I. Sawhill (Eds.), *The future of children: Postsecondary education in the United States* (Vol. 23, pp. 137–163). Princeton: Princeton-Brookings.

Fox Garrity, B., Garrison, M., & Fiedler, R. (2010). Access for whom, access to what? The role of the "disadvantaged student" market in the rise of for-profit higher education in the U.S. *Journal of Critical Education Policy Studies, 8*(1), 203–244.

Ginder, S., & Kelly-Reid, J. (2013). *Postsecondary institutions and cost of attendance in 2012–13; degrees and other awards conferred, 2011–12; and 12-month enrollment, 2011–12.* Washington, DC: U.S. Department of Education.

Hansmann, H. (1981). The rationale for exempting nonprofit organizations from corporate income tax. *The Yale Law Journal, 91*(1), 54–100.

Hart, O., Shleifer, A., & Vishny, R. (1997). The proper scope of government: Theory and an application to prisons. *Quarterly Journal of Economics, 112*, 1127–1162.

Kinser, K. (2006). From main street to wall street. *ASHE Higher Education Report, 31*(5), 1–146.

Knapp, L., Kelly-Reid, J., & Ginder, S. (2012). *Enrollment in postsecondary institutions, Fall 2011; financial statistics, fiscal year 2011; and graduation rates, selected cohorts, 2003-2008.* Washington, DC: U.S. Department of Education.

Marginson, S. (2011). Higher education and public good. *Higher Education Quarterly, 65*(4), 411–433. doi:10.1111/j.1468-2273.2011.00496.x.

Marwell, N., & McInerney, P. B. (2005). The nonprofit/for-profit continuum: Theorizing the dynamics of mixed-form markets. *Nonprofit and Voluntary Sector Quarterly, 34*(1), 7–28.

Picone, G., Chou, S.-Y., & Sloan, F. (2002). Are for-profit hospital conversions harmful to patients and to Medicare? *Journal of Economics, 33*(3), 507–523.

Pusser, B. (2006). Higher education, markets, and the preservation of the public good. In D. Breneman, B. Pusser, & S. Turner (Eds.), *Earnings from learning: The rise of for-profit Universities* (pp. 23–49). Albany: State University of New York Press.

Pusser, B., & Doane, D. (2001). Public purpose and private enterprise: The contemporary organization of postsecondary education. *Change, 33*(5), 18–22.

Rhoades, G. (2012). Closing the door, increasing the gap: Who's not going to (Community) college? Tuscon: Center for the Future of Higher Education (pp. 1–22).

Samuelson, P. A. (1954). The pure theory of public expenditure. *The Review of Economics and Statistics, 36*(4), 387–389.

Starr, P. (1989). The meaning of privatization. In S. Kamerman & A. Khan (Eds.), *Privatization and the welfare state.* Princeton: Princeton University Press.

Steinberg, R. (1987). Nonprofit organizations and the market. In W. Powell (Ed.), *The nonprofit sector: A research handbook* (pp. 118–138). New Haven: Yale University Press.

Suchman, M. C. (1995). Managing legitimacy: Strategic and institutional approaches. *Academy of Management Review, 20*(3), 571–610. doi:10.5465/amr.1995.9508080331.

Tierney, W. G., & Hentschke, G. C. (2007). *New players, different game: Understanding the rise of for-profit colleges and universities.* Baltimore: The Johns Hopkins University Press.

Trow, M. (1996). Trust, markets, and accountability in higher education: A comparative perspective. *Higher Education Policy, 9*(4), 309–324.

Turner, S. (2006). For-profit colleges in the context of the market for higher education. In D. Breneman, B. Pusser, & S. Turner (Eds.), *Earnings from learning: The rise of for-profit universities* (pp. 51–68). Albany: State University of New York.

Winston, G. (1999). Subsidies, hierarchy, and peers: The awkward economics of higher education. *Journal of Economic Perspectives, 13*(1), 13–36.

For-Profit Higher Education in the UK: The Politics of Market Creation

Jonathan White

On 9 September 2010, David Willetts, the new Universities Minister in the UK's recently formed Conservative and Liberal Democrat Coalition government, made a major speech to Universities UK, the umbrella organisation that purports to represent British universities. Willetts used his speech to set out for the assembled university heads the policies that the Coalition would be pursuing in higher education. There would have to be cuts to deliver on the Treasury's austerity policies, he said. Universities would have to remodel themselves to become smarter, leaner businesses, more focused on their students as customers. They would also have to recognise that the world was changing and that there was a new player at the table:

> Internationally, for-profit higher education providers are becoming more significant. They are a natural response to the global hunger for higher education and better qualifications. Unencumbered by the weight of history, these providers can grow quickly and change fast…The acid test for HE providers is whether they offer excellent teaching and a high-quality experience for students. If they can do that, at a fair price, then it doesn't matter whether they are old universities or new ones; for profit or not for profit.

J. White (✉)
University and College Union, London, UK
e-mail: jwhite@ucu.org.uk

T. McMillan Cottom, W.A. Darity, Jr. (eds.), *For-Profit Universities*,
DOI 10.1007/978-3-319-47187-7_3

> They have something to contribute and should have the chance to do so. That is the case for a more open market.[1]

It was the responsibility of a government that sought value for money and prioritised the interests of the student customer, Willetts argued, to remove the obstacles to such providers entering the market.

In this essay, I will examine how the UK Coalition government has pursued this vision of opening up English higher education to private providers.[2] I will argue that the Coalition government's de-regulatory policies are not, as Willetts would argue, a logical response to market developments, conceived of as quasi-natural phenomena. Instead they are part of a political project to create a market in higher education, and are designed in part to foster a growing for-profit sector in England in the interests of a determinate group of higher education companies closely tied to Anglo-US finance capital.[3]

In the first part of the essay, I will survey, briefly, the private sector in England, examining the growing prominence of the for-profit companies and showing how they are making inroads into the publicly regulated higher education sector, laying claim to a growing share of the public's funding contribution. I will then situate the Coalition government's policies in higher education within the context of the longer waves of public sector reform aimed at marketising, privatising and financialising services. These reforms are now being accelerated under the justification of the austerity fiscal policies being pursued in the UK. In the third I'll examine how the Coalition's policy agenda has been developed by and serves the interests of a small group of education companies closely tied to finance capital. I will then go on to examine the ownership structure of this group of companies in more detail, showing how key for-profit companies are being consolidated under the control of transnational higher education companies and private equity funds. In the final section, I return to the political sphere to examine the set of struggles set in motion by the Coalition's marketisation policies, and to speculate briefly on the future of the UK for-profit sector.

The UK Private Sector and the Growth of the For-Profit Providers

For-profit higher education forms part of a small but growing private sector mostly based in England and operating at the margins of the established higher education 'eco-system' in the UK. UK higher education continues to be dominated by quasi-public universities and colleges, subject to their own dynamics and transformations. In 2012, in England alone, there were 128 publicly funded higher education institutions, including 115 universities.[4] These institutions are legally independent charitable corporations or charitable companies. For public accounting purposes, used to calculate public debt, they are classed as 'private sector'. Yet they have been, until recently, overwhelmingly dependent on public funds administered on behalf of the government by funding councils established by statute. In addition, they are regulated in line with charitable and public good objectives and to date have been subject to public sector rules about transparency, information provision and equality. As the Coalition government has radically altered the form of the state's subsidy for higher education, shifting a large amount of it into the payment of upfront loans on behalf of students, so the debate has reopened about whether or not UK universities and colleges are discernibly public institutions. Yet they do continue to rely on public subsidies, many of them depend on substantial research grants, and they fall within a regulatory framework that is markedly more oriented to the public good and open to public scrutiny than the private sector.

The private sector has historically been defined by its lack of access to public funds, either as a consequence of legal impediments or as a consequence of an active choice not to accept the regulatory 'burden' that seeking access to public funding would entail. Private higher education in the UK is concentrated in England and comprises a diverse array of institutions, numbering in the hundreds. Yet there are distinct subgroups emerging that will be familiar to a US audience: a range of generally small religious colleges; much larger providers offering pathway courses into higher education for international students; career colleges offering degree level and sub-degree level courses to international and domestic UK and EU students. No one knows how many students study in the private sector. As they were, until recently, accessing no public subsidies, no agency was tasked with collecting any data. The best estimates put the sector as numbering at least 50,000 students and probably more. This is dwarfed by the publicly regulated student body, which numbers more than 2 million, but, as we will see, this is changing rapidly. The private sector student body is currently dominated by international students, though a combination of tighter visa controls and shifting policy in England toward domestic students is leading many career colleges to reorient themselves toward the 'domestic' market.[5]

Under the Coalition government, the for-profit sector is beginning to make inroads into the previously publicly regulated domestic student market. We can get a sense of this from recently published figures on the growth in the numbers of students accessing courses which entitle them to public subsidies. As Table 1 shows, in the short period since the Coalition government came to power in 2009/10, the number of students at private higher education institutions accessing public subsidies in the UK trebled from just over 4000 to more than 12000.[6]

Similarly, the volume of public subsidy flowing to the private sector has more than trebled in the same period, shooting up from £29 million in 2009/10 to more than £100 million in 2011/12. In 2010, the government took a decision to double the amount of loan each student could access. This will come onstream in 2013 and this is likely to result in an even sharper spike in the volume of subsidy flowing toward the private sector. This still represents a very small overall market share but the trend and the rate of change are nonetheless impressive (Fig. 1).

The potential benefits to be gained from access to international students and now increasingly, from public subsidies also appears to be leading to the sector's reconfiguration. A sector previously characterised by a profusion of small specialist providers in professional pathways is being increasingly dominated and consolidated by a handful of growing for-profit companies.

For-profit companies have established themselves firmly within the international student market and, using Kevin Kinser's typology, these companies are increasingly 'shareholder' firms as opposed to 'enterprise' firms. Five for-profit companies have established between them around 40

Table 1 Growth in student support costs at alternative providers, 2007/8 to 2012/13

Academic year	*Total financial support paid to students at private providers*
2007/8	£15,156,700
2008/9	£17,780,600
2009/10	£22,097,100
2010/11	£33,006,000
2011/12	£100,069,600
2012/13	£269,739,458

Source: The Private Providers' Designation Bonanza: A UCU Briefing (UCU, February 2014), https://www.ucu.org.uk/theprivateprovidersdesignationbonanza

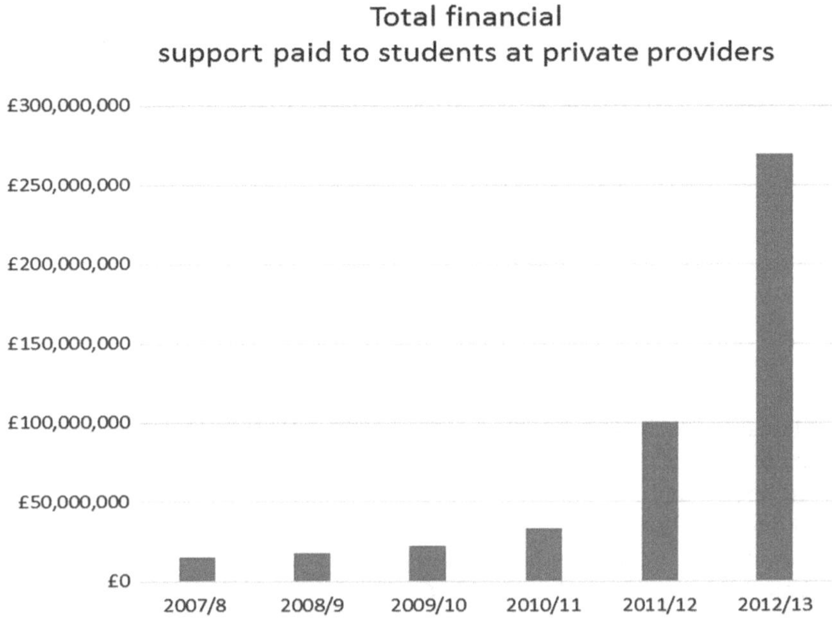

Fig. 1 Total loans and grants paid out to students enrolled with private providers, 2007/8 to 2012/13 (Applying Student Number Controls to Alternative Providers with Designated Courses, Annex A, pp. 23–26)

partnerships with UK Universities.[7] Study Group, Kaplan International Colleges, INTO University Partnerships, Navitas International Colleges and Cambridge Education Group are all now either subsidiaries of transnational parent companies or have significant private equity backing. It's a similar story with the more domestically oriented career college sector. This sub-sector has traditionally included both for-profit and not-for-profit companies, while even the for-profit companies have tended to conform more to the enterprise model, being small and privately owned. However, with the sales of BPP to Apollo Global and the College of Law to Montagu Private Equity, the expansion of Kaplan's Holborn College, and the entry of Pearson College into the market, the 'shareholder' model is clearly asserting itself within the private sector.

As they consolidate the private sector, these expansive for-profit companies are taking a greater share of the growing volume of public support flowing into toward private providers. Analysis of the Student Loans Company's statistical releases for 2011 and 2013 shows this clearly. Tables 2 and 3 show how a handful of subsidiaries of bigger for-profit companies or private equity funds is capturing a growing share of the emerging market. In two years, the total paid to alternative providers increased by almost 500%. Forty six percent of this vastly increased payout was captured by the subsidiaries of just five companies.

So, while the UK for-profit sector as yet remains a far remove from that which has emerged in the US, the key trends are clear. The private sector is making increasing incursions into the pool of subsidies that have traditionally been reserved for publicly regulated universities and colleges, while the becoming itself increasingly dominated by a handful of expansive for-profit companies. These trends are not simply a 'natural response to demand', as David Willetts would argue. Neither are they merely symptoms of a series of secularly conceived meta-processes like the 'heating up of competition', the 'digital revolution' or 'globalisation'.[8] Instead, as the next section shows, they are the consequence of deliberate government policy, shaped by determinate economic interests operating in a dynamic interaction with the forces described above.

Table 2 Totals paid to for-profit subsidiaries in 2011 as a proportion of the total paid to alternative providers

Provider	*Owned by*	*Total (£) paid in maintenance loans, tuition feel loans and grants*
Greenwich School of Management	Sovereign Capital	28,078,764
BPP University Ltd	Apollo Global	10,373,026
BIMM Ltd	Sovereign Capital	5,539,072
SAE Institute	Navitas	1,847,300
KAPLAN Holborn College	Kaplan	1,315,046
The University of Law	Montagu Private Equity	143,342
Total paid to above for-profit subsidiaries		47,296,550
Total paid to all alternative providers (including maintenance loans, tuition fee loans and grants)		123,139,680
% of total paid to all alternative providers		38%

Source: Student Loans Company, Supplementary Tables – Payments by Higher Education Provider published on 21 January 2015. Calculations by UCU

Table 3 Totals paid to for-profit subsidiaries in 2013 as a proportion of the total paid to alternative providers

Provider	*Owned by*	*Total (£) paid in maintenance loans, tuition feel loans and grants*
St Patrick's International College	Global University Systems	126,389,598
London School of Business and Finance Ltd	Global University Systems	68,125,295
Greenwich School of Management	Sovereign Capital	98,044,983
BPP University Ltd	Apollo Global	16,462,427
BIMM Ltd	Sovereign Capital	15,216,297
SAE Institute	Navitas	6,565,323
KAPLAN Holborn College	Kaplan	3,104,499
The University of Law	Montagu Private Equity/Global University Systems	2,557,221
Pearson College Ltd	Pearson plc	772,800
Total paid to above for-profit subsidiaries		337,238,443
Total paid to all Alternative providers (including maintenance loans, tuition fee loans and grants)		723,598,097
% of total paid to all Alternative providers		46%

Source: Student Loans Company, Supplementary Tables – Payments by Higher Education Provider published on 21 January 2015. Calculations by UCU

Higher Education and the Long Waves of Public Service Reform

The current government's reform of higher education need to be positioned in the context of the long waves of policy-making since 1979, whose general trajectory and often explicit intention has been to transform the operation of public services by reshaping them along market lines. These waves of policy-making have all been underpinned by different varieties of neoliberal ideology, which conceptualises markets as the most efficient way of distributing resources and views public services as inefficient state monopolies. Neoliberal public sector reform, pushed forward with varying degrees of conviction and determination by successive governments, can be seen to enact a series of mutually reinforcing processes that marketise public services. Marketisation is achieved through the transformation of the state into a commissioning agent, enforcing market discipline on service providers through the use of competitive funding mechanisms. Under such pressure, services are fragmented to enable their commodification, the repackaging of services into contracts to be tendered for. Perhaps most importantly, services are reconfigured as commodities that can be priced and sold to customers, while labour has market-like discipline imposed on it through the use of human resource techniques derived from New Public Management theories. The logic of these processes drives services inexorably toward full privatisation and financialisation, together with their transformation into financial assets that can be traded by the financial sector. First, the logic of competition and 'contestability' lays the groundwork for the entry of 'new providers' from the private sector who can offer to run services at lower cost. Second, the new providers must be encouraged to compete to break existing monopolies through the removal of regulatory barriers that entail costs to them, as well as the provision of subsidies to underwrite the 'risk' they take in moving into new, previously non-market areas. Finally, as public services are taken over by private providers, new assets are created that can be traded by the financial sectors and services and public revenue streams become increasingly financialised.[9]

In higher education, such policies have been pursued by successive Conservative, New Labour and now, Conservative-led Coalition governments. But the formation of the Coalition government has seen a marked acceleration in the marketisation, privatisation and financialisation of higher education, particularly in England, informed by a rigorous, if not entirely coherent, neoliberal vision derived from Milton Friedman and Friedrich Hayek. The government's English higher education reforms are complex and far reaching and I cannot do justice to them or their profound implications here.[10] Very briefly though, since coming to power in 2010, the government has attempted a root and branch restructure of higher education to make it function more like a market. In late 2010, it radically reshaped the way in which higher education is funded, cutting 80% of the teaching grant distributed to higher education institutions and enabling them to charge up to £9000 in tuition fees. At the same time, the government moved to increase the supposed 'sovereignty' of the student consumer by relaxing, to some degree, controls on recruitment. Institutions were told that they could recruit unlimited numbers of students performing at the highest levels, though this would be in the context of an overall cap on student numbers. The student's contribution is subsidised by a government loan with a relatively progressive income-contingent repayment structure. This last feature was forced on the government by the political outcry and the pressure exerted on its Liberal Democrat coalition partners by a swiftly mobilised student movement. The loan scheme is widely seen to entail unsustainable liabilities on the government which is now anxious to shift them onto the private sector by selling the loan book to private investors.[11] But the move to tuition fees has achieved part of its intended ends by placing greater competitive pressure on institutions. This competitive pressure has been heightened by the government's moves to make it easier for new private providers, and, more especially, for-profit providers to enter the new higher education 'market'.

On becoming Universities Minister, one of David Willetts's early acts was to widen a loophole that allowed students attending courses at private providers to access publicly subsidised student loans. Private providers, including for-profit companies, had been defined by their inability to access public funding through the distribution of teaching grant. In April 2011, in what appeared to be an act designed to 'pump-prime' the private sector, the amount of loan each student could access was doubled, from £3000 to £6000, leading private providers with the ability to fund rapid expansion to apply to have more of their courses deemed eligible for these subsidies. Private companies were given further encouragement by the fact that access to these subsidies came without any of the regulatory strings associated with the grants distributed to universities and colleges by the Higher Education Funding Council of England (HEFCE), the arms-length quango with statutory responsibility for allocating and regulating the use of public funds in higher education. Private providers who wanted their courses designated as worthy of public support through the loans scheme had only to apply direct to the Department of Business, Innovation and Skills (BIS), whereupon they could expect to have it approved with minimal scrutiny. Furthermore, unlike publicly regulated universities and colleges, the vast majority of these providers were then subject to no independent quality assurance scrutiny. In effect, the minister for Universities appeared to be stimulating the growth of a 'shadow' higher education sector, unregulated, opaque and dominated increasingly by for-profit companies.[12]

Willetts also announced, in 2011, that the government intended to legislate to radically de-regulate the higher education sector. Key parts of this legislation included proposals to bring private providers into direct competition with established universities and colleges by allowing them to compete on an 'equal' basis for centrally administered and controlled student places. Other measures were aimed at removing perceived regulatory 'barriers' to entry for new providers. These included measures to allow new providers easier access to degree-awarding powers and university title, essentially the kitemarks of quality and prestige in the UK university system. Also included were proposals to allow non-teaching institutions to award degrees, seen as a direct approach to Pearson, and proposals to make it easier for existing universities to change their corporate form. This last was designed to allow institutions whose powers were set down and limited by statute to move more simply into private company forms which would make it easier for them to access private finance or even attract private buyers.[13] In October 2012, the government announced that it would be including in the 2013 budget proposals to grant to for-profit companies the same tax exemptions that apply to not-for-profit education providers.[14]

Since the formation of the Coalition government in 2010, therefore, there has been a radical attempt to open up the market to new, for-profit providers. In the following section, I'll examine the evolution of this reform agenda in more detail, showing how policy on the de-regulation of higher education has been formed by a close nexus of right-wing politicians, consultancy firms, and a handful of Anglo-US private providers and private equity firms, closely tied to Anglo-US finance capital.

Making Policy on For-Profit Higher Education in the UK

David Willetts set out the Conservative Party's approach to higher education reform as early as 2008, stating that the party would 'welcome private providers' interest in higher education' and cited their growing international role: 'Internationally, private providers are extending choice, widening participation and responding to employers' needs'. In May 2009, he pledged that as a 'believer in supply-side reform', if the Conservatives came to power 'they would look to remove barriers to new entrants to the sector'. It was quite clear, even then, that the Conservatives had their eyes on the example of the US for-profit sector. In August 2009, as Apollo Global completed its acquisition of BPP, Willetts was quoted saying 'there are American university chains that are looking to come into Britain, talk of mergers between British and American universities. India is looking at links. I think it's ripe for these kind of supply-side reforms'.[15]

When it came to the concrete detail of how to achieve this 'supply-side' reform, the government was able to draw on proposals mapped out for it by think tanks and consultancies with an established record in public service reform and serving the interests of private sector public service providers and the City of London's financial sector. The key policies were effectively replicated in a series of supposedly independent reports. For example, the commercial legal consultancy Eversheds was commissioned by BPP to write a report on how to encourage private providers into the market. Their report, written by Eversheds partner Glynne Stanfield, included proposals to allow private providers access to publicly subsidised student loans, make it easier to buy out struggling universities, lower the regulatory burden on new entrants and make it easier to access degree awarding powers and university title. The report also called for for-profit providers to enjoy the same exemption from paying Value Added Tax (VAT) on education services as is enjoyed by not-for-profit institutions.[16] These policies were strikingly replicated within a report from 2010 by the right-wing think tank Policy Exchange titled 'Higher Education in the Age of Austerity', including the proposals on VAT exemption. Very similar proposals were made for the vocational and adult learning sector by the consultancy firm KPMG, one of four multinational consultancy firms operating in Britain with an established record in promoting outsourcing, public-private partnerships and private finance initiatives as a more efficient way of delivering public services.[17] Eversheds, meanwhile, have also been marketing themselves as consultants to universities and colleges trying to orient themselves in the new market. Glynne Stanfield has produced a series of broadly similar reports for university and college sector lobbying bodies, including almost identical proposals on how to lever in private equity funding by creating for-profit arms of not-for-profit entities.[18]

During 2012, at a time of growing public and political debate around the growing role of for-profit providers in UK education, the Institute of Economic Affairs, an orthodox Hayekian neoliberal think tank with roots in the Thatcher governments of the 1980s, published a report titled 'The Profit Motive in Education: Continuing the Revolution'. This featured a chapter on higher education, written by Daniel L. Bennett, Adam R. Lucchesi and Richard K. Vedder, who will be known to US audiences as researchers based at the Center for College Affordability and Productivity, indicating the interaction between neoliberal advocates and think tanks on either side of the Atlantic. Their essay provided an apology for the record of the US for-profit system, acknowledging the problems of 'impropriety' and 'rent-seeking behaviour', but ending, nonetheless, with a rousing defence of its achievements in 'expanding capacity and competing with the traditional higher education sector by offering career oriented and vocational programmes that are in high demand'. It has been able to do, this they argued,

> in large part because it is driven by a profit motive that has proved effective and attracted resources from capital markets. This is in sharp contrast to the government sector, which is largely dependent on non-competitive taxpayer subsidies that have been used to fund lavish university spending that is no longer economically sustainable.

The chapter finished by recommending that the government press ahead with 'incentivising the creation of new, privately owned or privately financed institutions by reducing existing barriers to entry and the amount of bureaucratic red tape required for a startup. In addition, the privatisation of financially struggling institutions should be encouraged.' As well as reinforcing the key message that for-profit is more efficient, this indicated that the growing public debate on both sides of the Atlantic around the record of US for-profit providers was becoming a problem that the advocates of neoliberal reform need to address.[19]

Finally, under the Coalition government, private providers and private equity funds looking to move into the higher education sector, alongside other areas of public services, have enjoyed untrammelled access to the heart of government. The Conservative Party's dependence on the UK's enormous financial sector is well known. In 2010–11, it was revealed that more than a quarter of its funding came from private equity funds, investment banks and hedge funds. Private Equity fund managers play key advisory roles in the government, exploiting the growth of 'independent advisors' from industry in all government departments. In 2012, the Secretary of State for education, Michael Gove, with responsibility for UK schools, made the recently ennobled Lord Nash a minister in his department. John Nash had formerly been an adviser to Gove and to the Chancellor of the Exchequer, George Osborne. His role in both departments was to advise on public sector reform. Nash was also a significant donor to the Conservative Party and the founding partner of Sovereign Capital, a UK private equity fund with stakes in a series of companies which have benefited from the deregulation and privatisation of social care, welfare, health care, schools, colleges and universities.[20]

In late 2011, it was also revealed that David Willetts had held a series of meetings with Anglo-US private providers in higher education and Anglo-US private equity funds. The list of companies he met with, some of them on several occasions, included: Apollo and their subsidiary BPP;

Education Management Corporation and their owners Goldman Sachs; Kaplan; Laureate; Pearson; Warburg Pincus; Sovereign Capital; Duke Street Private Equity; Providence Equity Partners; Silverfleet Capital, and Exponent. While Willetts's meetings were not secret, it is striking how many household names from the giant US for-profit sector made the effort to meet the minister. It is also highly significant that such a number of private equity fund representatives met with Willetts to discuss higher education.[21]

What this suggests is that policy-making in UK higher education has been captured by a close-knit group of transatlantic corporate and particularly financial interests, a phenomenon that is itself part of a deeper process whereby neoliberalism is institutionalised through state capture by corporate and more especially financial interests.[22] In the next section, I will look in more detail at the ownership structures of the emerging for-profit higher education companies and highlight their increasingly transatlantic and financialised character.

The Ownership of UK For-Profit Higher Education Companies

As Table 4 below shows, the ownership of the significant UK for-profit sector is itself increasingly passing under the control of a relatively small group of US, UK and Australian-based education and publishing companies.

US for-profit companies have maintained some operations in the UK since 2000. For example, Career Education Corporation operated the American InterContinental University in London between 2001 and 2013, finally agreeing to sell it, ironically, to the not-for-profit Regent's College that year as a result of persistent losses. Similarly, from 2005 onwards, Kaplan has steadily developed a growing portfolio of operations in the UK, including its Law School, Holborn College and a growing number of International Colleges with partnerships with UK universities to recruit and teach international students. In 2006, after the New Labour government had relaxed the requirements on acquiring degree awarding powers, Kaplan UK announced that it was 'within four months' of making an application, which would have made it the UK's first for-profit degree-awarding body. In the event, Kaplan never made the application, but Kaplan UK's Chief Executive, Peter Houillon maintains that the company ultimately wants to apply for these powers again at a time when it is a less onerous process. In the meantime, Houillon has professed himself to

Table 4 Acquisition or founding of UK private providers by transnational parent companies

Private provider operating in UK	*Main business*	*Parent company*	*Acquisition*
American Intercontinental University London	Pathway provider/ international students	Career Education Corporation	2001
Holborn College	Career college/ Domestic students	Kaplan Inc.	2005
Kaplan Law School	Career college/ Domestic students	Kaplan Inc.	2007
Kaplan International Colleges	Pathway provider/ international students	Kaplan Inc.	2007
BPP University College	Career college/ Domestic students	Apollo Global (Apollo Inc/ Carlyle Group)	2010
SAE International Ltd	Pathway provider/ international students	Navitas	2011
Arden University (formerly, Resource Development International)	Career college/ Domestic students	Capella Education Company	2011

be more enthusiastic in the immediate term at the prospect of acquiring a struggling university.[23]

In the end, it was BPP who became the first for-profit company with degree awarding powers, a decision made in 2008, again enabled by a New Labour administration that, at that time, was de-regulating public services with some enthusiasm. BPP's acquisition two years later by Apollo Global for £368 million marked a new level of interest from US companies in the UK's potential as a market for for-profit higher education. In the press release announcing the purchase, Apollo Global said that they view BPP as

> a strategic and unique opportunity to expand its international educational services offerings to the UK and Europe and believes that the opportunities in the UK education market and BPP's leading brand, together with the depth and breadth of talent of BPP's management team and employee base, make BPP an attractive investment.

The acquisition would 'provide Apollo Global with access to life-long learning programmes in the professional education sector, establish a significant

UK and pan-European platform and expand the range of advanced degrees and cross border educational opportunities it offers its students.'[24] In July 2011, Capella Education announced that it was buying the UK online higher education provider Resource Development International (RDI), for £9.3 million. The sale would include the payment of a further £4 million if RDI was successful in its application for degree awarding powers.[25]

Finally, Pearson's transatlantic education empire has also expanded into UK higher education. In a manner that mirrors the Washington Post Group's trajectory, Pearson's initial emphasis on publishing has been overtaken by its penetration of the education market. In 2003, Pearson bought the examination awarding body Edexcel, which awards qualifications at secondary school level as well as in vocational education and in non-degree-level higher education. It was widely recognised that the Coalition government's enthusiasm for the idea of detaching the power to award degrees from the need to have any teaching staff was part of an attempt to encourage Edexcel to move into higher education. This would have enabled the entry of other new providers into the sector, delivering degrees awarded by Edexcel and, hopefully, having the effect of driving down fees across the sector. When the government abandoned its legislation, this proved impossible. It was little surprise when Pearson announced in August 2012 that they were opening a new for-profit college of their own with degrees validated by a UK university. As one commentator put it, this could be seen as a 'hedge', allowing them to build up their own teaching experience if it proved impossible to detach degree awarding powers from the need to teach.[26]

Arguably just as important as the movement of transnational Anglo-American education corporations into UK higher education has been the growing domination and consolidation of the for-profit sector by private equity funds. This can be seen clearly in Table 5 below. In 2010, the international student 'pathway' provider Study Group International was bought by Providence Equity, part owners of Education Management Corporation. In 2011, the Greenwich School of Management was bought by John Nash's fund, Sovereign Capital, which also owns the Brighton Institute of Modern Music. As we saw above, the two companies between them accounted for around a third of all the publicly subsidised loan and grant support handed to the private sector in 2011/12. The same year also saw a new fund set up as a vehicle for UK and European higher education acquisitions, University Ventures. University Ventures was the brainchild of Ryan Craig, former director at Bridgepoint Education and

Table 5 Acquisition or founding of UK private providers by private equity funds

Private provider operating in UK	*Main business*	*Private equity owners*	*Acquisition*
Cambridge Education Group	Pathway provider/ international students	Palamon Capital	2007
Study Group International	Pathway provider/ international students	Providence Equity	2010
British and Irish Modern Music Institute (BIMM)	Career college/ Domestic students	Sovereign Capital	2010
Greenwich School of Management	Career college/ International and domestic students	Sovereign Capital	2011
University of Law	Career college/ Domestic students	Montagu Private Equity	2012
HE Online Ltd	N/A	University Ventures	2011
INTO University Partnerships	Pathway provider/ international students	Leeds Capital Partners (20% stake)	2013
Cambridge Education Group	Pathway provider/ international students	Bridgepoint Capital	2013

former employee of Warburg Pincus. In January 2013, INTO University Partnerships, another pathway provider targeting international students, announced that it had sold a 22% stake to Leeds Equity Partners. Finally, and most spectacularly, in November 2012, the charitable private higher education company College of Law was bought and turned into a for-profit company by Montagu Private Equity, a UK-based fund specialising in acquiring public service providing companies.[27]

As well as providing capital for the expansion of for-profit providers, private equity funds are also positioning themselves as the saviours of embattled ‘public’ universities. Eversheds’ partner Glynne Stanfield, who has worked hard to sell the idea of universities reshaping their legal form and operations to attract private finance, claimed to be aware of five universities in talks with private equity funds. It is notable that none of these negotiations have so far come to public fruition, yet the point remains that as Matt Robb, Senior Principal of the consultancy firm the Parthenon Group puts it, the UK higher education sector is seen as a ‘Treasure Island’ for for-profit providers.[28]

The argument of this essay has been that the trends in UK higher education noted at the outset – the sharply increasing volume of public subsidy flowing to the private sector and the growing domination of that private sector by a handful of for-profit companies – are not, as some would have us think, simply interesting and secular educational phenomena, to which policy-makers have to respond, in much the same way that 'globalisation' and 'internationalisation' are misconceived as disembodied processes over and above the actions of human or social agents. They are the more or less intended consequence of deliberate policies, shaped and lobbied for by think tanks, consultancy firms and private companies closely tied to determinate fractions of Anglo-US finance capital and delivered by politicians deploying orthodox neoliberal ideas to reshape public funds into private profit streams. In the final section of this essay, I will briefly examine how the government's attempts to create an open market for for-profit providers have fared.

The Politics of Market Creation in UK Higher Education

As the critical literature on public service reform has argued, markets have to be politically created. Contrary to many strands of neoliberal theory, markets rarely function purely. even in commercial sectors (banking being an obvious recent example), let alone in the non-market public sector. Certainly, the Coalition government's reforms in higher education spectacularly failed to create market behaviour in critical ways and they are still attempting to manage the consequences of this failure. For example, when the government raised the cap on the tuition fees universities could charge to £9000, after cutting university teaching grants, it confidently predicted that a market in prices would organically emerge. Instead, institutions keen to replace their lost funding and defend their prestige all set their fees at or around £9000. This only gave added impetus to the government's drive to lever in private providers so that they could act as a competitive pressure on prices. Similarly, the creation of a student voucher scheme – long the dream of the neoliberal education reformers – has been hampered by the political limits placed on the Coalition government. A rapidly mobilised student movement was able to put severe political pressure on the Conservatives' coalition partners, the Liberal Democrats. The Liberal Democrats had gone into the election courting the student vote by promising not to raise tuition fees. Only a few months later, the government they formed part of was doing precisely that. Such were the political strains on the newly formed government that a compromise was reached. Fees would be paid upfront by the government and repaid by students via a relatively progressive income-contingent repayment structure. This new loan scheme is set to produce ballooning government liabilities over the next decades years, while by some estimates more than 40% of the debt may never be repaid, with the taxpayer picking up the cost. For a government that has set out to reduce public debt, there is a clear political imperative to pay off some of the borrowing needed to finance the loans and to move some of the loan liabilities off the public balance sheet. This is leading the government to try to find a way of monetising a portion of the loan book by selling it off to third party investors.[29]

The Coalition's attempts to de-regulate the sector in favour of private and for-profit providers have run into similar problems. The response to these proposals from the university lobbying bodies themselves has been strangely muted. The university sector is highly fragmented, testament in part to the variety of different kinds of institution in UK higher education. The subdued response may also be a function of the extent to which legally independent institutions used to arguing for their 'autonomy' from government, have found it easy to internalise the competitive drives imported into the sector by the marketising policies of successive governments. Rather than present a united critique of government policy, for example, universities have greeted hugely radical and widely disliked policies with docility, preferring to pursue their own immediate institutional self-interests by engaging consultants to help them reshape themselves for the new environment. In response to the government's de-regulatory measures, Universities UK, the umbrella organisation that attempts to unite all universities, confined itself to a mild reference to worries about 'cherry picking' private providers.[30] It was only really UCU which identified the strategic threat posed by for-profit companies.

From the time that the government announced its intention to legislate, the union mobilised its membership around a focused campaign aimed at raising the public profile of the issue and putting political pressure on a Coalition already highly sensitive on higher education issues. The campaign attempted to pull in wider sector bodies, with mixed success, but was successful in shifting the terms of public debate away from vague discussions of public and private onto a focused attention on for-profit companies. This task was made immeasurably easier by the existence of the transnational connections with US for-profit companies and private equity firms, discussed above, while the fact that the US Senate's HELP committee was at that time investigating for-profit companies and issuing a succession of highly damaging reports, only helped to reinforce the union's message.

The campaign drew on the full range of lobbying techniques including the publication of regular reports, petitions, press stories and letter-writing. As a consequence, a succession of media stories linked Universities Minister David Willetts to the lobbying agenda of UK and US for-profit companies and drew attention to the record of US for-profit companies.[31]

The union was able to build significant political awareness of the for-profit threat and to create unease within the Coalition government itself. UCU enjoyed support from sympathetic and influential Labour MPs, but the union also targeted the Coalition's junior partners, the Liberal Democrats who were by this point highly sensitive on higher education issues. More than 3000 members contacted their MPs, asking them to support a Parliamentary motion warning of the danger posed by for-profit providers. By July 2011, this motion had attracted the support of 133 MPs, including key Liberal Democrats. The union also organised for the PBS documentary 'College Inc', to be shown in the House of Commons and made sure all MPs were made aware of the documentary's key points.[32]

By December 2011, political tensions over higher education were becoming apparent in the Coalition. In January 2012, a leaked report in the press revealed that the government's planned bill to deregulate higher education was being left out of the legislative programme.[33] From that point, the government has been forced to engage in a far more complicated process by which it attempts to pursue its deregulatory policies without legislation. In practical terms, this means seeking to bend the byzantine higher education regulatory infrastructure that has evolved over the years to suit a very different set of ends. The same combination of complexity and political resistance from the UCU has also resulted in the proposals to grant tax breaks to for-profit providers being at least temporarily shelved.[34]

Speculation and Summary

At the time of writing, the government is still doing all in its power to create a higher education market that favours for-profit education, but it is doing so in conditions that are not of its choosing and in a sector where the potential threat posed by for-profit companies is far better understood than it was when the government came to power. UCU continues to believe that for-profit higher education is toxic. In the political environment of mid 2013, our job is to press for a regulatory framework that recognises the risks entailed by the drives associated with the need to satisfy shareholders and which regulates such companies more tightly.[35]

Looking to the future, it is very likely that England will have an established for-profit sector in the next few years. How far that sector is able to grow will be determined partly by the capital it is able to mobilise, but it will also be shaped by politics – both the micro-politics of developing a regulatory sector with the agencies that exist, and the macro-politics of the general election, which is due to take place in 2015. If the Conservatives win an outright majority, we can expect the return of de-regulatory legislation. It is less clear what a Labour victory would mean, but at the least, it is unlikely to entail policies that would allow the rapid expansion of the for-profit sector.

One distinct possibility for future developments is that for-profit companies might look to build more partnerships with existing universities and colleges. One of the long-term consequences of marketisation in UK higher education has been the internal recomposition of universities around a neoliberal business model and their increasing subjection to new forms of financial dependency. This process has been sharply accelerated by the Coalition's de-regulatory policies. A recent UCU report surveyed some of the ways in which this 'internal privatisation' is manifesting itself, including: the outsourcing of 'non-core' functions (mostly support services but increasingly also some academic functions); public-private partnerships with for-profit companies; new experiments in bond-finance; and even the contemplation of private equity buyouts.[36] It may be that the competitive pressures in the system are already enough to give for-profit companies an alternative way of operating and one that requires less work than setting up their own colleges. It may also be that the real prize for for-profit companies now is to work out how to use the UK higher education system as a platform for breaking into Asia and in particular India. This presents UCU, and indeed anyone concerned with defending and advancing the idea of education as a public service, with several challenges. While we cannot take our eye off the messy micro-political regulatory battle over the for-profit companies, we also have to start to think about how we – and the public – can exercise some leverage over the behaviour of our existing institutions. And finally, we have to start to develop international strategies that mirror those of the for-profit companies and their finance capital backers.

In summary, in this paper, I've tried to argue for the need to put politics and political economy back into the discussion of for-profit higher education. While many commentators and policy-makers persist in describing the emergence of for-profit providers as though it were a quasi natural response to market stimuli, I've tried to show that the emergence of the small but fast-growing for-profit sector in the UK is in fact the product of politics. I've argued that the neoliberal public service reform policies pursued by the Conservative and Liberal Democrat Coalition government in higher education were developed and replicated by consultants and right-wing think tanks, working in the interests of US and British for-profit companies. As happened in the US, these for-profit companies are being consolidated, and the sector increasingly dominated by a small group of hugely powerful and wealthy transnational education companies and private equity funds tied to Wall Street and the City of London and enjoying easy access to the Coalition government. Finally, I've argued that in spite of this, the way that the government's reform programme has developed also shows the importance of politics. The Coalition government's attempt to create a market in the UK higher education sector has been hampered by a range of factors. Not the least of these has been the government's own internal political tensions and weakness on the issue of higher education, aggravated by resistance both from students and higher education staff unions. This ongoing struggle will play a crucial role in determining the development of for-profit higher education in the UK.

Notes

1. David Willetts, 'Speech to the Universities UK Annual Conference', 9 September 2010.
2. Higher education policy is devolved to the nations in the UK, so while funding is set in Westminster, the devolved nations have control over key aspects of higher education policy. Tuition fee policy, for example, is radically different in Wales and Scotland. While many of the wider processes of marketisation and the creation of competitive pressures are common to the whole of the UK, operate most strongly in the English context, where the Coalition has been able to legislate most freely.
3. It should be borne in mind throughout that the author is not writing as an academic investigator but was and is a protagonist in the events described throughout, being Deputy Head of Campaigns for the University and College Union and leading for the organisation on issues around marketisation and privatisation. The essay is therefore explicitly 'partisan' in approach.
4. Though in November 2012, the government announced that 10 colleges of higher education would be allowed to call themselves universities, using the newly relaxed criteria. In addition, the government allowed the College of Law to call itself a university, using an entirely different route, through changing its name at Companies House. For the institutions funded by the Higher Education Funding Council of England (HEFCE), see: http://www.hefce.ac.uk/whatwedo/invest/unicoll/ (accessed 28 June 2013).

5. This section draws on R. Middlehurst and J. Fielden, Private Providers in UK Higher Education: Some Policy Options (Higher Education Policy Institute, 2011); J. Fielden, R. Middlehurst and S. Woodfield, The Growth of Private and For-Profit higher education providers in the UK (Universities UK, 2010).
6. Subsidies here refer to the package of student loans and maintenance grants that can now be claimed by students at these private providers.
7. Fielden, Middlehurst and Woodfield, Growth of Private and For Profit higher education, p. 26. For Kinser's typology of for-profit institutions, see K. Kinser, From Main Street to Wall Street: The Transformation of For-Profit Higher Education (ASHe Higher Education Report, V. 31, No. 5 (San Francisco, Jossey Bass, 2006)).
8. For an example of this kind of analysis, see Michael Barber, Katelyn Donnelly and Saad Rizvi, An Avalanche is Coming: Higher Education and the Revolution Ahead (IPPR, March 2013), pp. 9–18.
9. For key critical studies of neoliberal public sector reform in the UK context, see Colin Leys, Market Driven Politics: Neoliberal Democracy and the Public Interest (Verso, London, 2002), Allyson Pollock, NHS plc: the privatisation of our health care. 2nd ed. London (Verso, London, 2005); Dexter Whitfield, Public Services or Corporate Welfare: Rethinking the Nation State in the Global Economy (Pluto, London, 2001); Ben Fine and David Hall, 'Contesting Neoliberalism: Public Sector Alternatives for Service Delivery', Milan European Economy Workshops Working Paper n. 2010–27 (September 2010). See also the work of the Public Services Research Institute at the University of Greenwich (PSIRU), http://www.psiru.org/.
10. The nature of these reforms is very well explained and critically analysed in Andrew McGettigan, The Great University Gamble: Money, Markets and the Future of Higher Education (Pluto Press, 2013) and Roger Brown and Helen Carasso, Everything for Sale: The Marketisation of UK Higher Education (Routledge, 2013).
11. Aditya Chakrabortty, 'Raise interest rates on old student loans, secret report proposes', The Guardian, Thursday 13 June 2013; http://www.guardian.co.uk/money/2013/jun/13/raise-interest-rate-student-loans-secret-report.
12. Hannah Richardson, 'Ministers 'rush to approve private degree courses'' BBC, 12 July 2012, http://www.bbc.co.uk/news/education-18812103 ; John Morgan, 'Private Bodies Saddle Up for State Subsidies', Times Higher Education 12 July 2012, http://www.timeshighereducation.co.uk/420545.article.
13. The government's planned legislation was outlined in two documents published by the Department of Business, Innovation and Skills (BIS): Students at the Heart of the System (June 2011) and A New, Fit-for-

Purpose Regulatory Framework for the Higher Education System (August 2011).

14. See Andrew McGettigan, 'The Budget and Universities', Critical Education Blog, 22 March 2012, http://andrewmcgettigan.org/2012/03/22/the-budget-and-universities/ ; VAT: Consideration of the case to extend the education exemption to for-profit providers of Higher Education. HMRC Consultation document, 12 September 2012.
15. David Willetts, press release: 'Ministers must focus more on universities': 4 September 2008; http://www.timeshighereducation.co.uk/406516.article; Melanie Newman, 'For-profit growth predicted if US giant buys UK's BPP',Times Higher Education, 14 May 2009, http://www.timeshighereducation.co.uk/406516.article ;Gaby Hinsliff, 'How do we tell the Good Universities from the Bad?' The Observer, 2 October 2009, http://www.guardian.co.uk/education/2009/aug/02/university-degree-comparison-oxford.
16. Glynne Stanfield, Report on the involvement of the private sector in higher education in England, Eversheds report for BPP, (November 2009); Simon Baker, 'Willetts signals boost for external providers' Times Higher Education, 24 June 2010, http://www.timeshighereducation.co.uk/412183.article.
17. Higher Education in the Age of Austerity: the role of private providers (Policy Exchange, 2010). Delivering Value for Money through Infrastructural Change (KPMG, 20 May 2010).
18. See the following reports, all written by Glynne Stanfield: Developing Future University Structures: New Funding and Legal Models, (Eversheds report for Universities UK, 2009); Preparing Colleges for the Future (Eversheds report for 157 Group, 2010); Collaborations and Mergers in HE: Lessons Learned and Future Prospects (Eversheds report for the Leadership Foundation (2011)).
19. Daniel L. Bennett, Adam R. Lucchesi and Richard K. Vedder, 'For Profit Higher Education in the United States', in James B Stanfield (ed.), The Profit Motive in Education: Continuing the Revolution (Institute of Economic Affairs, 2012), pp. 135–136.
20. Public Service Or Portfolio Investment: How Private Equity Funds Are Taking Over Post-secondary Education (University and College Union, September 2012), pp. 13–18.
21. Hannah Richardson, 'David Willetts met with for-profit university firms' BBC website 2 October 2011, http://www.bbc.co.uk/news/education-14987073 ; John Morgan, 'Willetts meets with private equity firms', Times Higher Education, December 2011, http://www.timeshighereducation.co.uk/418548.article; John Morgan, 'Universities could be in private hands 'in six months'', Times Higher Education, 13 October 2011, http://www.timeshighereducation.co.uk/417767.article.

22. The institutionalisation of neoliberalism through privatisation and financialisation is explored in Fine and Hall, 'Contesting Neoliberalism' while the connections between privatisation, state capture and corruption are made in David Hall, Corruption and Public Services, (PSIRU report, November 2012), http://www.psiru.org/.
23. Donald MacLeod, US firm bids to open UK university, The Guardian, 21 November 2006, http://www.guardian.co.uk/business/2006/nov/21/highereducation.newuniversities19922012; Harriet Swain, 'Boom time for private universities', The Guardian, 26 October 2010, http://www.guardian.co.uk/education/2010/oct/26/higher-education-private-university-boom.
24. 'Recommended all cash offer for BPP Holdings plc by Apollo UK Acquisition Company Limited, a wholly-owned subsidiary of Apollo Global, Inc'. Press release: 8 June 2009.
25. 'Capella Education Company Acquires Resource Development International Ltd', Bloomberg, 15 July 2011, http://www.bloomberg.com/apps/news?pid=newsarchive&sid=aGK2I_wPxz5I.
26. Sean Coughlan, 'Publisher Pearson launches UK degree course', BBC website, 14 August 2012, http://www.bbc.co.uk/news/education-19245788; Andrew McGettigan, 'Pearson BSc', Critical Education Blog, 14 August 2012, http://andrewmcgettigan.org/2012/08/14/pearson-bsc/.
27. UCU, Public Service or Portfolio Investment, pp. 1–12, 45–52; 'INTO announces major investment by leading US equity firm', INTO Press release, 15 January 2013, http://www.into-corporate.com/en-gb/news/press-releases/2013/into-announces-major-investment-by-leading-us-equity-firm.aspx.
28. Jonathan Bacon 'Academic Pursuits', Education Investor, October 2011, pp. 24–27. Matt Robb, 'Here be Treasure, but sector unprepared for private raiding parties', Times Higher Education, 12 May 2011.
29. The problems with the loan scheme have been identified by analysts from all sides of the policy debate. See for example, John Thompson and Bahram Bekhradnia, The cost of the Government's reforms of the financing of higher education (HEPI report, 25 Oct 2012); Nicholas Barr, Breaking the logjam, Submission to the Business, Innovation and Skills Committee, May 2011; Andrew McGettigan, False Accounting: Why the Government's Higher Education Reforms Don't Add Up (Intergenerational Foundation, May 2012), and 'Why Privatise Student Loans?', The Guardian, 16 June 2013, http://www.guardian.co.uk/commentisfree/2013/jun/16/why-privatise-student-loans-andrew-mcgettigan.
30. 'Universities UK comment on moves to open sector to private providers', 13 April 2011.

31. See for example, Hannah Richardson, 'David Willetts met with for-profit university firms' BBC website 2 October 2011, http://www.bbc.co.uk/news/education-14987073; Jason Beattie, 'Secret government talks with US private education firms sparks fears of uni privatisations', Daily Mirror, 30 May 2011, http://www.mirror.co.uk/news/uk-news/secret-government-talks-with-us-private-education-131479; Daniel Boffey, 'Risk to UK universities posed by private sector is being ignored, say critics', Observer, 22 May 2011, http://www.guardian.co.uk/education/2011/may/22/risk-damage-uk-universities-ignored; Graeme Paton, 'Professors warn over expansion of private universities', The Telegraph, 7 December 201, http://www.telegraph.co.uk/education/universityeducation/8881937/Higher-education-Professors-warn-over-expansion-of-private-universities.html; John Morgan, 'Willetts meets with private equity firms', Times Higher Education, December 2011, http://www.timeshighereducation.co.uk/418548.article; John Morgan, 'Universities could be in private hands 'in six months'', Times Higher Education, 13 October 2011, http://www.timeshighereducation.co.uk/417767.article.
32. Much of the union's campaigning activity is captured on its 'Fighting the White Paper' Blogsite, which can be seen here: http://whitepaper.web.ucu.org.uk/. See also http://www.ucu.org.uk/stopprivatisation. The parliamentary motion was an 'Early Day Motion' (EDM). These are largely symbolic but used as a way of testing opinion in Parliament on an issue. For the EDM on for-profit providers, see http://www.parliament.uk/business/publications/business-papers/commons/early-day-motions/edm-detail1/?session=2010-12&edmnumber=1999.
33. Rupert Winnett and Graeme Paton, 'American-backed private universities plan dropped', The Telegraph, 23 January 2012, http://www.telegraph.co.uk/education/universityeducation/9034279/American-backed-private-universities-plan-dropped.html. The government's admission that it was not legislating was announced in Written Ministerial Statement, David Willetts, Minister of State for Universities and Science, Higher Education Update, 11 June 2012, http://www.parliament.uk/documents/commons-vote-office/June_2012/11-06-12/1.BIS-Higher-Education-Update.pdf.
34. John Morgan, 'Willetts urged to ditch for-profit VAT exemption', Times Higher Education, 12 December 2012, http://www.timeshighereducation.co.uk/422109.article; John Morgan, 'Government changes course on for-profit VAT', Times Higher Education, 20 March 2013, http://www.timeshighereducation.co.uk/news/government-changes-course-on-for-profit-vat/2002713.article.

35. At the time of writing, the government has just published its attempt to work with the Higher Education Funding Council for England to create a regulatory framework without legislation. See David Willetts, 'Written Ministerial Statement: Higher Education Regulatory Reforms', http://www.hefce.ac.uk/media/hefce/content/news/news/2013/HE_Regulatory_Reforms_Written_Ministerial_Statement.pdf.
36. Lost in Translation: The Internal Privatisation of Our Colleges and Universities and the Threat to the Public Interest (University and College Union, 2013), http://www.ucu.org.uk/media/pdf/7/s/ucu_lostin-translation_may13.pdf.

For Profit U Through the Eyes of IPEDS: Warts and All

Victor M.H. Borden

According to the institutional data collections maintained by the National Center for Education Statistics of the U.S. Department of Education, "Private for-profit" institutions are "private institutions in which the individual(s) or agency in control receives compensation other than wages, rent, or other expenses for the assumption of risk." This definition comes from the Integrated Postsecondary Education Data System (IPEDS), through which the federal government has been tracking U.S. higher education activity since 1987. One impetus for developing IPEDS was expanding the domain of "tracked" institutions to include the large array of vocationally oriented postsecondary institutions, the majority of which are "Private, for-profit," that were not included in the predecessor HEGIS system (Fuller 2011).

This chapter provides a descriptive analysis of "Private, for-profit" institutions, hereinafter referred to as For-Profit, within the full landscape of postsecondary institutions included in the "IPEDS Universe." This universe

Note: The analysis reported in this chapter was completed in 2013 when the most recently available national data pertained to the 2011–12 academic year. The most notable change since this time has been a general decline in enrollments at For-Profit institutions. Thus, this analysis represents the point in time when For-Profit enrollments had reached their historical high point.

V.M.H. Borden (✉)
School of Education, Indiana University, Bloomington, IN 47405, USA
e-mail: vborden@iu.edu

T. McMillan Cottom, W.A. Darity, Jr. (eds.), *For-Profit Universities*,
DOI 10.1007/978-3-319-47187-7_4

currently numbers 7,737 "institutional entities," among which 3,432 (44%) are in the For-Profit category. We consider in this chapter, the subset of 7,012 institutions that are eligible to distribute federal aid (that is, Title IV-eligible, which includes the provision of being accredited by a regional, national or specialized agency recognized by the U.S. Department of Education), based in the United States (excluding those in U.S. commonwealths and protectorates), open to the public (excluding military service academies), and that enrolled students in Fall 2011. Forty-seven percent of this group (3,279) is in the For-Profit category.

The "Warts and All" subtitle of this chapter refers to the vagaries and nuances that result from collecting standardized data through a national system. One of the larger warts is illustrated through a consideration as to the nature of an institutional entity. Consider as examples, Ivy Tech Community College within the state of Indiana and the University of Phoenix. Prior to this year, Ivy Tech Community College was represented within IPEDS through 14 entities that, more or less, represented the regional components of this statewide Community College. As of this year, Ivy Tech reports as a single statewide institution. The University of Phoenix is represented in IPEDS by 78 institutional entities, including 77 "place-based" campuses that enrolled a combined 96,537 students in Fall 2011 and a single entity for the "online campus," that enrolled 307,871 students in Fall 2011. Another aspect of this institutional entity confusion is exemplified by the mismatch between what is considered an entity within IPEDS as compared to other federal, regional and state systems. Even the Office of Postsecondary Education, another branch of the U.S. Department of Education, maintains a list of OPE ID numbers that do not align perfectly with IPEDS unit ID numbers (Steele 2011).

Despite the warts described thus far and the others to come, the data collected through IPEDS is relatively reliable and, more importantly, authoritative. Response rates to the collection are close to 100 percent due to the penalties for non-compliance: fines and possible loss of Title IV status and, therefore, access to federal aid programs. The National Center for Education Statistics in partnership with the Association for Institutional Research, has developed a comprehensive training and support network that includes online webinars, video tutorials, and face-to-face training that is offered throughout the country (see https://nces.ed.gov/ipeds/InsidePages/JoinIn?pageid=37 for further details). Although it is important to understand the limitations and vagaries of IPEDS data (or any such system), the data provide a valuable, comprehensive source of information regarding U.S. higher education institutions

The Sectors of U.S. Postsecondary Education

The descriptive analysis in this chapter uses the IPEDS characterization of institutional sector, as a framework for placing For-Profit institutions within the broader postsecondary education landscape. Sector is a composite of two other distinctions: control of institution and institutional level. The For-Profit distinction comes entirely from the control variable, which distinguishes this category from institutions that are either "Public" (operated by publicly elected or appointed school officials and which is supported primarily by public funds) or "Private, not-for-profit" (the individual(s) or agency in control receives no compensation, other than wages, rent, or other expenses for the assumption of risk). We will use the terms, Public and Non-Profit to label the other two categories.

Institutional level distinguishes between institutions that are "four or more years," "at least 2 but less than 4 years," or "less than 2 years (below associate)." This designation, which we will characterize as Four-Year, Two-Year, and Less Than Two-Year, is based entirely on the highest degree or award conferred by the institution. This definition also reveals an important nuance within IPEDS. Over the last 20 years, many "Community Colleges" have begun to offer a limited number of bachelor's degrees, which places them in the four-year category. Some, like Miami Dade College, have changed their name to reflect this transition (dropping the word, "Community"). Others, like Seattle Community College, have not.

For-Profit Institutions Within the IPEDS Universe

The analysis begins by examining the most general aggregate statistics related to For-Profit institutions as compared to Public and Non-Profit Institutions: The number of institutions, their total enrollment, and the number of degrees and certificates awarded. We then explore in more depth a few key characteristics of the enrolled student body, the levels of degrees and certificates awarded, and overall staffing characteristics. Except for the historical trend data, we use the most recent data available publicly through IPEDS at the time this chapter was written. For the most part, these data represent the 2011–12 academic year (enrollment, degree completions and staffing). The institutional characteristic information is slightly more recent, being the first file released in the 2012–13 collection. Two slightly older files include the student financial aid data, reflecting the 2010–11 academic year, and the graduation rate data, which reflects the status, as of August 2011, of students who entered institutions in Fall 2005.

Institutional Enrollment Trends

The number of for profit institutional entities within the IPEDS collection increased from 685 in 1991–92 to the current total of 3,279. Correspondingly, overall enrollment increased from about 0.3 to 2.3 million. However, this apparent growth is confounded by changes in the number and types of institutions that reported through the IPEDS collection. This change was a result of changes in penalties for not doing so. The change affected the for-profit institutions most significantly, since the vast majority of Public and For-Profit institutions were previously responding.

Table 1 shows the overall changes in number of institutional entities and total fall semester "headcount" enrollment within For-Profit, Public, and Non-Profit institutions. The figures for 1990–91 are included with the proviso just noted. The increase over the last ten years, when the repercussions for not reporting remained the same, provides a more authentic view of change. Over this ten-year period, the number of For-Profit institutions increased by 43 percent and went from representing slightly more than one-third of all institutions (37%) to just under one-half (47%). The numbers of Public and Non-Profit institutions declined slightly over this time period.

Table 1 Trends in number of institutions and total enrollment by control, academic years 1991–92, 2001–02 and 2011–12

	Academic year 1991–92[a]		*Academic year 2001–02*		*Academic year 2011–12*		*% Change from 2001 to 02*
Number of institutions							
For-profit	**685**	**14%**	**2,287**	**37%**	**3,279**	**47%**	**43%**
Public	1,968	41%	2,052	33%	1,931	28%	-6%
Non-profit	2,132	45%	1,890	30%	1,802	26%	-5%
Total	4,785		6,229		7,012		13%
Total enrollment							
For-profit	**326,961**	**2%**	**752,326**	**5%**	**2,330,545**	**11%**	**210%**
Public	11,515,942	78%	12,330,860	76%	15,096,557	71%	22%
Non-profit	2,889,011	20%	3,176,494	20%	3,944,759	18%	24%
Total	14,731,914		16,259,680		21,371,861		31%

[a]The Title IV Eligibility status was not included in 1991 but very few non-Title IV institutions reported at that point in time

Although For-Profit institutions outnumber those in the other two control categories, they include many small institutions, as we shall see shortly. Thus despite constituting over one-third of the institutions in 2001–02, the enrollment market share was only five percent. In contrast, Public institutions comprised exactly one-third of all institutions in 2001–02 but enrolled more than three-quarters (76%) of all students. The slightly less numerous (30% of institutions) and moderately-sized Non-Profit group held a 20 percent market share of enrollment.

Enrollments at For-Profit institutions have more than tripled since 2001–02 resulting in a current market share of 11 percent. Although total enrollments increased by more than 20 percent for both Public and Non-Profit institutions, as a group, their market shares declined by 5 and 2 percentage points, respectively. Thus is appears that For-Profits have eroded the market share of Public institutions, more so than Non-Profit institutions.

Current Institutions, Enrollments and Awards by Sector

The overall market shares of institutions and enrollments shown in Table 1 mask large differences by institutional level. The top two panels of Table 2 illustrate this point. The first data column of the display carries over the 2011–12 numbers from Table 1 and the remaining columns disaggregate these totals by institutional level. Within the Four-Year category, Non-Profit institutions dominate the numbers, due to the many relatively small, private, liberal arts colleges. There are slightly more For-Profit, Four-Year institutions than Public, Four-Year institutions, although the enrollments are skewed toward the Public institutions, which have 60 percent of the market share, compared to just under 30 percent for Non-Profits and 12 percent for For-Profits. Among Two-Year institutions, Public institutions slightly outnumber For-Profit institutions and the Non-Profits are very few in number. Public, Two-Year institutions have the dominant market share of student enrollment at 93 percent. In contrast, the Less Than Two-Year category, which includes institutions that award only postsecondary certificates and no degrees, is dominated by For-Profit institutions in terms of both number of institutions and enrollments.

The third panel of Table 2 provides a different enrollment metric: 12-month FTE enrollment. This measure takes into account students who enroll throughout the year (12-month) and the "enrollment intensity" of

Table 2 Institutions, enrollments and awards by sector, 2011–12

	Overall		*Four-year*		*Two-year*		*Less than two-year*	
Number of institutions								
For-profit	**3,279**	**47%**	**743**	**25%**	**996**	**45%**	**1,540**	**84%**
Public	1,931	28%	683	23%	1,027	47%	221	12%
Non-Profit	1,802	26%	1,558	52%	171	8%	73	4%
Total	7,012		2,984		2,194		1,834	
Total enrollment								
For-profit	**2,330,545**	**11%**	**1,569,999**	**12%**	**463,901**	**6%**	**296,645**	**80%**
Public	15,096,557	71%	8,054,577	60%	6,983,618	93%	58,362	16%
Non-profit	3,944,759	18%	3,881,951	29%	46,954	1%	15,854	4%
Total	21,371,861		13,506,527		7,494,473		370,861	
12-month FTE enrollment								
For-profit	**2,543,283**	**14%**	**1,478,416**	**12%**	**681,375**	**12%**	**383,492**	**85%**
Public	11,890,074	66%	7,065,932	58%	4,773,658	87%	50,484	11%
Non-profit	3,664,820	20%	3,592,142	30%	56,206	1%	16,472	4%
Total	18,098,177		12,136,490		5,511,239		450,448	
Degrees conferred								
For-profit	**424,543**	**11%**	**352,418**	**12%**	**72,090**	**10%**	**35**	**100%**
Public	2,316,727	62%	1,693,362	56%	623,365	89%	–	0%
Non-profit	982,455	26%	975,160	32%	7,295	1%	–	0%
Total	3,723,725		3,020,940		702,750		35	
Certificates awarded								
For-profit	**427,380**	**42%**	**31,884**	**23%**	**180,316**	**28%**	**215,180**	**84%**
Public	543,513	53%	69,949	51%	442,018	70%	31,546	12%
Non-profit	58,008	6%	35,535	26%	13,445	2%	9,028	4%
Total	1,028,901		137,368		635,779		255,754	

students. This more encompassing metric increases the overall market share of For-Profit institution enrollments from 11 to 14 percent, primarily due to differences at the Two-Year and Less than Two-Year levels.

The last two panels of Table 2 examine degrees conferred and certificates awarded. The market share of degrees conferred tracks closely with enrollment market share among Four-Year institutions. However, the For-Profit institutions have a higher market share of (Associate's) degrees at the Two-Year Level relative to their enrollment market share. In a later section we review graduation rates to see if this is because they complete more students than do Public institutions. There is also a slight aberration in the small number (35) of degree conferrals among For-Profit, Less Than Two Year institutions which, by definition, should not confer any degrees. Yet another wart, albeit a very small one. Public institutions have the largest market share of certificate conferrals, primarily due to activity at the Four-Year and especially Two-Year levels. For-Profit institutions dominate the certificate numbers in the Less Than Two-Year category, consistent with their market share of institutions and enrollments in this category.

Institutional Size

When viewed by sector, that is, the nine cells defined by the crossing of control x level, the single largest group of institutions is represented in the Non-Profit, Four-Year cell (1,558). The second largest sector group, in terms of number of institutions, is represented in the For-Profit, Less Than Two-Year cell (1,540). Public institutions command the market shares of enrollments in the Four-Year and Two-Year categories, well-beyond their institutional number market shares. This suggests significant differences in institutional size by category. Table 3 illustrates these differences, overall and for the Four-Year and Two-Year levels, combined (due to small differences between these levels) and the Less Than Two-Year Level institutions. The vast majority (90%) of For-Profit institutions enroll fewer than 1,000 students, total. At the Less Than-Two Year level this includes more than two-fifths that enroll fewer than 100 students. This category includes many one-program institutions that award one or just a few types of certificates (e.g., culinary schools, cosmetology schools, etc.). The average small size of For-Profit institutions stands in contrast to the fact that the top two institutions in total enrollment are in the For-Profit category: The University of Phoenix-Online Campus (307,871) and Ashford University (74,596).

Among the Less Than Two-Year level category, the distributions by enrollment size of Public and Non-Profit institutions are similar to For Profit institutions. In contrast, the distribution of institutions by enrollment size differs among all three control categories in the combined Four-Year and Two-Year group. Very few Public institutions (11%) enroll fewer than 1,000 students, although more than one-third enroll between 1,000 and 5,000 students and 60 percent between 1,000 and 10,000. The Public sector includes the largest percentage of large institutions, with 30 percent enrolling more than 10,000 students and 12 percent more than 20,000. The dominant size categories among Non-Profit, Four-Year and Two-Year institutions are in the 1,000–4,999 (41%) and 100–999 range (38%), respectively.

Table 3 Distribution of enrollment size by control, Fall 2011 headcount enrollment

	For-profit	*Public*	*Non-profit*
Overall			
<100	**28%**	5%	12%
100–999	**62%**	15%	38%
1,000–4,999	**9%**	33%	40%
5,000–9,999	**0.5%**	21%	6%
10,000–19,999	**0.3%**	16%	3%
20,000–49,000	**0.2%**	10%	1%
50,000+	**0.1%**	1%	0.1%
Four-year and two year			
<100	**14%**	1%	11%
100–999	**68%**	10%	38%
1,000–4,999	**16%**	37%	41%
5,000–9,999	**1.0%**	23%	6%
10,000–19,999	**0.6%**	18%	3%
20,000–49,000	**0.5%**	11%	1%
50,000+	**0.2%**	1%	0.1%
Less than two-year			
<100	**43%**	43%	52%
100–999	**56%**	52%	47%
1,000–4,999	**1%**	5%	0%
5,000–9,999	**0%**	0%	1%

Student Characteristics

Table 4 examines four general student characteristics by sector: the percent of students that enroll full-time; percent female; percent minority; and the percent of undergraduate-level students age 25 or older. With regard to full-time proportions, students at For-Profit institutions are similar in profile to students at Non-Profit institutions when viewed across all institutional levels. This aggregate profile again masks significant differences by institutional level. Specifically, Four-Year, For-Profit institutions have the lowest proportion of full-time students, although still a significant majority (67%), compared to three-quarters at Public and Non-Profit institutions. In contrast, the vast majority of For-Profit students at Two-Year and Less Than Two-Year institutions enroll full-time, compared to a minority of Public, Two-Year students and just half of Public, Less Than Two-Year students. The Non-Profit profile is similar to the For-Profit one in these categories, but it should be remembered that there are relatively few Non-Profit institutions at these levels.

Table 4 Key student characteristics, Fall 2011 enrolled students

	Percent full-time	*Percent female*	*Percent minority*[a]	*Pct. ugrads age 25+*
Overall				
For-profit	**74%**	**65%**	**53%**	**65%**
Public	57%	56%	39%	31%
Non-profit	75%	58%	32%	23%
Four-year				
For-profit	**67%**	**63%**	**50%**	**73%**
Public	73%	55%	35%	21%
Non-profit	75%	58%	31%	23%
Two year				
For-profit	**89%**	**65%**	**57%**	**51%**
Public	39%	57%	44%	40%
Non-profit	80%	67%	46%	47%
Less than two year				
For-profit	**83%**	**77%**	**60%**	**50%**
Public	50%	57%	37%	50%
Non-profit	61%	66%	63%	71%

[a]The numerator (number of minority students) included students reported as American Indiana or Alaskan Native, Black or African American, Asian, Native Hawaiian or Other Pacific Islander, and Two or More Races. The denominator includes all of those students plus students reported as "White." Students of unknown race/ethnicity and Non-Resident Alien (that is, foreign) students were excluded from both the numerator and denominator of this figure

Women students represented the majority within all sectors. For-Profit institutions enroll a larger majority overall and within most sectors (with the exception of the small Non-Profit, Two-Year sector). For-Profit, Less Than Two Year institutions are especially dominated by women with more than a three-quarters majority.

For-Profit institutions at all levels enroll a "majority-minority" student population, with one-half or more of the aggregate population representing students of color. As noted in the table footnote, this calculation excludes foreign students and students of unknown race/ethnicity. The minority-majority is largest in the Less Than Two Year level category, followed closely by the Two-Year and then a exactly 50 percent in the Four-Year category. Minority representation at Public and Non-Profit institutions, although smaller than at For-Profit institutions, is above the general U.S. population representation of minorities, which for the 2010 census was 31 percent (using the same method of calculation).

Nearly two-thirds of all For-Profit students enrolled in undergraduate level programs are aged 25 or older, compared to just under one-third of Public institutions and less than one-quarter of Non-Profit institution students. This pattern is most exaggerated among Four-Year institutions, where the percent of age 25 plus students is nearly three quarters, compared to just over 20 percent of Public and Non-Profit students. The differences are much smaller in the Two-Year category and non-existent between For-Profit and Public institutions in the Less-Than Two-Year category (where the very tiny Non-Profit group has the oldest students). In fact, For-Profit institutions enroll the most non-traditional-age undergraduates at the Four-Year level and relatively smaller proportions at the Two-Year and Less Than Two-Year, a pattern that is mirror image of the age pattern for Public Institutions, where increasing proportions of older students are found at the Two-Year and Less Than Two Year levels.

Student Financial Aid

The National Center for Education Statistics recently expanded the amount of information collected regarding student financial aid. Starting with the 2010–11 collection, institutions report basic financial aid statistics for their entire undergraduate student population. We summarize a few key statistics from this new collection in Table 5.

Table 5 explores the percent of students who received aid and the average amount among recipients of federal Pell Grants (need based); grants for all sources (need or merit based); and subsidized and unsubsidized federal loans. More than three of five For-Profit students (over 60%) receive Pell Grants overall and at each level. This eligibility rate is nearly double the rate for students at Public and Non-Profit institutions, suggesting that For-Profit institutions serve a larger proportion of low socioeconomic status students. Although the rate of eligibility is much higher, the average grant amount is very similar across control and level categories. When other grant aid is considered, including those from other federal, state, institutional and private sources, the percent receiving and average amount received are skewed dramatically among students enrolled at the generally more expensive Non-Profit, Four-Year institutions. However, there is also an increase in percent receiving and average amount received among students enrolled at Public, Four-Year institutions. It is interesting to note that the percentage receiving aid increases considerably but not average amount received among students enrolled at Public, Two-Year institutions.

Table 5 Student financial aid: Grants and federal loans distributed to undergraduate students, academic year 2010–11

	Pell grants		*Grant aid, any source*		*Federal loans*	
	Pct. receiving	*Avg. amount*	*Pct. receiving*	*Avg. amount*	*Pct. receiving*	*Avg. amount*
Overall						
For-profit	**63%**	**$4,047**	**71%**	**$4,665**	**71%**	**$7,826**
Public	36%	4,068	54%	5,475	31%	6,407
Non-profit	34%	4,020	75%	14,630	58%	7,496
Four-year						
For-profit	**60%**	**$4,027**	**71%**	**$4,813**	**73%**	**$8,542**
Public	36%	4,237	58%	6,873	46%	6,870
Non-profit	33%	4,028	75%	14,863	58%	7,515
Two year						
For-profit	**69%**	**$4,190**	**73%**	**$4,728**	**73%**	**$7,238**
Public	36%	3,919	50%	3,992	18%	5,315
Non-profit	59%	3,824	75%	5,839	60%	6,845
Less than two year						
For-profit	**65%**	**$3,905**	**68%**	**$4,181**	**64%**	**$6,540**
Public	28%	3,804	39%	3,968	16%	6,013
Non-profit	42%	3,889	46%	4,604	24%	6,165

Nearly three-quarters of For-Profit students obtain federal loans to pay for college. The loan-taking rate is similarly high for For-Profit students at Four-Year and Two-Year institutions but slightly lower for students at Less Than Two-Year institutions. Students at Non-Profit institutions also have relatively high loan-taking rates (about 60%) within the Four-Year and Two-Year categories. Public institution students exhibit the lowest rates with slightly less than 50 percent at Four-Year institutions and less than 20 percent taking federal loans at Two-Year institutions. For-Profit students average the highest loan amounts at just under $8,000 overall, with the highest average among those attending Four-Year institutions. The rates for students enrolled at Non-Profit institutions is just slightly below the For-Profit averages. For students at Public Four-Year and Two-Year institutions, average loan amounts are about $1600 to $1800 lower.

Viewed at the aggregate level, students enrolled at For-Profit institutions consume 21 percent of the total of Pell Funds and 23 percent of federal loans as represented in the data collected through the IPEDS Student Financial Aid collection, as shown in Table 6. Because these data pertain to only undergraduate students, the enrollment market share is slightly higher within the For-Profit sector (13%) compared to the market share represented in the total enrollment reported in Table 1. The discrepancy between enrollment market share and aid share is even larger for federal loans where the 13 percent of students enrolled at For-Profit institutions account for 23 percent of the total loan distribution.

Graduation Rates

Perhaps one of the more contentious measures collected through IPEDS, the "150% Graduation Rate" examines the percentage of students who receive a degree or other formal award from the institution at which they start as a full-time, first-time student, within a time period that is 1.5 times the nominal degree time period (for example, 6 years for a 4-year bachelor's degree and 3 years for a 2-year associate's degree). It is beyond the scope of this chapter to describe fully all the warts related to this measure, but the most important to keep in mind is that its usefulness is related to the extent to which students enroll full-time (see Table 4 and related discussion), and the amount of student mobility (transfer) among institutions. For certificate programs, and even in the case of some associate's and bachelor's degrees, the time frame may vary and so does the tracking period (e.g., receiving a 3-year certificate or associate's degree in 4.5 years). Table 7 summarizes the 150 percent graduation rate by sector and includes a contextual indicator as to the percent of all entering students in that sector who qualify to be included in the cohort and are therefore tracked to completion.

Despite the limitations noted here and many others that have been expressed (see, for example, the final report of the federally convened Committee on Measuring Student Success at https://www2.ed.gov/about/bdscomm/list/cmss-committee-report-final.pdf), Table 7 reveals

Table 6 Percent of total Pell Grants and federal loans relative to total enrollment by control

Pell Grants	*% of Total Enr*	*% of Pell funds*	*% of loan funds*
For-profit	**13%**	**21%**	**23%**
Public	73%	67%	57%
Non-profit	14%	12%	21%

Table 7 Graduation rates among the 2005 first-time, full-time cohorts

	Pct. In GRS cohort	*150% Grad. rate*
Overall		
For-profit	**61%**	**59%**
Public	44%	41%
Non-profit	70%	64%
Four-year		
For-profit	**57%**	**40%**
Public	60%	54%
Non-profit	71%	64%
Two year		
For-profit	**74%**	**63%**
Public	32%	22%
Non-profit	61%	57%
Less than two year		
For-profit	**85%**	**66%**
Public	55%	68%
Non-profit	57%	77%

that completion rates are relatively high among students enrolled at For-Profit institutions but mostly because of the completion rates at the Two-Year and Less Than Two-Year levels. For-Profit students at Four-Year institutions fare less well than their peers at Public and Non-Profit institutions. Completion rates are highest for students at Non-Profit institutions (which are generally more selective) and lowest among students at Public, Two-Year institutions. The contrast in completion rates at Two-Year For-Profit (63%) and Public (22%) institutions is most striking. It is informed, however, by the large difference in the percent of entering students who are included in the cohorts of these two types of institutions. For-Profit, Two-Year institutions appear to be more "completion oriented" than For-Profit, Public institutions that accommodate more casual (part-time) enrollees. It appears, though, that the opposite is the case among Four-Year institutions. It is possible that the relatively large number of online learners at the For-Profit two-year level impacts these figures. The thirty Four-Year, For-Profit institutions that reporting having exclusively online programs account for slightly more than one-quarter of total enrollments at For-Profit, Four-Year institutions (half of which is attributable to the University of Phoenix-Online Campus). Many of these institutions are relatively new and so do not yet have graduation rate data available.

The five that do report a composite 150 percent graduation rate of 18 percent. By comparison, there are currently nine Non-Profit, Four-Year institutions that enroll students into exclusively online programs. Although the one of these that reports graduation rates (Western Governors University) has a similarly low rate (18%), these institutions account for less than two percent of all Non-Profit, Four-Year institution enrollments. In the Public sector, there are currently two exclusively online institutions within the IPEDS Universe—Penn State's World Campus and Colorado State's Global Campus—but neither of these yet reports even enrollments.

Degree and Certificate Completions

The penultimate products of postsecondary education are the degrees and certificates awarded upon successful completion of academic programs. By definition, bachelor's and graduate-level degrees are offered only by Four-Year institutions. Table 8 shows the number of these degrees awarded by the For-Profit, Public, and Non-Profit institutions in the IPEDS universe. Noting the lag between entry and completion, the market shares of these degrees cannot be directly compared to the market share in more recent overall enrollments. Thus the 7 percent bachelor's degree share among For-Profit institutions, although lower than its 11 percent total enrollment share, may partially reflect the lower market share from 4 to 6 or more years ago when these students began their undergraduate careers. On the other hand, the lower graduation rate among For-Year, For-Profit institutions just noted also likely contributes. We also see this effect within the Non-Profit group, which has the highest graduation rates and therefore claims a larger market share of bachelor's degree conferrals relative to its market share of enrolled students. Four-Year, For-Profit institutions have their greatest degree market share among Master's degrees conferred (11%). However, graduate degrees are still mostly the domain of Public and Non-Profit institutions, at about equal levels.

Associate's degrees and pre-baccalaureate level certificates are awarded by institutions in every sector. For-Profit institutions play a much larger role in associate's degree conferrals, accounting for 38 percent of the total, with nearly two-thirds of these being conferred by Four-Year, For-Profit institutions. Public institutions confer about three-quarters of all Associate's degrees with the vast majority (83%) conferred at Two-Year institutions. Pre-baccalaureate certificates are reported according to the nominal length of the program (that is, how long it takes to complete

Table 8 Bachelor's and higher degrees conferred by control, academic year 2011–12

	Bachelor's degrees		*Post-Bac. certificates*		*Master's degrees*		*Doctoral degrees*	
Number of degrees								
For-Profit	**132,602**	**7%**	**3,432**	**6%**	**79,447**	**11%**	**5,724**	**3%**
Public	1,127,398	63%	23,884	45%	348,623	46%	84,727	50%
Non-Profit	525,600	29%	25,563	48%	323,554	43%	79,483	47%
Total	1,785,600		52,879		751,624		169,934	

if pursued full-time). The most numerous type of certificate are those that require at least one but less than two years to complete. For-Profit institutions award the majority share of this type of certificate (54%) with slightly more than half of those being awarded by Less Than Two-Year institutions and relatively few at Four-Year institutions. The Public institution share of this type of certificate is predominantly affiliated with Two-Year institutions, which exceed Two-Year For-Profit institutions in total production. The shorter, less than one-year certificate is the next most numerous types just slightly lower than the 1–<2 year certificates in total production. Public sector institutions account for two-thirds (67%) of the shorter-length certificate awards, with the vast majority and nearly one-half of the total, conferred at Public, Two-Year institutions. Among For-Profit institutions, Less Than Two Year institutions award the bulk of these short-term certificates. The least numerous type of pre-baccalaureate certificate is those that require at least two but less than four years to complete on a full-time basis. These certificates are conferred at one-tenth the rate of the other two, shorter-length certificates, with For-Profit institutions accounting for more than two-fifths (62%) of these, primarily through activity at Two-Year, For-Profit institutions (see Table 9).

Staffing

We conclude this descriptive analysis with a brief look at several staffing variables, summarized in Table 10. The first of these, the Student/Faculty Ratio, is among the more wart-laden measures within the IPEDS realm. Institutions are provided fairly complex instructions for the calculation and, unlike most other derived IPEDS variables, institutions do not report the data that goes into calculating the ratio and so it is not possible to

Table 9 Associate's degrees and certificates awarded by sector, academic year 2011–12

	Overall		*Four-year*		*Two-year*		*Less than two-year*	
Associate's degrees								
For-profit	**206,770**	**20%**	**134,649**	**43%**	**72,086**	**10%**	**35**	**100%**
Public	755,979	74%	132,614	42%	623,365	89%	–	0%
Non-profit	53,818	5%	46,531	15%	7,287	1%	–	0%
Total	1,016,567		313,794		702,738		35	
Less than one-year certificates								
For-profit	**139,347**	**30%**	**7,946**	**18%**	**51,228**	**16%**	**80,173**	**82%**
Public	304,611	67%	31,320	72%	259,803	82%	13,488	14%
Non-profit	13,671	3%	4,035	9%	5,199	2%	4,437	5%
Total	457,629		43,301		316,230		98,098	
One to less than two-year certificates								
For-profit	**258,266**	**54%**	**20,115**	**53%**	**103,477**	**37%**	**134,674**	**86%**
Public	203,960	43%	12,986	34%	173,008	62%	17,966	11%
Non-profit	13,451	3%	4,878	13%	3,982	1%	4,591	3%
Total	475,677		37,979		280,467		157,231	
Two to less than four-year certificates								
For-profit	**26,335**	**62%**	**391**	**12%**	**25,611**	**66%**	**333**	**78%**
Public	11,058	26%	1,760	55%	9,206	24%	92	22%
Non-profit	5,323	12%	1,059	33%	4,264	11%		0%
Total	42,716		3,210		39,081		425	

examine the consistency or reliability of this figure. Further discussion of these vagaries can be found in Borden (2011). With these provisions in mind, Table 10 shows that reported Student/Faculty ratios are lowest at Non-Profit, Four-Year and Two-Year institutions but fairly similar between For-Profit and Public institutions (slightly higher for For-Profit Four-Year institutions but slightly lower for For-Profit Two-Year institutions).

The next two staffing variables—the percent of faculty who are full-time and the percent among full-time faculty who are in tenure track positions (either tenured or tenure-eligible)—reveal greater differences between the For-Profit, Public and Non-Profit institutions. Among Four-Year institutions, For-Profit institutions employ mostly part-time faculty and those who are full-time are predominantly not tenure-eligible. Within Two-Year institutions all types of institutions employ a majority of part-time faculty and, in fact, the Public institutions have the smallest proportion of Full-Time Faculty. However, among the full-time faculty in the Two-Year sector, the majority of those in Public and Non-Profit institutions

Table 10 Key staffing characteristics by control, Fall 2011

	Faculty/student ratio	*Pct. full-time faculty*	*% FT fac on track*	*Staff/ faculty ratio*
Overall				
For-profit	**18.0**	**20%**	**2%**	**2.08**
Public	18.5	52%	66%	1.67
Non-profit	12.9	57%	62%	1.98
Four-year				
For-profit	**20.1**	**15%**	**2%**	**1.49**
Public	18.2	67%	71%	1.97
Non-profit	12.8	57%	62%	1.98
Two year				
For-profit	**18.7**	**42%**	**1%**	**2.00**
Public	20.0	32%	53%	1.04
Non-profit	12.3	48%	6%	2.13
Less than two year				
For-profit	**16.6**	**67%**	**19%**	**436.23**
Public	12.6	78%	0%	84.97
Non-profit	17.3			

are tenured or tenure-eligible whereas hardly any For-Profit, Two-Year institution faculty are tenure-eligible. The final measure—non-academic staff to faculty ratio—is generally highest at private institutions, both For-Profit and Non-Profit. The Public, Two-Year sector has a notably lower staffing level than all other sectors. Less Than Two-Year institutions have rather anomalous staffing measure values, especially the non-academic staff to faculty ratio among For-Profit institutions. This final wart relates to at least two nuances. First, many of the individuals directly involved in instruction at these institutions may be categorized as non-academic staff, given the vocational nature of the programs and the "everyone does everything nature" of such relatively small institutions. Second, and relatedly, the IPEDS collections were generally designed to accommodate institutions offering more traditional academic programs. Institutions with entirely or predominantly vocational programs often have difficulties numerically summarizing their programs, resources, and activities according to the variable definitions included within IPEDS. Reporting staff at all types of institutions will tell you that complying with such standardized accountability schemes often requires fitting round pegs into square holes. For the Less Than Two-Year Institutions, it may be more like fitting round pegs into a black hole.

Conclusion

The descriptive data provided in this chapter is intended to serve as a context for reading and interpreting the rest of this volume. The common lore regarding postsecondary institutions, and especially For-Profit institutions, includes some assumptions and myths that are not necessarily borne out by the data. Despite their limitations, IPEDS data reveals some interesting findings. Every individual will pick up on a point or two that runs counter to their prior beliefs. For example, before conducting this analysis, I expected to see a lower rate of full-time attendance at For-Profit, Two-Year institutions. The high rate of full-time attendance and the correspondingly high completion rate was a surprise to me. Indeed, many of my prior perceptions of the For-Profit sector were skewed toward the relatively few extremely large, Four-Year For-Profit institutions, like the University of Phoenix and Ashford University. In the larger scheme, these are rather anomalous For-Profit institutions. They account for a large number of enrollments but not so many completers. Most significantly, they represent only a small fraction of the 3,279 For-Profit institutions included in this analysis.

For-Profit institutions serve disproportionately large numbers of minority, older, and lower socioeconomic status. However, they do not serve the majority of any of these groups. Students at For-Profit, Two-Year institutions are far more likely to complete their degree or certificate programs than their peers at Public, Two-Year institutions. When doing so, they are also likely to encumber a higher student loan debt. It is therefore critical that these students obtain jobs with wages high enough to allow them to repay this debt.

These are just some of the findings that stand out to me from this analysis. One issue that I did not address, given space limitations, are differences in enrollments across academic programs. Part of the reason for not doing so is the fairly limited program-level information available through IPEDS (primarily completions with some limited enrollment data). I will leave it to the other authors of this volume to explore these and other critical issues related to For-Profit institutions.

References

Borden, V. M. H. (2011). *Suggestions for improvements to the student-to-faculty ratio in IPEDS.* U.S. Department of Education Washington, DC: National Postsecondary Education Cooperative. Retrieved August 1, 2013, from http://nces.ed.gov/npec

Fuller, C. (2011). *The history and origins of survey items for the integrated postsecondary education data system*, (NPEC 2012–833). U.S. Department of Education. Washington, DC: National Postsecondary Education Cooperative. Retrieved August 1, 2013, from http://nces.ed.gov/pubsearch

Steele, P. (2011). *Suggestions for improvements to the collection and dissemination of federal financial aid data* (NPEC 2012–834). U.S. Department of Education. Washington, DC: National Postsecondary Education Cooperative. Retrieved August 1, 2013, from http://nces.ed.gov/pubsearch

Social Capital Development and For-Profit Post-secondary Education: A Planned Study

Thomas A. Mays

Introduction

As for-profit institutions have experienced dramatic growth, research has inadvertently lagged, in part due to deficiencies in data collection and reporting. Whereas a body of in-depth research on for-profit institutions is lacking, several questions have been asked through the mainstream press, the academic community, and more recently, the United States Senate Committee on Health, Education, Labor, and Pensions (2012). Among the questions raised are serious inquiries into graduation rates, loan default rates, economic returns, and questionable enrollment practices (Belfield 2013; Blumenstyk and Richards 2011; Deming et al. 2011, 2013; Johnson 2011; Gorski 2010; Office of Student Financial Assistance Programs 2011; S. Rep. No. 112-37 2012; Yeoman 2011). As governments inquire and researchers delve into these relevant areas, attention also should be directed to the social effects of for-profit institutions, specifically the influence of education on social capital development. The purpose of this paper is to first, provide background literature on social capital and education, and second,

T.A. Mays (✉)
Miami University, Middletown Campus,
Middletown, Ohio
e-mail: maysta@miamioh.edu

T. McMillan Cottom, W.A. Darity, Jr. (eds.), *For-Profit Universities*,
DOI 10.1007/978-3-319-47187-7_5

describe the work completed in developing an instrument and research protocol for studying social capital development in post-secondary institutions.

Post-secondary education is sought as a vehicle for individuals to improve their standing in society. Data have shown that a host of economic and non-economic benefits arise as an individual's education increases (Baum et al. 2010; Carnevale et al. 2011; Perna 2005). But deeper questions of equity and social effects of higher education must be asked, specifically of for-profit institutions. It is difficult to research for-profit institutions in a meaningful way, in part due to their proprietary nature as some researchers have found a lack of institutional cooperation (Tierney and Lechuga 2010) or have considered the lack of rich data (Chung 2012).

Social capital theory provides an alternative lens in researching the effects of for-profit institutions. While economically oriented research may provide an understanding of the financial impacts of education, a social capital perspective can grant insight into the complex interrelations of education, students, and communities. This is important because the internal and external connections that individuals make with others can affect other forms of capital (Bourdieu 1986; Coleman 1988). Exploring for-profit institution outcomes through social capital theory provides an opportunity to study key social questions from an interdisciplinary perspective, allowing for economists, academics, policy makers, and other disciplines to research the topic using a shared framework (Grootaert and van Bastelaer 2001).

Social capital is difficult to study due partly to the nuance found in the various definitions and conceptualizations that its proponents have applied. Furthermore, many researchers have discussed the multidimensional nature of social capital (Adler and Kwon 2002; Coleman 1988; D'Agostino 2010; Grootaert et al. 2004; Helliwell and Putnam 2007; Sandefur et al. 1999; Stone 2001; Woolcock 2002). These dimensions generally include the constructs of groups, networks, and trust. The complexities in using social capital theory should not deter researchers; however, it should foster a greater push to clearly identify and outline research intentions and definitions.

In a simplified construct, social capital in higher education can be reflected in the relationships that students have with faculty, staff, administrators, other students, and those from outside the institution. These relationships may grant access to information or other resources that the student could not otherwise attain. While a student's social capital develops throughout life, the college experience can provide fertile ground for developing not only a cache of social capital, but also the skills for future social capital development.

A challenge for researchers and policymakers is uncovering and understanding how the differences between various types of institutions affect learning and development outcomes. The National Center for Education Statistics (NCES) categorizes post-secondary institutions by sectors. These sectors are identified by institutional control, and they include public, private nonprofit, and private for-profit categories. Sectors are further divided into subcategories including two-year, more than two-year but less than four-year, and four-year (NCES n.d.). A significant difference between these institution categories, or types, is how they are funded. As of 2013–2014, public four-year institutions collected 20.6% of their revenue from tuition and fees, while private nonprofit four-year institutions collected 29.5% from tuition and fees (NCES 2015b, c). In comparison, for-profit four-year institutions collected 89.8% of their revenue from tuition and fees (NCES 2015d). Data for two-year institutions include the tuition and fees portion of revenue of 15.9%, 70.5%, and 86.9% for public, private, and for-profit intuitions respectively (NCES 2015b, c, d).

In addition to for-profit institutions relying on tuition and fees for a greater percentage of their revenue, students have also been more likely to take on debt compared to their private nonprofit counterparts. Payea, Baum, and Kurose (Payea et al. 2013) reported that during 2011–2012, for-profit students used debt to finance 37% of tuition and fees. This compared to 30% for public four-year students, 20% for four-year private students, and 19% for two-year public students (Payea et al. 2013). While three-year student loan default rates for students of two-year for-profit institutions were found to be lower than their public two-year counterparts (17.7% versus 19.1%), 14.7% of four-year for-profit students defaulted on their loans, compared to 7.6% of students from four-year public institutions (NCES 2015b, c, d). These data should raise economic and social concerns.

In this paper, I include a brief review of the for-profit industry, an exploration into social capital theory, and a presentation of the literature on social capital and higher education. Next, I present a quantitative social capital instrument, the subsequent pilot, and a planned methodology and revised instrument for future research. My guiding research questions include:

- How does social capital develop on campus?
- How do students perceive the effect of higher education on social capital development?
- What is the relationship between institution type and social capital development?

To measure social capital, I adapted a survey instrument from Grootaert et al.'s (2004) Social Capital Integrated Questionnaire (SC-IQ). Instead of applying the full questionnaire, I began with what Grootaert et al. (2004) defined as the core questions. Adaptations to the core questions include cultural and linguistic changes to address the intended survey population in addition to new items measuring participant academic credentials and perceptions of education and social capital. After piloting the first instrument adaptation and engaging in additional research, I have further modified the instrument and research methodology, expanding from a quantitative study to one using mixed methods in a case study format. The modified instrument was used to collect data from multiple campuses at a public Midwestern university (Mays 2016). Beginning with a literature review, this paper reports the development and modification of an instrument and method for studying social capital in higher education.

Literature Review

For Profit Institutions of Higher Education

Both popular press criticism and an overall lack of understanding of for-profit institutions require a push for new academic research. In 2012, the Senate Committee on Health, Education, Labor, and Pensions concluded the necessity of improving reporting and accountability in the for-profit higher education market. Much of the scrutiny has focused on the for-profit industry's low graduation rates and high loan default rates (Belfield 2013; Blumenstyk and Richards 2011; Gorski 2010; Johnson 2011; Yeoman 2011). The stale economy and enhanced scrutiny may have contributed in part to the recent contraction in for-profit enrollments (Blumenstyk 2013). Given the critical eye that has been placed on for-profit education, both Tierney (2011) and the Senate committee (2012) have stated that for-profit institutions must become an integral part of the higher education system in order for the United States to achieve its post-secondary education goals.

By 2009, the for-profit higher education industry had grown, with for-profit institutions enrolling 9% of all post-secondary students and encompassing 39% of all post-secondary institutions (Hentschke et al. 2010). After reaching a peak of 11.3% in 2010, the for-profit share of the student population had decreased to 9.1% in 2014 (NCES 2015a). The longer term increase in growth could be partially due to the flexible and convenient scheduling, customer service orientation, and in-demand career education programs offered by for-profit institutions (Floyd 2007). However, the recent declines in the share of students attending for-profit institutions also may be related to negative reports, including the previously referenced Senate committee report (2012). Figure 1 illustrates the share of all students at Title IV institutions by institution control.

Much of the research and reporting on for-profit institutions focuses on economic metrics, yet little research exists examining the influence of for-profit institutions on student social capital development. Related social questions include the number of high-risk students who attend for-profit institutions. Swail (2009) found that for-profit institutions enrolled a greater percentage of high-risk students than do traditional institutions. Utilizing NCES Beginning Postsecondary Student study data from 2003, Swail (2009) reported that for-profit college students were older than students attending other types of institutions. In addition, for-profit students were more likely to be members of minority groups, receive Pell Grants, and exhibit multiple risk factors such as having children or working while attending school. Using National Longitudinal Study and Postsecondary

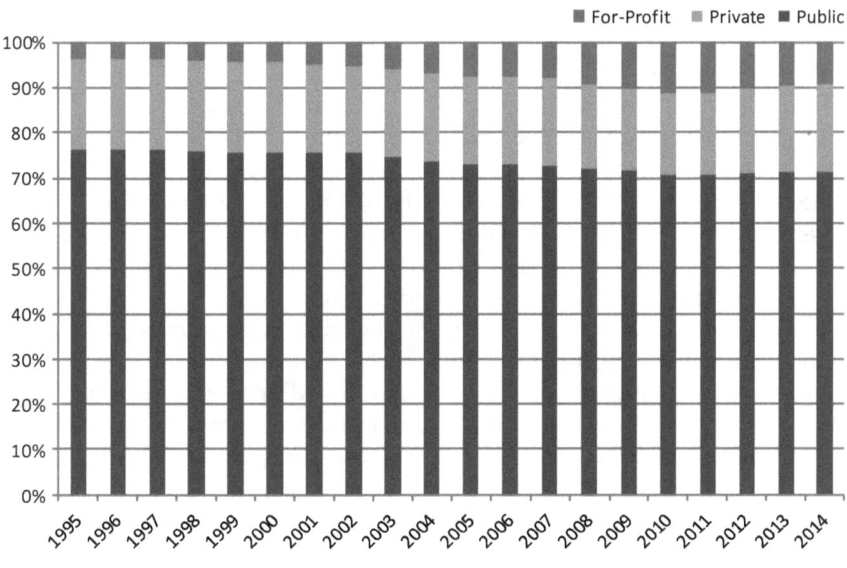

Fig. 1 Enrollment as a percentage of total postsecondary enrollment, Title IV institutions, 1995–2014
(*Source*: NCES (2015a))

Education Transcript Study data, Chung (2012) similarly found greater minority and female representation in for-profit institutions as well as a correlation between family socioeconomic level and school selection. Students of families from lower socioeconomic strata tended to select for-profit institutions over community colleges or four-year nonprofit schools (Chung 2012).

Researchers should examine the social structure of these institutions and if these structures are conducive to the development of socially productive citizens. Tierney (2011) noted that early for-profit institutions recognized a potentially large target market in nontraditional students. These students were in search of a convenient education, not the expanded set of student life options offered by traditional institutions. Students certainly should be able to select an institution that will best meet their needs and goals (Tierney 2011). However, the social effects of higher education is also in question. Perhaps some students, specifically those who have already accumulated a cache of social capital, are only in need of career training and knowledge development. But many students, especially those with high-risk characteristics, may require a greater return on their education that stretches beyond accumulation of knowledge.

Social Capital Definition and Theory

While the definition of social capital varies by researcher, many definitions share several general elements. Social capital definitions often include the premise of membership in groups and networks, and the outcomes, actions, or behaviors of agents within those groups and networks. The following discussion falls far short of a comprehensive review of social capital theory; however, the presented views do form a variety of perspectives that have largely informed my research perspective.

According to Coleman (1988), social capital exists in both individuals and organizations, and has both economic and noneconomic capacities. He lists various sources of social capital including the closeness of ties, an individual's associations with organizations, community openness, and shared beliefs between individuals. He emphasized the interaction of individuals in social capital theory; specifically, that social capital was involved in an individual's relationships. "Social capital, however, comes about through changes in the relations among persons that facilitate action" (Coleman 1988, p. S100). Synthesizing the definitions of other social capital researchers, Woolcock (1998) referred to social capital as

"... the information, trust, and norms of reciprocity inherent in one's social networks" (p. 153). In summarizing social capital, Lin (2001) remarked, "The premise behind the notion of social capital is rather simple and straightforward: investment in social relations with expected returns in the marketplace" (p. 19).[1]

The various definitions of social capital have their own nuance, yet common themes are identifiable. The social capital definitions of Bourdieu (1986), Coleman (1988), Woolcock (1998), Woolcock and Narayan (2000), Lin (2001), and Adler and Kwon (2002) share similarities regarding the concepts of memberships and outcomes or manifestations. The terms found in the literature that reflect membership include "social relations" (Lin 2001, p. 19; Adler and Kwon 2002, p. 23), "social structures" (Coleman 1988, p. S98), "social networks" (Woolcock 1998, p. 189), and "networks" (Woolcock and Narayan 2000, p. 226). Membership generates outcomes. Research has included the terms "flow" and "solidarity" (Adler and Kwon 2002, p. 23), "expected returns" (Lin 2001, p. 19) "actions" (Coleman 1988, p. S98), "norms of reciprocity" (Woolcock 1998, p. 189), and "act" (Woolcock and Narayan 2000, p. 226). Bourdieu's (1986, 1998) description of social structure and habitus reflect a deeper concept of membership and outcomes.[2] He claimed that social capital networks develop both consciously and unconsciously through relationships. In addition, Bourdieu (1986) discussed the volume of an individual's social capital, which is based not only on the size of an individual's social network, but the amount of economic, symbolic, and cultural capital possessed by the individual and within the individual's network.

In an interesting example of social capital in a family network, Coleman (1988) described a school district where Asian families acquired two copies of each text book. Purchasing multiple copies allowed the mother to simultaneously learn their children's subjects, with the intention of tutoring them throughout the academic year. In this case, membership in the family resulted in social capital manifestations in the form of a strong parental commitment to education for their children. The children's social capital was enhanced by their network connection to their parents.

The literature adds depth to the social capital discussion through the concepts of bonding, bridging, and linking forms of social capital. Adler and Kwon (2002) described bonding forms of social capital as those that enhance the cohesiveness of a community. Grootaert et al. (2004) defined bonding social capital as "ties to people who are similar in terms of their demographic characteristics, such as family members, neighbors, close friends, and work colleagues" (p. 4). Bridging capital has been defined as connections to people who do not reflect similar demographic characteristics (Grootaert et al. 2004). Adler and Kwon (2002) noted that bridging forms of social capital may enhance an individual's relationships with others. Additionally, Putnam (2000) described bridging social capital as inclusive, providing the Civil Rights movement as an example. Bridging can help groups and networks create ties with other groups and networks. Conversely, the development of bonding social capital can be exclusive as individuals focus on building ties with members within the community, ignoring outside groups and networks. However, bonding can lead to enhanced solidarity within the group. While both of these forms of social capital can have positive and negative influences, Putnam (2000) noted that bridging can avail a community to outside resources.

Woolcock (2002) characterized linking capital as "the capacity to leverage resources, ideas, and information from formal institutions beyond the community" (p. 26). Woolcock and Sweetser (2002) furthered that linking ties included connections with individuals from political or higher socioeconomic classes. The researchers claimed that access to all three forms of capital is favorable for individual well-being (Woolcock and Sweetser 2002).

The social capital literature also includes multiple measures of social structures including trustworthiness, obligations, and openness (Coleman 1988). Trustworthiness is an important part of social structures, and without trust between group members, the social network can weaken. Individuals who feel obligated to the group, or whose members feel obligated to each other, can strengthen the social structure. These dynamics can also affect the flow and amount of information within the group. Social networks may also include members who are connected to each other in more than one way, including as coworkers, neighbors, or religious congregants (Coleman 1988). Similarly, Putnam (2000) measured social capital through community memberships, volunteering, socialization, trust, and activity in the community.

Social capital is not a simple asset to be accumulated. Woolcock (1998) stressed that social capital should be observed from a cost and benefit perspective. For example, can membership in a community group become so intense as to cause more social harm than good? Could group-think be an outcome of an intensely close social network? According to Putnam (2000), social capital can lead to both positive and negative results, and Woolcock (1998) stated social capital should be discussed in terms of optimization, not maximization.

Considering Woolcock's (1998) argument to focus on optimizing social capital, practical questions arise of how to implement optimization strategies within academic institutions. What kinds of social capital are being developed on and off campus as well as formally and informally? Will the forms of social capital that are being developed help create a positive social structure for students and their communities? How will the social capital that students develop during school help them in utilizing other forms of capital in the future? Walpole (2003) found that students of lower socioeconomic status (SES) experienced less social capital development than their higher SES peers. This was measured through student involvement in campus groups as well as students engaging faculty in their homes. While low SES students experienced less social capital development, they accumulated greater amounts of economic capital by working more hours per week than high SES students. This difference in the activities where time was spent during the week influences what kind of capital develops. Walpole (2003) also found that low SES students who engaged in interactive and group activities were more likely to attend graduate school. Considering these dynamics, policymakers and administrators should explore providing additional social capital development opportunities for students of all socioeconomic strata (Walpole 2003).

Lin (2001) described four aspects of social capital that translate well to studying post-secondary institutions. The four aspects include information, influence, social credibility, and reinforcement. The breadth and depth of an individual's social network influence the flow of information, thus a stronger social network could lead to an individual learning about new opportunities. Certain social relationships could also lead to an ability to influence decision makers. In addition, an individual's social credentials are established and enhanced through their network relationships including claims to resource accessibility and the individual's usefulness to the organization. Reinforcement is understood through the acceptance of the individual by the group based on that individual's value to the group (Lin 2001). Considering these four aspects of social capital in a higher education context underscores the necessity of students to develop social capital during their college experiences. For example, students experience positive outcomes from interaction with faculty, staff, and administrators (Çelik and Ekinci 2012; Kim and Sax 2011). These kinds of supportive growth environments may be developed through interdisciplinary learning communities that promote developing diverse social, academic, and professional relationships.

Woolcock (1998) noted that social capital has become misunderstood, even simplified to the point that it requires critical examination of how social capital is currently studied. Furthermore, the diversity in social capital theory has led to increasing confusion of what exactly social capital is or does. Is social capital the cause, effect, or both the cause and effect of economic and social rewards? Can social capital beget additional social capital? To further complicate the study of social capital, Woolcock (1998) stated that social capital has become politicized. As one side states that government should be the catalyst for spawning social capital growth, the other proclaims that social capital growth emanates from the private sector. Even with these disagreements, social capital theory can serve as a valuable tool for studying, analyzing, and improving both traditional and for-profit institutions.

Social Capital Research and Education

Families, peers, communities, institutions, and their structures influence students throughout their academic journeys. The scope and power of this influence has been a topic of study that has led to a growing field of educational research focused on social capital variables. Researchers interested in studying the complex phenomena inherent in post-secondary student experiences should examine the social capital and education body of literature to gain insight on possible research methods.

Research on social capital and education has included a range of measures and methodologies, including social capital as the dependent as well as the independent variable. Several researchers have examined family structure and behaviors and education-related variables (Astone and McLanahan 1991; Coleman 1988; Perna and Titus 2005; Ravanera and Rajulton 2010; Sandefur et al. 1999), while other researchers have focused on institutional structures and culture (Avery and Daly 2010; Çelik and Ekinci 2012; Walpole 2003), or the influence of peers and their families (Cherng et al. 2013). Additional focal areas have included the effect of service-learning projects (D'Agostino 2010) as well as the effect of education on political involvement and citizenship (Helliwell and Putnam 2007; Nie et al. 1996; Persell and Wenglinsky 2004).

Coleman (1988) compared the dropout rates of public, private, independent, and religious schools. He found the highest dropout rates in public schools (14.4%) and the lowest rates in Catholic schools (3.4%) and in non-Catholic religious schools (3.7%) (Coleman 1988, p. S115). According to

Coleman (1988), this could be the result of social network closure, which fosters the development of group norms. When a social network experiences closure, members share accountability and responsibility for each other. Coleman (1988) uses the example of a group of several families, where the "... parents' friends are the parents of their children's friends" (p. 106). Multiplex relationships might also have an effect; wrapped around the school network is the church network, and both networks are likely to have relatively greater degrees of closure (Coleman 1988).

Also researching family structures, Ravanera and Rajulton (2010) added to Coleman's research that complete family structures led to lower school dropout rates. Ravanera and Rajulton (2010) drew from several perspectives of social capital thought including Bourdieu (1986), Lin (2001), and Coleman (1988). Ravanera and Rajulton's (2010) concern when considering the determinants of outcomes was that prior research focused only on the internal family structure, ignoring broader explorations of social capital. The researchers summarized the various views of capital, dividing them into attributes of individuals and attributes of social groups like communities (Ravanera and Rajulton 2010).

Ravanera and Rajulton (2010) found that married mothers with intact families held a greater trust in people and of the community. Married mothers also experienced a larger informal network, a greater confidence in institutions, and higher instances of memberships in organizations. Conversely, single mothers were found to have less extensive networks. Lone mothers, who already lack support networks, also held less confidence in institutions (Ravanera and Rajulton 2010).

Sandefur, Meier, and Hernandez (Sandefur et al. 1999) studied educational transitions and social capital, finding that family structure, residential stability, and Catholic school attendance positively affected educational attainment. Similarly, Meier (1999) studied the quality of social capital, finding that families who invest in social capital are more involved in school, and their investments led to enhancements in extracurricular activities and religious school attendance. Alternatively, research has found that students living in households with a single parent or a stepparent experienced negative academic outcomes on grades, attendance, and attitudes toward education (Astone and McLanahan 1991).

While the previous studies included research on family structures, the following studies examined influences within the institution including network group participation and organizational commitment. Similar to Walpole's (2003) findings, Avery and Daly (2010) studied formal networks within the institution. They found that students who were able to develop social capital through on-campus employment, student organizations, and faculty interaction improved their chances of completing their degree. This, in part, led Avery and Daly (2010) to develop an alternative model that tied resilience with self-efficacy and engagement with social capital, and the sum of these factors influenced degree attainment. A significant finding was that "students' resilience, or abilities to rebound from adverse situations, in combination with their self-efficacy, or their belief that they could do what was required of them, was common among all of the students" (Avery and Daly 2010, p. 33). Because of the importance of social capital in degree attainment, Avery and Daly (2010) suggested that institutions should teach students the positive effects of social networks. Additionally, research by Çelik and Ekinci (2012) suggests that the organizational commitment of teachers and administrators had a positive influence on student achievement. The research presented thus far supports the theory that social capital-based student support structures, whether formal or informal, family based or institutional, are a key aspect for improving academic outcomes.

Putnam (2000) drew attention to social capital's role in education, finding that students from states with higher levels of social capital experienced better academic performance than students from states with lower levels of social capital. Even more interesting, states with higher measures of informal social capital experienced a higher rate of positive academic outcomes when compared to states with higher levels of formal forms of social capital. In other words, trust became a more significant factor than memberships in official groups. Putnam (2000) also found that as civic engagement and parental support increased, misbehavior decreased.

Treating social capital as a dependent variable, Helliwell and Putnam (2007) studied education and the social capital dimensions of participation and trust. They concluded the importance of education is a factor in enhancing socialization and political involvement. An individual's level of education was found to positively affect social participation and trust (Helliwell and Putnam 2007). In general support of these findings, Huang, van den Brink, and Groot (Huang et al. 2008) reported in a meta-analysis of social capital and education research that education had a positive effect on social participation.

In a summary of social capital and education research, Dika and Singh (2002) reviewed research studies exploring the link between social capital and educational factors, noting a significant weakness in social capital and education research resides in the lack of theoretical and empirical evidence. This could be due to misunderstandings about social capital based on research focused on conceptualizations instead of the sources of social capital (Dika and Singh 2002). The reviewed research also simplified or ignored factors such as inequality and institutional discrimination. Dika and Singh (2002) suggest that Bourdieu's approach could address these omissions.

Kinser (2006) noted a lack of research focusing specifically on for-profit post-secondary education and social outcomes, citing Persell and Wenglinsky (2004) as an exception. Persell and Wenglinsky (2004) found that students who began their higher education with comparable civic engagement behaviors split based on attending for-profit versus public community college. Specifically, community college students were found to vote, engage in community service, and become more politically active than their peers at for-profit institutions. In a comparison of the costs and benefits of two-year for-profit education and a community college education, Cellini (2012) mentioned the social returns to education, stating "there are no studies that differentiate between the social returns to various types of colleges" (p. 173).

While not focused on for-profit institutions, Gumport (2000) noted the changes that occur when institutional management increases in importance, and the overall movement of higher education as an industry. Similarly, Bok (2003), Ruch (2003), and Davis (2011) have written about educational institutions' change in focus. The connection is based in a concern that a profit-centric model may negatively influence education, especially regarding social welfare. These issues lead to questions of stratification, both with a student's initial choice of institution, as well as resulting economic effects later in the student's life. Loury (1995) observed, "Inequality in the endowments of social capital in their communities of origin generally implies inequality in the outcomes that otherwise equally competent persons can achieve" (p. 105).

Lareau (2011) observed families with different socioeconomic backgrounds, finding that parental understanding and expectations in terms of the secondary school process varied by socioeconomic class. Middle class youth were more likely to have parents who attended college, meaning they had firsthand knowledge of the process and could offer assistance. Middle class parents were also concerned with maximizing their children's activities in the interest of improving their chances of college admission. Conversely, working class families communicated confusion over the process (Lareau 2011). How should colleges and universities, including for-profits, address these issues as they are reflected in their student bodies?

Bourdieu's (1998) social capital theory included an accounting of various forms and volumes of social capital. Much of his focus was not on the outcomes of education in terms of social capital development, but on social capital's effect on the education of entering students. Students possessing different levels of social capital when beginning school may have different experiences and outcomes. Bourdieu (1988) commented that sustained social inequality was based on inherited capitals.

> Thus, the school institution, once thought capable of introducing a form of meritocracy by privileging individual aptitudes over hereditary privileges, actually tends to establish, through the hidden linkage between scholastic aptitude and cultural heritage, a veritable *state nobility*, whose authority and legitimacy are guaranteed by the academic title. (Bourdieu 1998, p. 22)

Research has involved the effects of several factors including socially related family and organizational factors influencing education and education's impact on social capital formation. The complex relationships raise legitimate concern on how to properly define and research social capital, specifically regarding measurement and methodology. The following section describes the original instrument designed by Grootaert et al. (2004), how it was adapted for the initial pilot, and the subsequent updates completed after the pilot.

Instrument and Methods Evaluation

Several studies and methods were reviewed in the process of identifying an appropriate framework for researching the social effects of for-profit institutions on students and communities. Based on the complex nature of social capital, I found the six dimensional framework and SC-IQ instrument developed by Grootaert et al. (2004) provided the appropriate breadth and depth of social capital measures for the study. Several other researchers have used the six dimensional framework including Sheingold, Hahn, and Hofmeyer (2013), Lu, Yang, and Yu (2013), and Schoenacher (2009).

The initial research design included a comparison of institution types using a modified version of the SC-IQ instrument. The SC-IQ is organized around six identified dimensions of social capital. A subset of the

SC-IQ, dubbed the Core Questions, formed a substantial portion of the pilot instrument presented in this paper. The purpose of the pilot instrument was to measure participant social capital, academic credentials and institution type, and participant perceived effects of education on social capital. Based on the pilot, modifications were made to the instrument and methodology. The revised protocol, involving a mixed methods case study design, was used to more fully understand the social capital phenomenon at the studied institution.

SC-IQ Framework and Survey

Grootaert et al. (2004) defined their interpretation of social capital along three views. First, social capital represented the resources an individual could access based on their relationships. Second, social capital can be based on involvement in formal and informal networks. Third, social capital can be derived from relationships with authority figures. While the instrument was developed for use in studying social capital and poverty, the views reflected critical elements of social capital which have been reported in the literature, and mirrored my thoughts on the intended outcomes of a post-secondary education.

The social capital model includes six dimensions: (1) groups and networks, (2) trust and solidarity, (3) collective action and cooperation, (4) information and communication, (5) social cohesion and inclusion, and (6) empowerment and political action. The first three dimensions are defined as measures of social capital; groups and networks are considered a measure of structural social capital, trust and solidarity a measure of cognitive social capital, and collective action and cooperation a measure of underlying social capital. The last three dimensions are considered manifestations of social capital, with social cohesion and inclusion as well as empowerment and political action reflecting outcomes (Grootaert et al. 2004).

The SC-IQ is a 97-item quantitative instrument built to collect data on the six dimensions of social capital. Grootaert et al. (2004) also presented a core questions instrument with 27 items. These core questions were adapted for use in the pilot instrument. Grootaert et al. (2004) noted that alteration of the instrument would be appropriate to account for demographic, linguistic, or cultural differences. The researchers also recommend that the instrument be used in conjunction with a second instrument, such as a household survey, as well as given in a pretest and posttest format

Table 1 Social capital dimensions and education related examples

Social capital dimension	*Example*
Groups and networks	Groups, clubs, classes, friends
Trust and security	Willingness to help others on campus; Trust in others
Collective action and cooperation	Volunteerism; Involvement on campus; Expectations of involvement
Information and communication	Frequency and medium of communication
Social cohesion and inclusion	Campus diversity; Access to resources; Crime and violence
Empowerment and political action	Voting habits; Petitioning the administration

Note: Adapted from Grootaert et al. (2004) with educational context added by the research

with the intention of using the results to evaluate social projects. The original SC-IQ was based on prior surveys which demonstrated reliability and validity. Additionally, a panel of external advisors provided input. The SC-IQ was also piloted in Albania and Nigeria. Table 1 includes the six social capital dimensions and education related examples.

Pilot Instrument and Evaluation

The first section of the pilot instrument includes all 27 items in the SC-IQ identified as core questions. The SC-IQ questions were modified for audience appropriateness as well as to reflect a research focus on education and social capital. Words reflecting cultural and social designations not commonly used in the United States were removed. Furthermore, questions were modified to address the different technologies generally used in the United States compared to the SC-IQ's intended population. After the SC-IQ questions, academic experience items were added, including highest level of education completed, institution type (public, private, and for-profit subcategories), perceived importance of a college education, and perceived effects of college on social capital.

The pilot instrument was administered at a private research university in the Midwest. I used convenience sampling to select participants from two graduate courses in education, and 16 surveys were completed. The response rate was much lower than anticipated due in part to a narrow data collection timeframe. However, the responses helped identify issues with the instrument and led to several modifications as well as a review of the research methodology.

Modified Instrument and Methods

Reviewing social capital and education research, Dika and Singh (2002) noted general weakness in empirical support. Dika and Singh (2002) specifically described social capital as a complex phenomenon. Furthering the social capital complexity argument, Dudwick, Kuehnast, Jones, and Woolcock (Dudwick et al. 2006) remarked that a research approach that uses both quantitative and qualitative paradigms better addresses the phenomenon. Specifically, Dudwick et al. (2006) stated, "Qualitative methods and open-ended responses tilt the balance of power and expertise away from the researcher toward respondents and community members. Such methods are vital for examining complex issues of causality, process, and context" (pp. 3–4). The qualitative approaches described by Dudwick et al. (2006) were designed to complement Grootaert et al.'s (2004) instrument.

Based on the recommendations provided by Dudwick et al. (2006), a mixed methods approach was used for the study to better explore the complex phenomenon of social capital in higher education. In addition to distributing the revised SC-IQ instrument, qualitative data was collected through observations on campus as well as interviews with students and faculty. Student interview participants were selected to provide a variety of backgrounds and experiences including gender, home campus, degree and major, and time spent in college. A basic qualitative approach described by Merriam (2009) was followed, and the online software package Dedoose was used for coding and analysis. Note the findings are not presented in this paper and have not been published as of press time (Mays 2016).

The revised instrument included reworded items in both the SC-IQ core questions section as well as the section on the perceived effects of education on social capital. These revisions addressed national and cultural issues as well as clarified items that may have been confusing to participants during the initial pilot. Additionally, several additional items from the full SC-IQ instrument were added to enhance dimensions that were previously underrepresented.

The instrument was distributed to a random sample of 2,000 students attending a public Midwestern university. A total of 63 surveys were fully completed. While the SC-IQ items involved a variety of data types including both quantitative and qualitative data, the items involving participant perceptions of college and social capital used a five point Likert scale. Internal consistency results for the Likert scale items are reported in Table 2. The Communication and Information items will be reviewed for the next iteration of the instrument.

Table 2 Internal consistency results of college impact on social capital development survey items

Subscale	*Number of items* $n=$	*Cronbach's alpha score* $\alpha=$
Overall	29	0.920
Groups and networks	6	0.792
Trust and security	5	0.827
Information and communication	3	0.632
Collective action and cooperation	5	0.898
Social cohesion and inclusion	4	0.746
Empowerment and political action	4	0.927

Future Direction

While the instrument discussed in this paper was used to collect cross sectional data, future research should also involve a longitudinal approach, including a sample of high school seniors who are followed through their collegiate careers and into post-collegiate adulthood. This approach could provide an opportunity to follow the development of social capital through a student's post-secondary and early adult professional life. In addition, new research should involve the subdivision of each dimension of social capital. For example, the groups and networks dimension should be subdivided into social, community, religious, professional, and academic. Subdividing the dimensions and focusing on forms of social capital could lead to improved research outcomes as schools and communities may focus on providing support structures and opportunities to develop areas lacking in the student experience.

A key in studying social capital and education is to create a model categorizing the dimensions of social capital, the level or volume of social capital in each dimension, and the positive or negative effect of social capital based on stakeholder perceptions. Also, it should be understood that social capital can be constricted by a limited capacity. Additional items may be required to measure the perceived positive or negative effects of specific dimensional characteristics. Future research should encompass both quantitative and qualitative methodologies. The complex relationships and the disagreements within social capital theory demand a more comprehensive research approach.

Conclusion

The issues framing the presented approach to studying social capital and for-profit institutions are relevant to traditional institutions of higher education as well. While for-profit institutions continue to maintain a significant position in higher education, they must increasingly avail themselves to eternal data collection and research efforts. The instrument and mixed methods approach described in this paper represent a foundation for future study. Although the development of an instrument measuring social capital, academic outcomes, and institution type marks a key step in gathering and analyzing data on the social effects of for-profit institutions, the strength of the instrument will depend upon the clear mapping of questions to elements in the social capital model.

Within the framework of higher education, some see the vast majority of higher education becoming more business oriented (Bok 2003; Davis 2011; Gumport 2000; Ruch 2003). This corporatization of higher education stretches the important social questions of education from for-profit institutions to all of higher education; thus the question of social capital formation and development is significant to all of higher education. Implications tie to questions of stratification in higher education and the effect on class mobility.

Studying social capital is not an easy task. However, social capital can provide unique insight into for-profit higher education institutions by uncovering how these institutions fit into the social fabric of their communities. Woolcock (1998) stated the following:

> The challenge for development theorists and policy-makers alike is to identify the mechanisms that will create, nurture, and sustain the types and combinations of social relationships conducive to building dynamic participatory societies, sustainable equitable economies, and accountable developmental states. (p. 186)

Woolcock's (1998) warnings on social capital research should resonate with researchers and policy makers who need to avoid simplifying and politicizing social capital. It should be respected as multifaceted, complex, and evolving. Even while respecting its complexity, researchers also must be careful when inferring causation in their findings. The abstract nature of social capital and its measurement using proxies adds difficulty to research efforts. Stone (2001) noted the importance of separating social capital from its outcomes, then understanding the relationships between the dimensions of social capital as well as with the outcomes of social capital. Woolcock (1998) noted that focus should be given to understanding the nature of relationships in a changing economy, that social relations are not static, but dynamic.

As the for-profit post-secondary education industry continues to grow, additional efforts will be made to assess their outcomes as measured by more traditional metrics. A significant part of future for-profit research must also include not just the measurement of social capital but also what it means to individuals, institutions, communities, and class mobility. How can students, specifically those from disadvantaged socioeconomic strata, develop and leverage social capital while in college? What institutional and community structures need to be developed and nurtured to foster and enhance beneficial social capital formation? For-profit institutions will remain a key aspect of higher education in the United States. As such, research efforts should focus on how to improve institutions of all types, especially given the aggressive higher education goals set for the country.

Notes

1. Lin (2001) described the *marketplace* as including economic, political, and community markets.
2. "To each class of positions, there corresponds a class of habitus produced by the social conditioning associated with the corresponding condition and, through the mediation of the habitus and its generative capability, a systemic set of goods and properties, which are united by affinity of style" (Bourdieu 1998, p. 22). With its foundation formed in early childhood, habitus is developed through an individual's social structures and cultural surroundings. It becomes a part of how individuals view their world, and it influences every aspect of their lives. In terms of class habitus, members of the same social class share similar individual habitus (Bourdieu 1998).

References

Adler, P., & Kwon, S. (2002). Social capital: Prospects for a new concept. *The Academy of Management Review, 27*(1), 17–40.

Astone, N., & McLanahan. (1991). Family structure, parental practices and high school completion. *American Sociological Review, 56*(3), 309–320.

Avery, C., & Daly, A. (2010). Promoting equitable outcomes for high-risk college students: The roles of social capital and resilience. *Journal of Equity in Education, 1*(1), 20–50.

Baum, S., Ma, J., & Payea, K. (2010). *Education pays 2010: The benefits of higher education for individuals and society*. College Board Advocacy and Policy Center. Retrieved from http://trends.collegeboard.org/downloads/Education_Pays_2010.pdf

Belfield, C. (2013). Student loans and repayment rates: The role of for-profit colleges. *Research in Higher Education, 54*(1), 1–29.

Blumenstyk, G. (2013, February 3). For-profit colleges take a step back to regroup. *Chronicle of Higher Education*. Retrieved from http://chronicle.com/article/For-Profit-Colleges-Take-a/136961/

Blumenstyk, G., & Richards, A. (2011, March 18). Many for-profits are 'managing' defaults to mask problems, analysis indicates. *The Chronicle of Higher Education*. Retrieved from http://chronicle.com/article/Many-For-Profits-Are/126689/

Bok, D. (2003). *Universities in the marketplace: The commercialization of higher education*. Princeton: Princeton University Press.

Bourdieu, P. (1986). The forms of capital. In J. Richardson (Ed.), *Handbook of theory of research for the sociology of education* (pp. 46–58). Westport: Greenwood Press.

Bourdieu, P. (1998). *Practical reason: On the theory of action*. Cambridge: Polity.

Carnevale, A. P., Rose, S. J., & Cheah, B. (2011). *The college payoff: Education, occupation, lifetime earnings*. Washington, DC: Georgetown University, Center on Education and the Workforce. Retrieved from http://www9.georgetown.edu/grad/gppi/hpi/cew/pdfs/collegepayoff-complete.pdf

Çelik, V., & Ekinci, A. (2012). The effects of social capital on school success. *International Journal of Social Sciences and Education, 2*(1), 211–223.

Cellini, S. (2012). For-profit higher education: An assessment of costs and benefits. *National Tax Journal, 65*(1), 153–180.

Cherng, H., Calarco, J., & Kao, G. (2013). Along for the ride: Best friends' resources and adolescents' college completion. *American Education Research Journal, 50*(1), 76–106.

Chung, A. (2012). Choice of for-profit college. *Economics of Education Review, 31*(6), 1084–1101.

Coleman, J. (1988). Social capital and the creation of human capital. *The American Journal of Sociology Supplement: Organizations and Institutions, 94*, S95–S120.

D'Agostino, M. (2010). Measuring social capital as an outcome of service learning. *Innovative Higher Education, 35*(5), 313–328.

Davis, T. (2011). In this age of consumerism, what are the implications of giving students what they want? Have it your way U. In P. Magolda & M. Baxter Magolda (Eds.), *Contested issues in student affairs: Diverse perspectives and respectful dialogue* (pp. 85–96). Sterling: Stylus Publishing.

Deming, D., Goldin, C., & Katz, L. (2011). *The for-profit postsecondary school sector: Nimble critters or agile predators?* (NBER working paper 17710).

Cambridge, MA: National Bureau of Economic Research. Retrieved from http://www.nber.org/papers/w17710

Deming, D., Goldin, C., & Katz, L. (2013). For-profit colleges. *Postsecondary Education in the United States, 23*(1), 137–163.

Dika, S., & Singh, K. (2002). Applications of social capital in education literature: A critical synthesis. *Review of Education Research, 72*(1), 31–60.

Dudwick, N., Kuehnast, K., Jones, V. N., & Woolcock, M. (2006). *Analyzing social capital in context: A guide to using qualitative methods and data*. Washington, DC: World Bank Institute. Retrieved from http://siteresources.worldbank.org/WBI/Resources/Analyzing_Social_Capital_in_Context-FINAL.pdf

Floyd, C. (2007). Know your competitor: Impact of for-profit colleges on the higher education landscape. *New Directions for Higher Education, 140*, 121–129.

Gorski, E. (2010, October 4). For-profit college students most likely defaulters as rates continue upward climb. *Community College Week, 23*(4), 8–9.

Grootaert, C., & van Bastelaer, T. (2001). *Understanding and measuring social capital: A synthesis of findings and recommendations from the social capital initiative* (Social capital initiative working paper No. 24). Washington, DC: The World Bank. Retrieved from http://siteresources.worldbank.org/INTSOCIALCAPITAL/Resources/Social-Capital-Initiative-Working-Paper--Series/SCI-WPS-24.pdf

Grootaert, C., Narayan, D., Jones, V. N., & Woolcock, M. (2004). *Measuring social capital: An integrated questionnaire* (World Bank working paper #18). Washington, DC: The World Bank. Retrieved from http://www-wds.worldbank.org/external/default/WDSContentServer/WDSP/IB/2004/03/23/000160016_20040323162541/Rendered/PDF/281100PAPER0Measuring0social0capital.pdf

Gumport, P. J. (2000). Academic restructuring: Organizational change and institutional imperatives. *Higher Education, 39*(1), 67–91.

Helliwell, J., & Putnam, R. (2007). Education and social capital. *Eastern Economic Journal, 33*(1), 1–19.

Hentschke, G., Lechuga, V., & Tierney, W. (2010). For-profit colleges and universities in a knowledge economy. In G. Hentschke, V. Lechuga, & W. Tierney (Eds.), *For-profit colleges and universities: Their markets, regulation, performance, and place in higher education* (pp. 1–21). Sterling: Stylus Publishing.

Huang, J., van den Brink, H., & Groot, W. (2008). A meta-analysis of the effect of education on social capital. *Economics of Education Review, 28*(4), 454–464.

Johnson, N. (2011). Phoenix rising: Default rates at proprietary institutions of higher education and what can be done to reduce them. *Journal of Law & Education, 40*(2), 225–235.

Kim, Y., & Sax, L. (2011). Are the effects of student–faculty interaction dependent on academic major? An examination using multilevel modeling. *Research in Higher Education, 52*, 589–615.

Kinser, K. (2006). *From main street to wall street: The transformation of for-profit higher education* (Association for the Study of Higher Education (ASHE) Higher Education Report). San Francisco: Jossey-Bass.

Lareau, A. (2011). *Unequal childhoods: Class, race, and family life.* Berkeley: University of California Press.

Lin, N. (2001). *Social capital: A theory of social structure and action.* New York: Cambridge University Press.

Loury, G. (1995). *One by one: From the inside out.* New York: Free Press.

Lu, J., Yang, J., & Yu, C. S. (2013). Is social capital effective for online learning? *Information and Management, 50*(7), 507–522.

Mays, T. (2016). *A multiple case study of social capital development at a public Midwestern University* (Unpublished doctoral dissertation). University of Dayton, Dayton.

Meier, A. (1999). *Social capital and school achievement among adolescents* (Paper No. 99-18). Madison: Center for Demography and Ecology, University of Wisconsin-Madison. Retrieved from http://www.ssc.wisc.edu/cde/cdewp/99-18.pdf

Merriam, S. (2009). *Qualitative research: A guide to design and implementation.* San Francisco: Jossey Bass.

National Center for Education Statistics. (2015a). Table 303.20. Total fall enrollment in all postsecondary institutions participating in Title IV programs and annual percentage change in enrollment, by degree-granting status and control of institution: 1995 through 2014. In U.S. Department of Education, National Center for Education Statistics (Ed.), *Digest of education statistics* (2015 ed.). Retrieved from http://nces.ed.gov/programs/digest/d15/tables/dt15_303.20.asp

National Center for Education Statistics. (2015b). Table 333.10. Revenues of public degree-granting postsecondary institutions, by source of revenue and level of institution: 2007–08 through 2013–14. In U.S. Department of Education, National Center for Education Statistics (Ed.), *Digest of education statistics* (2015 ed.). Retrieved from http://nces.ed.gov/programs/digest/d15/tables/dt15_333.10.asp

National Center for Education Statistics. (2015c). Table 333.50. Total revenue of private nonprofit degree-granting postsecondary institutions, by source of funds and classification of institution: 2013–14. In U.S. Department of Education, National Center for Education Statistics (Ed.), *Digest of education statistics* (2015 ed.). Retrieved from http://nces.ed.gov/programs/digest/d15/tables/dt15_333.50.asp

National Center for Education Statistics. (2015d). Table 333.60. Total revenue of private for-profit degree-granting postsecondary institutions, by source of funds and classification of institution: 2013–14. In U.S. Department of Education, National Center for Education Statistics (Ed.), *Digest of education statistics* (2015 ed.). Retrieved from http://nces.ed.gov/programs/digest/d15/tables/dt15_333.60.asp

National Center for Educational Statistics (NCES). (n.d.). *Integrated postsecondary education data system: Glossary*. U.S. Department of Education. Retrieved from http://nces.ed.gov/ipeds/glossary/index.asp?id=587

Nie, N., Junn, J., & Stehlik-Barry, K. (1996). *Education and democratic citizenship in America*. Chicago: The University of Chicago Press.

Office of Student Financial Assistance Programs. (2011, September 12). *Direct loan and federal family education loan programs: Institutional default rate comparison of FY 2007, 2008, and 2009 cohort default rates*. Department of Education. Retrieved from http://www2.ed.gov/offices/OSFAP/defaultmanagement/instrates.html

Payea, K., Baum, S., & Kurose, C. (2013). *How students and parents pay for college*. New York: College Board Advocacy and Policy Center. Retrieved from http://trends.collegeboard.org/sites/default/files/analysis-brief-how-students-parents-pay-college.pdf

Perna, L. (2005). The benefits of higher education: Sex, racial/ethnic, and socioeconomic group differences. *The Review of Higher Education, 29*(1), 23–52.

Perna, L., & Titus, M. (2005). The relationship between parental involvement as social capital and college enrollment: An examination of racial/ethnic group differences. *The Journal of Higher Education, 76*(5), 485–518.

Persell, C., & Wenglinsky, H. (2004). For-profit post-secondary education and civic engagement. *Higher Education, 47*(3), 337–359.

Putnam, R. (2000). *Bowling alone*. New York: Simon & Schuster.

Ravanera, Z., & Rajulton, F. (2010). Measuring social capital and its differentials by family structures. *Social Indicators Research, 95*(1), 63–89.

Ruch, R. (2003). *Higher ed, inc: The rise of the for-profit university*. Baltimore: Johns Hopkins University Press.

Sandefur, G., Meier, A., & Hernandez, P. (1999). *Families, social capital, and educational continuation* (Paper No. 99-19). Madison: Center for Demography and Ecology, University of Wisconsin-Madison. Retrieved from http://www.ssc.wisc.edu/cde/cdewp/99-19.pdf

Schoenacher, S. R. (2009). Building social capital through online class discussions: A little freedom goes a long way. *Journal of Educational Technology Systems, 37*(3), 291–304.

Sheingold, B. H., Hahn, J. A., & Hofmeyer, A. (2013). Hiding in plain sight: Building community graduate programs. *Contemporary Issues in Education Research, 6*(2), 265–272.

Stone, W. (2001). *Measuring social capital: Toward a theoretically informed measurement framework for researching social capital in family and community life* (Research Report No. 24). Melbourne: Australian Institute of Family Studies. Retrieved from http://www.aifs.gov.au/institute/pubs/RP24.pdf

Swail, W. (2009). *Graduating at-risk students: A cross-sector analysis*. Washington, DC: Imagine America Foundation.

Tierney, W. (2011). Too big to fail: The role of for-profit colleges and universities in American higher education. *Change: The Magazine of Higher Learning, 43*(6), 27–32.

Tierney, W., & Lechuga, V. (2010). Differences in academic work at traditional and for-profit postsecondary institutions: Policy implications for academic freedom. In G. Hentschke, V. Lechuga, & W. Tierney (Eds.), *For-profit colleges and universities: Their markets, regulation, performance, and place in higher education* (pp. 1–21). Sterling: Stylus Publishing.

United States Congress Senate Committee of Health, Education, Labor and Pensions. (2012). *For profit higher education: the failure to safeguard the federal investment and ensure student success* (Serial No. 112-37). Retrieved from http://www.gpo.gov/fdsys/browse/committeecong.action?collection=CPRT&committee=health&chamber=senate&congressplus=112&ycord=0

Walpole, M. (2003). Socioeconomic status and college: How SES affects college experiences and outcomes. *The Review of Higher Education, 27*(1), 45–73.

Woolcock, M. (1998). Social capital and economic development: Toward a theoretical synthesis and policy framework. *Theory and Society, 27*(2), 151–208.

Woolcock, M. (2002). Social capital in theory and practice: Reducing poverty by building partnerships between states, markets, and society. In *Social capital and poverty reduction: Which role for the civil society organizations and the state?* (pp. 20–44). United Nations Education, Scientific and Cultural Organization. Retrieved from http://www.unesco.org/most/soc_cap_symp.pdf

Woolcock, M., & Narayan, D. (2000). Social capital: Implications for development theory, research, and policy. *The World Bank Research Observer, 15*(2), 225–249.

Woolcock, M., & Sweetser, A. (2002). Social capital: The bonds that connect. *ADB Review, 34*(2), 1–26. Retrieved from http://web.archive.org/web/20100420121848/http://www.adb.org/Documents/Periodicals/ADB_Review/2002/vol34_2/social_capital.asp

Yeoman, B. (2011). The high rise of for-profit colleges. *Academe, 97*(3). Retrieved from http://www.aaup.org/AAUP/pubsres/academe/2011/MJ/Feat/yeom.htm

Stratification and the Public Good: The Changing Ideology of Higher Education

Gaye Tuchman

William G. Tierney has suggested, "[T]he definition of the 'public good' in general, and with regard to higher education in particular, is a protean notion than changes over time and has multiple facets to it. What the country expected of post-secondary education in the late nineteenth-century when largely one class of people received a degree is different from what we ought to expect from the kind of country we inhabit in the twenty-first century" (2010: 186).

The contemporary definition of racial, ethnic, and class diversity is indeed different than that of the late nineteenth-century. Then people identified what today we call ethnic groups as races; their distinctions within and among social classes also diverged from ours. Yet, by late nineteenth-century criteria—even by twentieth-century standards—higher education

Identifying footnote: I appreciate the help of Will Baker, Executive Director of New Haven's The [Mechanics] Institute Library, who located documents for me and showed me the library's records. I enjoyed very helpful conversations and emails with Will Baker, Tressie McMillan Cottom, Leigh Dale, Andrew Deener, and Bandana Purkayastha.

G. Tuchman (✉)
Department of Sociology, University of Connecticut, Storrs, CT 06269, USA
e-mail: gaye.tuchman@uconn.edu

T. McMillan Cottom, W.A. Darity, Jr. (eds.), *For-Profit Universities*,
DOI 10.1007/978-3-319-47187-7_6

was expanding and becoming more diverse. Then, as now, elite groups claimed that expanding educational opportunities gave members of the working-class and also of some racial/ethnic groups a measure of upward mobility; however, the schools designed for them also functioned as agents of social control. As Collins (1979) has argued, the historical expansion of education can be explained not as a technical response to the need for skilled labor, but as a bureaucratic response to cultural conflict—first, from the working classes, later from immigrants and women and also from African Americans. Educational stratification assuages demand from lower status groups for "access" while protecting the status of elite education.

In her introduction to this volume, Tressie McMillan Cottom notes that for-profit colleges and universities provide an apt contemporary example of what Collins (1979) discussed. The fastest growing segment of the tertiary educational sector, for-profit institutions provide (mostly occupational) training to roughly ten percent of the students enrolled in U.S. colleges. They also graduate a higher percentage of African Americans than any other higher-education sector. Additionally, they have the highest default-rate on student-loans.

I discuss two very different nineteenth-century institutions, mechanics institutes and historically black colleges and universities, to demonstrate how expanding educational opportunities, such as those supposedly provided by the for-profit industry, can be used as a mechanism of social control. Then as now, the United States was undergoing profound social change. The nineteenth-century experienced a significant shift from an agricultural to an industrial economy; it coincided with first wave of immigration. Today we have been moving from an industrial to a so-called knowledge economy and are experiencing a second wave of immigration. The students at the nineteenth-century mechanics institutes were white and from the elite sectors of the working class. Those at the nineteenth-century HBCUs were African-Americans who had been agricultural workers (often slaves) and were fiercely segregated from white industrial workers. They were said to form an elite group within the black segment of the American caste system.

As other essays in this volume note, the students attending for-profit schools today are anything but elite. The typical for-profit student in the United States is likely black or Latina and attending college since taking a multi-year break after high school. She—most likely she—has adult responsibilities: she may be a parent or responsible for a family; she often works and is juggling competing social roles. After graduation, she is likely to find a racially-typed and gender-typed job that qualifies her as a marginal member of the lower-middle class who is indebted by student loans.

I draw on both primary data and secondary sources about mechanics institutes, which were founded throughout the English speaking world from roughly 1825 through 1850, and also studies about the historically black colleges and universities (HBCUs) created by the 1890 Morrill Act. (Other HBCUs were established before that act.) Mechanics institutes were a form of further education said to have anticipated and encouraged the establishment of public schools. They spread rapidly in the early nineteenth-century, much as for-profit colleges have grown exponentially since the 1990s. Although the nineteenth-century terms differ from those used today, both may be said to have "brought science to the service of industry, answered the demand for technical education from the superior artisan and operative, performed important economic functions in an industrializing society, and [to have been]...the forerunners of the modern technological university" (Shapin and Barnes 1977).

However, the elite men who founded the British institutions and supported the American ones were not interested in promulgating social equality. Instead they seemed to argue that education enabled fractions of the "agricultural and industrial classes" to improve their work-skills and so their lives. As a result, they believed, these non-elite groups would strengthen the national economy, encourage social stability and so serve the social good. In the case of the mechanics institutes, "those who were interested in stabilizing their middle-class authority worked to stabilize class tensions by promoting a series of conceptual frameworks that effectively undermined oppositional notions of class" (Rice 2004: 146). I will suggest that when the Morrill Act of 1890 enabled the establishment of (more) HBCUs, the funders and sometimes the founders of those institutions were also engaged in social control. The HBCUs favored a particular model of racial stratification to control the upward mobility of African Americans.

Even as the spokespeople for the for-profit educational industry insist that they help their students to get better jobs and so to experience some social mobility, that industry reinforces contemporary class, race, and gender distinctions. Indeed, in the cases of the for-profit education industry and the nineteenth-century mechanics institutes and HBCUs, elites speak of social control as a public good.

What Is a Public Good?

Tierney (2010) has reminded us that the definition of a public good has varied historically. In the nineteenth-century, educators spoke of a public good as a phenomenon—procedure, practice, or entity—that contributed to the welfare of the collectivity.[1] Some aspects of that welfare appear to have been ineffable. For instance, education was said to increase the likelihood of upright behavior and decrease the probability of drunkenness and other forms of turpitude. Because it encouraged adherence to morality, education was said to be a public good.

Today educators and researchers are more likely to use a definition of the public good that is based in the emphasis of twentieth-century economics on individuals, markets, and payment s. That notion tends to exclude ideas—the ineffable. Rather, a public good is said to have three characteristics.[2]

1. It involves *nonexcludabiity*—nonpayers cannot be excluded from participation in a public good, such as a July 4th fireworks display;
2. It entails *nonrivalrous consumption*—because it is inefficient or impossible to exclude some people by holding it in a private meadow, even nonpayers could watch the show without increasing the show's cost or diminishing anyone else's enjoyment; and,
3. It involves *externalities*—one person's actions affect another person's well-being and the relevant costs and benefits are not reflected in market prices, as occurs when my neighbors benefit from my cleaning up my yard.

Fox Garrity explains that this definition emphasizes intent, because it discriminates between an externality that is created incidentally and one that is produced on purpose: "A public externality that results from the creation of a private good is not the same as a truly public good. For example the private good of being educated and being able to follow a scientific argument might lead to the public externality of a society that has some people who are able to follow that argument which might lead to closer examination of important issues in society. This is not the same as a truly public good such as space for debate or open access research meant to benefit society at large" (personal communication, email 10/04/2012).

However, many contemporary researchers abjure definitions of the public good as an externality. Discussing not-for-profit higher education, they decry the current trend to "replac[e] *value* in the economic sense for *values* as a moral compass" (Pusser et al. 2012: 6). Gumport (2000: 70) fears that "technical market imperatives [are running] wild, urging colleges and universities to adapt to short-term market demands, to redeploy resources (which include people; i.e. faculty), in an effort to reposition themselves within an increasingly competitive context. " And Kezar argues, "For much of the last hundred years, higher education in the United States can be seen as mirroring the communitarian belief system with its emphasis on such goals as developing leaders, serving the needs of regional and local communities, or acting as a social critic" (2004: 435), but in a "disturbing trend.... [t[he collective or public good, a historically important component of the charter between higher education and society, is being compromised" (ibid.: 429).

In their discussions, Gumport (2000), Kezar (2004), and Pusser et al. (2012) were criticizing not-for-profit higher education—traditional colleges and universities which, as defined by the U.S. tax code, are distinguished by their eleemosynary or charitable tradition (see Kinser 2006). Despite their tax status, they all argue, not-for-profit tertiary education is becoming increasingly corporatized. Their critical comments are particularly applicable to the for-profit industry, which has the explicit intent to increasing profits from quarter to quarter (Lee 2012).

The scholarly and popular literatures are blunt: In the United States of the 1990s and still today, the more tax monies became available to students in the form of loans, the more for-profit corporations sought to suck up the funds of their students, many of whom qualified for those loans (Cellini and Goldin 2012). These students are more likely than students in not-for-profit colleges to be members of racial minorities, more likely to be women, more likely to be older than traditional college students, more likely to drop out, and most likely to default on their loans. Equally blunt is the for-profits' abandonment of research, aspects of academic freedom (including tenure) and shared governance. The education literature reminds that these last research, academic freedom and shared governance highlight the activities of the faculty; they are said to be faculty-oriented.[3] They are also said to be irrelevant to for-profit education, which emphasizes "practical knowledge" that meets employers' needs and so enables graduates and certificate holders to get a job. Ironically, the literature identifies meeting employers' needs as a student-orientation. This approach to practical knowledge is the obverse of the philosophy practiced by the early nineteenth-century mechanics institutes, which assumed that their students should know the theoretical knowledge associated with the occupational skills they had mastered.

The Mechanics' Institutes

At the turn of the nineteenth-century and into the Victorian era, some wealthy Whigs sought to build national prosperity by founding mechanics' institutes to educate some elite sectors of the new working-classes. The first mechanics' Institute was founded in Edinburgh, Scotland in 1821. Other schools rapidly followed. Indeed, the schools were so popular that they spread from Scotland to the rest of Great Britain, to Canada and the United States, and somewhat later to such outposts as Australia and New Zealand. The founders intended the mechanics' institutes to serve "artisans," the term then applied to *elite* members of the working class. These included such skilled workers as journeymen, apprentices in such trades as printing and carriage-making, other skilled makers of things, and even physicians (see Shapin and Barnes 1977; Firth 2005; Rice 2000; Rice 2004). I will present data, some primary, most secondary, about some of the institutes in Britain and the United States.

By stressing national interests, those who founded the mechanics institutes were emphasizing the public good. Historians generally agree that the institutions were supposed to provide adult education in technical subjects associated with the skills of the artisans who wishes to join the institute. Historians also agree that these institutes were a response to galloping social change.

To identify the early nineteenth-century in Britain and the United States as a time of intense social change is to engage in vast understatement. It was an era of conflict between agriculture and industry, of such geographic movement from country to city that the literacy rate in England actually decreased, of intense upward and downward class mobility, of demographic transformation, and of dismal conditions for the poor. Ideologically, in England "the emerging discipline of political economy challenged an older discourse concerned with the preservation of a hierarchical socio-economic order" (Firth 2005). The people who challenged the older, agricultural order also tended to favor the establishment of mechanics institutes.

The political lines in England were pretty clear. Whigs, including Dissenters and Radical, and Tories debated the institutional structures appropriate as that once-agricultural nation experienced extensive demographic transformation. Whigs, who were pro-industry and the new factory economy, tended to favor the mechanics' institutes and to oppose the corn laws that had been designed to protect English and Irish agriculture by imposing high import duties on grains. Tories held the obverse political positions.

There was debate in the United States, too, but it was not as "clean;" that is, questions about social class, education, industry and agriculture were conflated with issues of race. For instance, in the 1830s through the 1850s, most of the civic leaders of New Haven, Connecticut supported the city's mechanics institute, but favored slavery, a practice associated with the agricultural South to which industrial New Haven had close economic ties. (Race was not implicated in the British debate, because it had exported colonists and imperialists to other continents rather than importing large numbers of their inhabitants as slaves.) Also, in the United States working-men rather than industrialists tended to found the institutes (Rice 2000, 2004; Borden 1904; Reinhardt 2005). However, within a decade of their establishment, members of the local elite usually dominated the membership and also served as the organizations' directors and officers. Within 15 to 20 years, the institutes founded to educate mechanics were dominated by the middle-classes and fewer artisans attended lectures and other events.

By subscribing for a small fee, members supported these institutions, which built libraries, held classes, and provided some recreation. A subscription was not cheap. Founded in 1854 after the inflationary California Gold Rush by such skilled workers as a stonemason, a contract carpenter, a blacksmith and the owner of a sawmill, the San Francisco Mechanics Institute was a late-comer to this adult-education movement, but its fees seem typical of the time: the "$5 initiation fee and the $12 yearly dues struck many San Franciscans as insurmountably high (Reinhardt 2005: 7).[4] Because members initially supported these enrichment activities, the mechanics' institutes are often associated with self-help (*e.g.* Briggs 2011). Some historians have considered mechanics institutes to be a success, because they encouraged self-help through education (*loc. cit.*). Others have argued that they are associated with the development of the ideologies that supported such publicly-funded schools. Although some of the institutes evolved into such institutions as public libraries, ultimately, other researchers have considered them to be a failure. Members of the blue-collar elite avoided them when middle-class office-workers embraced the lectures and classes. David Roh (2006) explained, "Despite its initial popularity, the Mechanics' Institute largely failed to capture the hearts and minds of the working class, and soon found that its facilities, lectures, and advanced classes appealed more to the bourgeoisie than the proletariat." The lower classes had generally left school by age 12; "they had more need of remedial educations than lectures on abstract theories." They were weary from a day of work. "The middle class simply took the Institutes over, coloring their purpose and character to the point that the working class had nothing to do with them." Although a few institutes survived the mid-nineteenth century, "many were converted into libraries, schools, intellectual recreation centers (i.e., chess clubs), and even cinema houses. (Roh 2006)."

In England, a few proponents of the mechanics institutes believed in education for education's sake. However, most advocates of the institutes emphasized the public good. In terms of current economists' criteria of public good, they fulfilled the criterion of intentionality. In part, they did so by advocating the promotion of prosperity and the intensification of social control. Opponents believed that further education was wasted on the working classes, since the welfare of the nation would trickle down from the wealthy to the lower classes. As the historical literature testifies, "[p]romoters of the Mechanics' Institutes believed that only education that increased the skill and productivity of [individual] workers could contribute to the twin goals of national prosperity and individual well-being." It would benefit the nation by bringing "science to the service of industry" (Shapin and Barnes 1977: 32). Rather than prosperity trickling down from the wealthy to the middle-classes and the poor, as Tories believed, Whigs felt that education would enable prosperity to spread from the middle. Doing so, it would serve the cause of the wealthy: "The master would be provided with a better mansion and the genuine nobleman with a palace" (Walker 1825: 22 quoted in Firth 2005: 9).

In a classic work, Richard Altick (1957) pointed out that members of both British schools of thoughts agreed that further education for workers could also be a means of social control. Both sets of proponents argued that education teaches moral restraint. "Like religion, it is a force for teaching the laborer 'ways of inspecting, ordering and evaluating his desires'" (Firth 2005: 10; cf. Shapin and Barnes 1977). Some industrialists also argued that the mechanics institutes would discourage drinking and carousing by providing morally sound alternatives, such as attending lectures and classes and using a library after work. Also, some of them maintained, education had political consequences: it might even help "safeguard working men from the deceptions of those who advocated collective action in strikes and civil disobedience as the most effective way to increase wages" (Brougham quoted in Firth 2005: 10). A laborer who felt that education offered him advancement and so a better future was a man who would comply with his employers' wishes.

It is noteworthy that these elite proponents of education for the working class did not regard the mechanics as their equals. They did not assume that the worth of a person is measured by character as opposed to earnings. Rather, their attitude toward laborers was indicated by the name of an 1816 British parliamentary committee, chaired by a proponent of the mechanics' institutes. It was "The Select Committee for the Education of the Lower Orders." In sum, even proponents of educating elite laborers believed that the mechanics institutes would help individual men to "advance" and that further education for these men would serve industry, the socio-economic elite, and the nation.

In the United States, the debate about education for workers used somewhat different terms. They revolved around the need to coordinate "head" and "hand," respectively represented by managers and mechanics (Rice 2004). American proponents argued that by educating skilled workers, the institutes would ward off class conflict, even though mechanization had decreased the wages of many skilled workers and many workers understood that "the possibility of moving up or making a living...[was] becoming undone" (ibid.: 6). Indeed, some historians argue that the American mechanics' institutes helped to smooth over the class conflicts that were to become endemic in nineteenth-century Europe.

In both countries, the institutes served several classes of white men—from apprentices and journeymen to members of the local elite. (At the time, the term "white" excluded such groups as the Irish Catholics who are today identified as members of a so-called white race.) Although women might attend lectures at some mechanics' institutes (Kreppel 2004) and at least one offered special courses for women,[5] women could not join. In the United States, neither could immigrants or African-Americans.

Consider the New Haven Institute. In 1826, eight young working men had founded that institute's as an educational society dedicated to the "intellectual and moral improvement of its members" through a shared book collection and mutual encouragement in writing and speech. From the mid-1830s through the Civil War, governed by members of the city's elite, the organization flourished as the democratic heart of intellectual life in New Haven. According to Will Baker (the librarian and executive director of the Institute Library in a personal communication May,

2013), in the nineteenth-century almost all of the members of the New Haven Young Men's Institute had English-sounding names. Although New Haven was an industrial city that attracted immigrants, Irish and Italian names did not begin to appear on the membership roles until after World War II.

In the United States, the politics and ideologies of the mechanics' institutes also captured the disputes among local elites. Again New Haven serves as a good example. Although New Haven was a northern city, its prosperity was tied to the South. It had large business interests there. The original home of Eli Whitney's cotton-gin factory (out-of-business in 1797), the location of his invention of cotton mills and his advocacy of interchangeable parts, as well as a leader in the production of carriages, guns, and clocks, New Haven had significant business ties to the south. Most members of New Haven's political elite favored slavery. Even those who were abolitionists did not claim that the races were equal. "Though black emancipation was in the realm of understanding, black equality simply was not" (Roper n.d.g.).[6] As William Alanson Borden the institute historian in 1904 explained, just before the Civil War, when speakers included men who made radical statements about the need to end slavery,

> A little friction was developed over some of the lecturers. New Haven was rather conservative in its religion and it had large business interests in the South. A decided exception was taken to some of the utterances of Theodore Parker, Archbishop Hughes, George B. Cheever, Henry Ward Beecher, and Wendell Phillips. After many meetings of the directors and much discussion, a compromise was affected and the names of Wendell Phillips and Theodore Parker were dropped from the list of lecturers and goodfellowship [sic] was restored (Borden 1904).

In sum, the local elites who controlled the mechanics' institutes were interested in promoting political harmony and preventing conflicts (including arguments relating to race and class) among white men. However, although the institutes' memberships came to be dominated by middle-class and elite white men, one could argue that participants were more diverse than, say, the young elite men who attended the many local denominational colleges founded throughout the United States in the early nineteenth-century—even though those colleges exhibited significant regional variation. One might view both the mechanics' institutes and the denominational colleges as early expressions of class stratification among white Americans. With the noteworthy exception of a few institutions, they not only promoted racial and gender segregation, but also promoted class stratification among white students.

Different sorts of people were to receive different sorts of education. By the last quarter of the nineteenth-century, when many mechanics institutes had become public libraries, "[t]he typical college of the period, because of its relatively isolated, local support, and limited means, tended to serve several functions, from preparatory education through classical and commercial courses" (Curran 2003 reviewing Geiger 2000). By the late nineteenth-century, higher education was a clearly stratified field, boasting both public and private not-for-profit colleges, colleges for men, for women, for African Americans, even some appealing to local ethnic groups, as well as for-profit establishments, such as trade schools. Contrary to Tierney's suggestion, throughout the nineteenth-century, classroom education beyond high school appears to have become more, not less diverse.

Educating Black Americans

In the nineteenth-century United States, African American students were simply others. In the north as in the south, few people thought that both black and white students were entitled to equal education. Compared to discussions of the Mechanics' Institutes, which had been designed to serve men, the debate about educating black Americans was gender-neutral, although in practice institutions intended for black Americans were more likely to have men than women as students.

Just as debates about the Mechanics Institutes underscored how upper-class men viewed the emerging working-class elite, so too the views of prosperous whites' dominated the American discourse about further education for black Americans. Quite simply, white legislators approved the bill that founded most historically black colleges and universities (HBCUs) and whites hogged the power and resources necessary to found and fund key institutions for black Americans. Black Americans made crucial contributions, but both before and after the Civil War, white people exercised power over the education of black Americans.[7]

Tuskegee University is a familiar example. Founded as the Tuskegee Institute by Booker T. Washington in 1881, its early history is riddled with the power exercised by whites. As reported on the Tuskegee University web site (Tuskagee University n.d.g.), a white politician, W. F. Foster, convinced the Alabama legislature to provide $2000 annually to pay teachers' salaries at a school for African Americans that was to be founded. These funds to establish the school as part of a deal Foster had made with Lewis Adams, a former slave and a black community leader. (In exchange for the school, Adams convinced members of the black community to reelect Foster to the state senate.) After consulting General Samuel Chapman Armstrong, the founder principal of the Hampton Institute, the white men who served as Tuskegee's first trustees hired Booker T. Washington as Tuskagee's first principal. Armstrong had advised them that he did not know of a qualified white candidate for the job, "but if they would be willing to take a coloured man, he had one whom he could recommend (Washington 2004: 85):" Booker T. Washington. As principal, Washington had to secure funds to buy land for the school and to build classrooms and dormitories. Members of the local black and white communities contributed, but when their donations could not suffice, he and his wife turned to raising money from northern white philanthropists .

In the South, debates about the Mechanics Institutes had centered on the bumpy transition from an agricultural to an industrial society. For instance, the Little Rock Mechanics Institute, founded in 1845 advocated free labor—for whites. Before the civil war, Its members "simply insisted that those with African blood could never possess the knowledge, skill, or work ethic necessary truly to replace white mechanics and artisans" (Pierce 2008: 222). After the war, discussion centered on maintaining elite artisanal jobs for white men and keeping those jobs closed to ex-slaves.

Arguments about educating black Americans concerned the centrality of agricultural workers to the South's economy, as Booker T. Washington documented in his autobiography. He explained that some whites feared that education would prompt black people to migrate to cities and so would have a negative impact on the agriculture-based Southern economy: "Some had the feeling that in proportion as the Negro received education, in the same proportion would his value decrease as an economic factor in the state. These people feared the result of education would be that the Negroes would leave the farms, and that it would be difficult to secure them for domestic service" (Washington 2004: 67.)

Such people, and we suspect others, had a visual image of an educated black men. "The white people who questioned the wisdom of starting this new school had in their minds pictures of what was called an educated Negro, with a high hat, imitation gold eye-glasses, a showy walking-stick, kid gloves, fancy boots, and what not--in a word, a man who was determined to live by his wits. It was difficult for these people to see how education would produce any other kind of a coloured man" (ibid.: 68)[8]

As well known, Washington believed that the Tuskegee Institute should devote itself to training students to do skilled labor. (He did not discuss them as competition for the members of mechanics institutes.) In his autobiography, he highlights such accomplishments as developing new agricultural practices and making bricks.[9] Washington was not alone in emphasizing the importance of training students to enter and to survive in the labor force. Improving the nation's economic well-being through college-level vocational training is, of course, the thrust of the 1862 Morrill Act, which established the land-grant universities, and the 1890 act which affirmed the importance of agriculture.

However, there are many ways to think about both agricultural and industrial education. W. E. B. DuBois (1903) suggested one of them when he spoke about educating the "talented tenth"—"the best of the race" who would serve as "the social leadership of the people." DuBois' vision of education went well beyond inculcating artisanal skills. He wrote: "If we make technical skill the object of education, we may possess artisans but not in nature men. Men we shall have only as we make manhood the object of the work of the schools—intelligence, broad sympathy, knowledge of the world that was and is, and of the relation of men to it—this is the curriculum of that Higher Education that must underlie true life." To DuBois, "On this is the foundation we may build bread winning, skill of hand and quickness of brain, with never a fear lest the child and man mistake the means of living for the object of life."

DuBois' statement is *not* a rejection of education as preparation for the labor force, but white philanthropists preferred to fund Booker T. Washington's vision than DuBois' more philosophic version. And they were certainly opposed to DuBois' notion that college should be free. (DuBois had written, "Negro schools should be a public burden, since they are a public benefit." They serve the public by increasing the economic productivity of blacks and so the taxes of towns, state and nation.) Although W. E. B. DuBois and Booker T. Washington disagreed with one another about the sort of education suitable for black Americans, each intended the education of black women and men to result in a public good. In both the philosophic terms popular in the nineteenth-century and the economic concepts of the twenty-first century, each man felt that education helped individuals, but was justified by its contribution to the collectivity. Indeed, they might have stressed education for blacks as a public good that aided whites as a group as well as blacks as a group—as a collective benefit—because they were aware that most white people did not care a fig about the uses of education for individual African Americans. Washington believed: "Any movement for the elevation of the southern Negro in order to be successful must have to a certain extent the cooperation of the southern whites. They control government and own the property—whatever benefits the black man benefits the white man" (Hawkins 1974 quoted in Lovett 2011: 37).

Conclusion

I have been telling a story about how in nineteenth-century America the stratification of further education was associated with intersectionality—the multi-dimensional stratification of race, class, and gender. (Gender was implicated in the mechanics' institutes assumption that women should not be members and in the disproportionate attendance of black men at the HBCUs.) The two sorts of workers' education that I have discussed, the mechanics institutes and the HBCUs, served very different students. The mechanics' institutes offered academic subjects to skilled (mostly) male workers. "The nineteenth-century curricula for HBCUs mostly reflected the religious and educational philosophy of Northern missionaries: religion, moral living, working with the hands, liberal arts, civic education, and loyalty to America" (Lovett 2011: 22). Obviously, although the HBCUs taught foreign languages, history, mathematics and the sciences, their curricula were not the educational equivalent to those offered in the Ivy League colleges, the denominational liberal arts colleges, or some of the programs found at other public colleges and universities. By and large, they were to prepare black students to work in and for their own communities. Even when colleges offered higher education for white ethnic groups, as was the case of the City College of New York, the intent of civic leaders was to transform the children of immigrants into good Americans and to place them in useful semi-professional jobs such as teaching where they might serve immigrant groups (Gorelick 1982).

Like these nineteenth-century institutions, the contemporary for-profit colleges are intended for adults. More important, these colleges and universities also maintain the stratification of higher education. Simply put, the people who attend them have different social characteristics than students at not-for-profit colleges (Chung 2012; cf. Cottom). As the character of labor force has changed—more women are in the labor force than men—

and the type of jobs for which the for-profit colleges train their students are, most often, feminized. Tthe profile of "the student" has changed as well. Unlike the nineteenth and twentieth centuries, when most colleges served men, contemporary for-profit schools tend to focus on working-class minority women, especially African American and Latino women.[10]

Additionally, whether by intention or not, the corporations that own them use education as a profitable form of social control: they train students for specific jobs and assume that as technological developments made their skills obsolete, students can simply return for more training (and pay for it). The for-profit institutions do not develop what DuBois (1903) had called "intelligence, broad sympathy, knowledge of the world that was and is, and of the relation of men to it." The focus of the for-profits remains on women, the working class or poor, and racial minorities, especially the educational loans for which they qualify.

To be sure, proponents of for-profit education do not speak of the "lower orders," although higher education is clearly stratified by social class. Instead, they emphasis that for-profit education is open to everybody and that increasing the availability of higher education will increase the competitiveness of American corporations in the global economy. Although a rich white man is as free to enroll in a for-profit university as is an economically struggling black woman, the for-profits' advertisements address the working class and feature a disproportionate number of people of color.

It is important to emphasize that today's for-profit colleges are more expensive than public colleges; both students who drop-out and students who graduate wind up in more debt than when they started. As well documented in such countries as Chile (Bernasconi 2012, Cabalin 2012), where for-profit educational institutions have become ever more important and students have protested the impact of loans on their lives, the corporations that own the schools are those most likely to gain economically and socially. These schools emphasize individual good and claim it is the "public good." Their notions and assumptions are very different from DuBois' concept of individual good. Their idea of the individual good includes mounting student debt and the short term possibility of access to jobs; the notion of the public good is restricted to the good of the owners and shareholders and rejects the idea that the public good includes nonmaterial gains. Thus contemporary for- profit education continues to sustain the boundaries of race, class and gender even as it presents itself as the institution that helps individuals overcome 'their race, class and gender disadvantage.' This new chapter in for-profit education creates new configurations of social divisions. At the turn of the twentieth century, higher education helped to mold what has been called the "business class." As Christopher Jencks and David Riesman explained, (2002) the late nineteenth-century professionalization of academia introduced a common culture to what had once been a fragmented mélange of religious schools, liberal arts colleges, land grant universities, and institutions that served different local elites. Because of the "professionalization of the academy," they argue, colleges "played as large a role in providing the young with specialized job skills.... [They] provide[d] firms with managers who shared a common culture." They stress: "*A national economy needs entrepreneurs and managers who have a fair amount in common. Without a common culture, they cannot anticipate one another's reactions or develop the kind of trust that makes cooperation possible*" (Jencks 2002: viii and ix, emphasis added). Jencks and Riesman are implying that the college curriculum served the public good by creating a new managerial class. That new managerial class confounded race and class, for African Americans and members of despised ethnic groups were segregated and trained to serve their own communities.

Higher education still confounds race and class, but in a different way. In the nineteenth-century, there were explicit provisions about race. The pre- and post-Civil War mechanics' institutes were openly for whites only. The 1890 bill establishing black land-grant colleges addressed the south when it required each state to show that race was not an admissions criterion or else to designate a separate land-grant institution for persons of color. Today, segregation is not as explicit. Such elite not-for-profit private universities as Harvard admit people of color—though they are disproportionately either immigrants, the children of immigrants, or "to a lesser extent, children of biracial couples marriages...[O]nly about a third of the [black] students were from families in which all four grandparents were born in this country" (Rimer and Arenson 2004). In other words, elite colleges maintain class distinctions in the guise of racial inclusion.[11]

Because the new ideology of higher-education emphasizes the individual good without working toward racial equality, it perpetuates the stratification of racialized ethnicity and so harms the public good. As the American class system shifts, as the rich get richer and everyone else get a smaller piece of the pie, the stratification of higher education continues to confound race and class. Claiming to advocate for disadvantaged individuals, the proponents of for-profit higher education simultaneously serve the corporate good.

Notes

1. Kezar (2004) speaks of this as communitarianism.
2. I draw heavily on the argument of Tyler Cowan (2010), http://www.econlib.org/library/Enc1/PublicGoodsandExternalities.html.
3. On faculty governance at for-profits, see Tierney and Hentschke (2007).
4. In contrast, according to The September 4, 1832 *Connecticut Journal*, at the New Haven Young Mechanics Institute (1832), "The payment of 25 cents monthly by persons, over eighteen years of age, and 18 cents by those younger, shall constitute membership... The executive committee shall have charges of all the property of the Institute, defray necessary expenses, and appropriate the surplus of funds for procuring teachers, (if practicable) books, apparatus for illustrating the sciences, &c."
5. In the 1830s, the New Haven Young Men's Institute offered a course in chemistry for women. One can interpret this series of classes as providing a theoretical background for cooking and baking.
6. Roper (n.d.g.) used these words to characterize disputes in the northern Connecticut town of Canterbury, where in 1833 Prudence Crandall was arrested for permitting an African-American girl to attend the school that she had founded to serve the daughters of the town's local (white) elite. Four weeks before the arrest, the Connecticut legislature had passed a statute forbidding integrated schools. After the trial resulted in a hung jury, white citizens harassed the Crandall family, the students, and the school; they attempted to set the school on fire and a group of white citizens eventually attacked the building with iron bars and clubs.
7. Three of the 131 HBCUs that exist today were founded in northern states before the Civil War. In 1909, prosperous white men were still supporting HBCUs, but also founded the National Association for Colored People.
8. There is, of course, a contemporary version of this image.
9. After several failed attempts at brickmaking, Washington "secured" fifteen dollars to buy a kiln that enabled the Tuskegee students to produce bricks of such fine quality that "[m]any white people who had had no contact with the school, and perhaps no sympathy with it, came to us to buy bricks because they found out that ours were good bricks. They discovered that we were supplying a real want in the community. The making of these bricks caused many of the white residents of the neighbourhood to begin to feel that the education of the Negro was not making him worthless (Washington 2004: 83)."
10. In most industrial countries, women are more likely to enroll in and graduate from college, partly because men without a degree have more occupational (and financial) opportunities (Dwyer et al. 2013). However the enrollment at for-profit colleges is even more skewed toward women.

11. Even classic statements about the transition from elite to mass and then to universal education do not address this pattern. See, for example, Trow (1974).

References

Altick, R. (1957). *The English common reader: A social history of the mass reading public.* Chicago: University of Chicago Press.

Baker, W. (2013, May 2). Personal communication.

Bernasconi, A. (2012, September 10). *The profit motive in higher education.* Insidehighereducation.com. http://www.insidehighered.com/blogs/world-view/andr%C3%A9s-bernasconi-profit-motive-higher-education

Borden, W. A. (1904, October 6). An historical sketch of the New Haven Young Men's Institute Delivered at the Seventy-Ninth Annual Meeting of the Association. Pdf. Property of The Institute Library, New Haven.

Briggs, A. (2011). Forward to the second mechanics' worldwide conference (pp. v, vi). In Bronwyn Lowden, compiler. 2011. Self-Help: Mechanics' worldwide conference, 2009. Donvale: Lowden Publishing Co.

Brougham, H. (1825). *Practical observations upon the education of the people.* London.

Cabalin, C. (2012). Neoliberal Education and Student Movements in Chile: Inequalities and malaise. *Policy Futures in Education, 10*(2).

Cellini, S. R., & Goldin, C. (2012). *Does federal student aid raise tuition: New evidence on for-profit colleges.* (Working Paper 17827). Washington, DC: National Bureau of Economic Research. Cottom, Tressie McMillan.

Chung, A. S. (2012). Choice of for-profit college. *Economics of Education Review, 31*(6), 1084–1101.

Collins, R. (1979). *The credential society: An historical sociology of education and stratification.* New York: Academic Press.

Cowan, T. (2010). Public goods and externalities. In D. R. Henderson (Ed.), *The concise encyclopedia of economics.* http://www.econlib.org/library/Enc1/PublicGoodsandExternalities.html. Downloaded 17 July 2012.

Curran, R. E. (2003). A New history of higher education in nineteenth century America: A Prolegomenon. http://www.h-net.org/reviews/showrev.php?id=7413. Downloaded 10 May 2013.

DuBois, W. E. B. (1903). "The Talented Tenth," from *The Negro problem: A series of articles by representative Negroes of to-day.* New York. http://www.yale.edu/glc/archive/1148.htm. Downloaded 24 July 2013.

Dwyer, R. E., Hodson, R., & McCloud, L. (2013). Gender, debt, and dropping out of College. *Gender & Society, 27, 30–55.*

Firth, A. (2005). "Culture and wealth creation: Mechanics' Institutes and the emergence of political economy in early nineteenth-century Britain." *History of*

Intellectual Culture 5 (1). http://www.ucalgary.ca/hic. Downloaded 10 Sept 2012.

Garrity, B. F. (2012, October 4). Personal communication, email.

Geiger, R. L. (Ed.). (2000). *The American College in the Nineteenth Century, Vanderbilt Issues in Higher Education*. Nashville: Vanderbilt University Press.

Gorelick, S. (1982). *City College and the Jewish poor: Education in New York, 1880–1924*. New York: Schocken Books.

Gumport, P. J. (2000). Academic restructuring: Institutional change and organizational imperatives. *Higher Education, 39*, 67–91.

Hawkins, H. (1974). *Booker T. Washington and his critics*. Lexington: Mass D.C. Heath and Co.

Jencks, C. (2002). Introduction. In D. Riesman & C. Jencks (Eds.), *The academic revolution*. Transaction Books.

Kezar, A. J. (2004). Obtaining Integrity? Reviewing and examining the charter between higher education and society. *The Review of Higher Education, 27*(4), 429–459.

Kinser, K. (2006). *From Main Street to Wall Street: The transformation of for-profit higher education: ASHE Higher Education Report* (Vol. 31 (5)). New York: Wiley Publishing.

Lee, S. (2012, August 9). The for-profit education industry, by the numbers. *ProPublica*. http://www.propublica.org/article/the-for-profit-higher-education-industry-by-the-numbers. Downloaded 24 July 2013.

Lovett, B. L. (2011). *America's historically black colleges and universities: A narrative history, 1837–2009*. Macon: Mercer University Press.

Pierce, M. (2008). The mechanics of Little Rock: Free labor ideas in antebellum Arkansas, 1845–1861. *Arkansas Historical Quarterly, LXVII* (Autumn): 221–244.

Pusser, B., Kempner, K., Marginson, S., & Ordorika, I. (Eds.). (2012). *Universities and the public sphere: Knowledge creation and state building in the era of globalization*. New York: Routledge.

Reinhardt, R. (2005). *Four books, 300 dollars, and a dream: An illustrated history of the first 150 years of the Mechanics' Institute of San Francisco*. San Francisco: Mechanics Institute.

Rice, S. P. (2000). *The mechanics' institute of the City of New York and the conception of class authority in early industrial America, 1830–1860* (pp. 269–298). New York: New York History.

Rice, S. P. (2004). *Minding the machine: Languages of class in early industrial America*. Berkeley: University of California Press.

Rimer, S., & Arenson, K. W. (2004, June 24). Top colleges take more blacks, but which ones?. *The New York Times*. http://www.nytimes.com/2004/06/24/us/top-colleges-take-more-blacks-but-which-ones.html?pagewanted=all&src=pm. Downloaded 23 June 2013.

Roh, D. (2006). *The Mechanics Institute*. http://transliteracies.english.ucsb.edu/post/research-project/research-clearinghouse-individual/research-reports/the-mechanics-institute. Downloaded 29 Sept 2012.

Roper, J. (n.d.g). *The struggle for equality by Connecticut blacks in the 18th and 19th century*. Yale-New Haven Teachers' institute. http://www.yale.edu/ynhti/curriculum/units/1981/cthistory/81.ch.03.x.html. Downloaded 5 Sept 2013.

Shapin, S., & Barnes, B. (1977). Science, nature and control: Interpreting mechanics' institutes. *Social Studies of Science, 7, 31–74.*

Tierney, W. G. (2010). The public good in a changing economy. In G. Hentschke, V. Lechuga, & W. Tierney (Eds.), *For profit colleges and universities: Their markets, regulation, performance and pace in higher education* (pp. 171–188). Sterling: Stylus Publications.

Tierney, W. G., & Hentschke, G. C. (2007). *New players, different game: Understanding the rise of for-profit colleges and universities*. Baltimore: Johns Hopkins University Press.

Trow, M. (1974). Problems in the transition from elite to mass higher education. Reprinted in Michael Burrage, (Ed.) (2010). *Martin Trow: Twentieth century higher education: Elite to mass to universal*. Baltimore: The Johns Hopkins University Press.

Tuskegee University. (n.d.g). http://www.tuskegee.edu/about_us/history_and_mission.aspx. Downloaded 10 Sept 2012.

Walker, J. (1825). *An essay on the education of the people*. London.

Washington, B. T. (2004). *Up from slavery: An autobiography*. LLC Sioux Falls: NuVision Publications.

Young Mechanics Institute. (1832, September 4). *Connecticut Journal*. Pdf. Property of The Institute Library.

Who Attends For-Profit Institutions?: The Enrollment Landscape

Rhonda Vonshay Sharpe, Steve Stokes, and William A. Darity, Jr.

Overview

For-profit educational institutions, particularly universities and other institutions of vocational and higher learning, have seen enormous, "almost exponential" growth in recent years (Coleman and Vedder 2008; see also Levine 1997; Breneman et al. 2006; Kamenetz 2005; Bennett et al.2010; National Center for Education Statistics 2011). The National Center for Education Statistics estimates that from 1998–99 to 2008–09, the number of associate's and bachelor's degrees conferred by for-profit postsecondary institutions grew by 125 and 400 percent respectively (National Center for Education Statistics 2011). The corresponding growth in associate and

R.V. Sharpe (✉)
Women's Institute for Science, Equity and Race,
Mechanicsville, VA, USA
e-mail: rhondavsharpe@wiserpolicy.org

S. Stokes
Brigham Young University, Provo, UT, USA
e-mail: steve.s.stokes@gmail.com

W.A. Darity, Jr.
Samuel DuBois Cook Center on Social Equity, Duke University,
Durham, NC, USA
e-mail: william.darity@duke.edu

T. McMillan Cottom, W.A. Darity, Jr. (eds.), *For-Profit Universities*,
DOI 10.1007/978-3-319-47187-7_7

bachelor degree conferrals from public universities was 33 and 29 percent over the same time period (Ibid.). Other research has shown that since 1976, for-profit enrollment has grown at an annualized rate of about 11 percent, much faster than the sector a whole (Coleman and Vedder 2008; Kamenetz 2005). While they are still a relatively small part of the overall higher education landscape, their size, scope and influence are rapidly expanding.

This rapid growth and rise in popularity has not gone unnoticed by lawmakers and regulators, nor has it been without controversy (Boardman 2012). While some believe that proprietary universities fill crucial gaps left by our traditional nonprofit and state-sponsored higher education system, others claim that these businesses are ineffective at best and unethical at worst, leaving poor, minority, and other nontraditional students with high levels of debt and low prospects of gainful employment (Kamenetz 2005; Carey 2010; Coleman and Vedder 2008; Bennett et al. 2010). Unfortunately the claims made by both camps largely are unsupported. Research on for-profit post-secondary school or the people who enroll in them is spare (Kinser and Levy 2005; Cellini 2010) . The most fully developed study thus far is Bennet et al. 2010 report for the Center for College Affordability and Productivity.

It is worth noting that for-profit education is by no means a new, novel or strictly American occurrence. As early as the Golden Age of Ancient Greece, competitive for-profit education was quite prominent and successful, particularly in Athens (Coulson 1999; Carey 2010; Bennett et al. 2010). Bennett et al. (2010) assert that in ancient Greece, "competition among the sophists was brisk and produced two beneficial outcomes for the consumers of education: affordability and quality" and, as a result, literacy rates were high among members of the citizen class, commerce flourished, and Athens ultimately became an intellectual and cultural powerhouse.

Over the proceeding centuries, the influence and prevalence of for-profit institutions waxed and waned, but the approach never disappeared completely (Coleman and Vedder 2008). Even within the structure of a more traditional university system there was a period where students' fees went directly to the professor whose lectures they selected; for example,Adam Smith lectured under precisely those conditions at the University of Glasgow in the eighteenth century. Social, political and economic forces often affected the prevalence, distribution and demand for private for-profit education services. In the 1890s at the apex of the Industrial Revolution in America, skilled labor was high in demand but short in supply. A standard narrative has it that bookkeeping, shorthand, teaching, medicine, law, the use of mechanical typewriters and stenographers, and other related skills were exceedingly valuable (Heckman 2000), particularly to women who often were excluded not only from traditional colleges but also from traditional labor-intensive employment opportunities (Kamenetz 2005; Breneman et al. 2006; Goldin and Katz 1999; Turner 2006). It is not surprising that this gap between the supply and demand for skilled labor spawned some of the nation's first for-profit "career colleges" (Kamenetz 2005).

After a brief decline in the first half of the twentieth century, proprietaary universities made a comeback in the 1970s, and continued to grow and expand over the next three decades. Frequently, this growth is attributed to the 1972 reauthorization of the Higher Education Act, which, among other things, permitted certain tuition subsidies like Pell Grants to be used at for-profit colleges and universities Bennett et al. (2010; Kamenetz 2005; Turner 2006). For example, S. R. Cellini found that in California, increases in federal and state tuition support encouraged students to enroll in for-profit programs, particularly in counties with high levels of poverty, where more students were eligible for need-based aid (Cellini 2010). Allegations of fraud and financial mismanagement in the 1980s and 1990s led to a series of high-profile Congressional hearings resulting in somewhat tighter regulations (Carey 2010; Kamenetz 2005). Today the largest of these publicly traded giants each rake in more than $4 billion annually (and more than $32 billion collectively), mostly in the form of tuition subsidies and grants, subsidized student loans, and other forms of federal tuition support (Kamenetz 2005; Carey 2010; Boardman 2012). Thus, these private profit-seeking institutions rely heavily either directly or indirectly on government spending.

Anecdote has it that the growth of for-profits over the past two decades also is closely associated with the rise and proliferation of the internet. As intuitive as it may sound, Breneman et al. (2006) report that such q connection is, "largely coincidental." Indeed, they show that distance (online) learning is not unique to for-profit universities, in the same way that face-to-face instruction is not unique to traditional brick and mortar public and private institutions.

Throughout their recent history, the general custom of for-profit post-secondary schools has been to provide *highly career-oriented training* to underserved (non-traditional student) populations. For profit-institutions give considerably less attention—nor even lip service—to a research mission or the principles of liberal arts education. Nevertheless, thus far their faculty have been drawn largely from traditional (nonprofit) institutions, although the expansion in for-profits has been sustained for a sufficient period of time that they now are able to "grow" some of their own faculty. Regardless, for-profit institutions generally seek to teach skills that are intended to make individuals work place ready for specific types of employment and deemphasize general intellectual knowledge and critical analysis of conventional perspectives within each field of specialization.

Indeed, critics lament the apparent lack of liberal arts training at for-profit institutions Bennett et al. (2010). For-profit curricula often push to the side courses in the humanities, fine arts, and social sciences in favor of business, engineering, and computer-related fields. Perhaps this is doue to the greater likelihood that certification in many technical skills (e.g. computer programming, culinary arts, and accounting) provides a verifiable and transparent signal to potential employers, whereas expertise in the arts, humanities and "soft" sciences sends a less reliable signal (Turner 2006).

In addition, for-profits routinely are criticized for having relatively high drop-out rates (some as high as 66 percent), tuition rates that are higher than their public counterparts, relatively high student loans default rates, and relatively low post-graduation employment rates (Boardman 2012; Staff 2012). DeVry University and the University of Phoenix, in particular, have exceptionally low degree completion rates—as low as 4 percent in some cases, while those for-profits at the upper end of the degree completion rate scale only achieve rates of approximately 75 percent Bennett et al. (2010).

Still there also is a high degree of variation in the graduation rates at traditional colleges and universities. Two year non-profit institutions also generally have notoriously low completion rates as do a number of traditional four year colleges. Historically black colleges and universities (HBCUs) often are singled out for their low graduation rates. At one point in the previous decade St. Augustine's University had a degree completion rate of a mere 8 percent Bennett et al. (2010).

While for-profit attendance does not assure students of successful degree completion, one can argue that there is an admirable egalitarianism associated with their virtually open enrollment policy. Moreover, a positive dimension of the low college completion rate means that for-profits do not function as "diploma mills"; high attrition could be seen as an indicator of quality control. Unfortunately, there is no agency that conducts an independent assessment of the quality of for-profits. In principle, quality assurance would be dictated by the labor market success (or failures) of their graduates—among those who do graduate. But there also is little data on the comparative job outcomes for graduates of for-profits versus graduates of traditional colleges and universities.

Stephanie Cellini (2012) argues that the greater expense of a two year education at the average for-profit than the average community college sets a higher bar for the requisite employment outcome to make it worthwhile for students. She estimates that net benefits for students would have to amount to an 8.5 percent annual gain in earnings to yield a net financial benefit for students from a for-profit education in contrast with the 5.3 percent annual gain needed to yield a net financial benefit from a traditional community college education.

For-profits appear to operate on a business model that is predicated on high rates of attrition and high rates of flows of new students year in and year out. Is this a successful business model? Again the jury is out in the absence of more information about the profitability of these institutions. We do know that the 15 largest of the for-profits that enroll close to 60 percent of all students at those institutions Bennet et al. (2010) typically have sustained operations for at least 15 years.

Non-traditional students are disproportionately drawn to for-profit programs. (Coleman and Vedder 2008; Turner 2006). Breneman et al. (2006) suggest that, "extending the market is the most accurate way to view the impact of the for-profits thus far... [especially to] students who, in many cases, would otherwise not enroll at all." This is particularly true for older, non-traditional adult students and students from ethnic/racial groups subject to discrimination who often are passed over in the admissions offices of traditional universities, particularly those admissions offices that generate "selective" student bodies. In addition, it is widely held that proprietary institutions are likely to be more flexible and responsive to demographic and economic changes, largely because they are unencumbered by bureaucratic political constraints (Turner 2006; Heckman 2000).

In reality, "neither extreme view is likely to be completely accurate" Bennett et al. (2010). As major players on the field of education, much about the performance and fate of for-profits remains to be seen. As the industry and corresponding empirical research develop, we will begin to see how these players might fit into and alter the established system of higher education not only in the U.S., but also globally (Cellini 2010).

Indeed, despite the controversy and importance of the subject, Breneman et al. (2006) point out that researchers often lack reliable information about, "the basic demographics of the for-profit sector of the higher education market… [and that] little empirical research has been devoted to a documentation of the changes in the number, distribution, and characteristics of for-profit education providers over the past three decades." Factors that may have contributed to this oversight include definitional ambiguities, a lack of publicly available representative data sets, the absence of transparent information from the institutions themselves and the fact that the industries' rise to prominence is a relatively recent occurrence (Kinser and Levy 2005; Cellini 2010). While research in this area is increasing and evolving y, this paper represents an attempt to augment what traditionally has been a deficiency in the literature. Specifically, we seek to identify the trends in enrollment at for-profit institutions by age, gender, and race using a particularly rich data set.

Data and Methodology

This study examines the trends in enrollment at for-profit institutions by enrollment level—undergraduate and graduate, by enrollment status—full-time and part-time, and age. The analysis by age includes the years 1995, 1997, 1999, 2001, 2003, 2005, 2007, 2009, and 2011. The analysis by gender and race is limited to the years 1995 thru 2011. The study addresses two broad research questions:

1. How have the demographics of students enrolled at for-profit institutions changed since 1995?
2. How has the market share of for-profits changed since 1995?

To address these research questions, we rely on data from Integrated Post-Secondary Educational Data System Enrollment Survey accessed via WebCASPAR. The sample is limited to undergraduate and graduate students who self-identified as black, white, Hispanic, Asian or Native American.

We resort to a direct descriptive analysis is used to answer the research questions. This study has several limitations. First, we do not examine the trends at any particular type of for-profit institution, e.g. vocational vs. academic; therefore, we do not isolate whether changes are broad or being driven by a smaller segment of for-profit institutions. Second, we do not have data on the educational history of students in the sample so we do not know if they transferred to a for-profit or completed all of their education at a for-profit institutions.

Findings: Who the Students Are at For-Profits

Our central finding is for-profit institutions have become a vital source of educational enrollment for black and Hispanic students at all ages. Therefore, these groups particularly affected by the advantages and disadvantages associated with for-profit education.

We begin with a discussion about enrollment trends at for-profit institutions by age. Of the 18–24 year old (traditional college age) students enrolled in college as full-time undergraduates, 6 percent were enrolled at for-profits in 2011 up from 1 percent in 1995 (See Table 1). Traditional college age students at for-profits were 1 percent of the full-time undergraduate enrollment in 1995 and 6 percent of the full-time undergraduate enrollment in 2011.

In 1995, 4 percent of all nontraditional students enrolled as full-time undergraduate students were at for-profit institutions. By 2011, the percentage of all nontraditional students enrolled as full-time undergraduates at for-profit institutions was 34 percent, an increase of 30 percentage points. For-profit institutions enrolled 13 percent of all full-time undergraduates in 2011, a significant increase from 2 percent in 1995.

Of the 18–24 year old (traditional college age) students enrolled in college as part-time undergraduates, 4 percent were enrolled at for-profits in 2011. This represents an increase from less than 1 percent in 1995. In 1995, 1 percent of all nontraditional students enrolled as part-time undergraduate students were enrolled at for-profit institutions. By 2011, the percentage of all nontraditional students enrolled as full-time undergraduates at for-profit institutions had grown to 10 percent. For-profit institutions enrolled 8 percent of all part-time undergraduates in 2011 up from 1 percent in 1995.

At the graduate level, full-time enrollment for students in the 18–21 age range actually declined at for-profit institutions, but increased at public and private nonprofit institutions. But for all other ages, full-time graduate enrollment rose at for-profits. Between 1995 and 2011, for-profit experienced increases in full-time enrollment at the graduate level that ranged from 9 times as many students among 22–24 year olds to nearly

Table 1 Undergraduate enrollment at for-profits by age

Full-time										
Age group	*Institutional control*	*1995*	*1997*	*1999*	*2001*	*2003*	*2005*	*2007*	*2009*	*2011*
18–19	Public Institutions	981,208	1,049,143	1,129,445	1,191,243	1,271,207	1,312,472	1,391,824	1,505,581	1,467,001
	Private: Nonprofit	344,034	364,744	387,291	397,421	413,781	432,828	450,406	466,035	475,074
	Private: For-Profit	18,744	26,968	28,359	30,438	36,686	44,184	45,692	63,833	62,280
20–21	Public Institutions	804,204	851,163	908,165	1,004,733	1,082,031	1,114,639	1,141,000	1,248,204	1,274,490
	Private: Nonprofit	302,968	318,848	338,418	362,325	395,623	411,302	424,217	442,338	460,254
	Private: For-Profit	14,397	20,439	23,962	28,665	37,205	51,014	60,059	90,005	92,377
22–24	Public Institutions	472,937	472,613	480,461	520,048	578,563	592,074	589,154	633,734	649,203
	Private: Nonprofit	113,053	110,567	115,543	124,914	138,878	144,129	146,493	150,051	155,917
	Private: For-Profit	12,806	20,616	24,261	28,384	41,134	62,987	74,686	115,037	119,171
Percent of 18–24 year olds	Public Institutions	74%	73%	73%	74%	73%	72%	72%	72%	71%
	Private: Nonprofit	25%	25%	24%	24%	24%	24%	24%	22%	23%
	Private: For-Profit	1%	2%	2%	2%	3%	4%	4%	6%	6%

Full-time

Age group	*Institutional control*	*1995*	*1997*	*1999*	*2001*	*2003*	*2005*	*2007*	*2009*	*2011*
25–29	Public Institutions	242,848	242,180	225,290	235,050	272,368	274,007	272,688	314,508	329,250
	Private: Nonprofit	51,476	52,276	50,772	52,765	59,308	63,628	64,814	69,801	71,040
	Private: For-Profit	11,708	21,704	25,526	32,626	48,102	83,559	100,575	160,806	163,169
30–34	Public Institutions	137,297	120,893	109,800	121,649	144,754	136,372	129,565	158,325	175,570
	Private: Nonprofit	29,363	28,710	27,710	31,280	35,637	35,675	36,451	40,924	43,517
	Private: For-Profit	7,144	12,686	15,919	22,219	32,319	56,853	67,972	113,737	119,723
35–39	Public Institutions	98,463	89,136	81,719	80,923	90,957	87,712	85,001	103,627	108,079
	Private: Nonprofit	22,647	22,777	22,333	23,039	25,839	26,619	28,195	30,298	31,059
	Private: For-Profit	5,102	11,415	12,167	16,620	22,001	41,349	50,044	83,379	84,986

(*continued*)

Table 1 (continued)

Full-time

Age group	*Institutional control*	*1995*	*1997*	*1999*	*2001*	*2003*	*2005*	*2007*	*2009*	*2011*
40–49	Public Institutions	96,220	93,148	89,586	94,131	111,256	103,947	96,010	119,891	132,079
	Private: Nonprofit	25,496	26,499	27,434	29,276	32,573	34,397	34,478	37,856	40,775
	Private: For-Profit	4,159	9,377	13,683	19,626	29,090	50,723	58,404	98,006	106,698
50–64	Public Institutions	17,841	19,865	21,854	23,993	31,358	32,040	32,681	45,039	52,538
	Private: Nonprofit	4,716	6,545	6,806	7,616	9,145	10,419	11,466	13,588	15,747
	Private: For-Profit	944	2,139	2,997	4,976	8,073	15,930	19,944	37,920	43,834
Percent of 25–64 year olds	Public Institutions	78%	74%	72%	70%	68%	60%	57%	52%	53%
	Private: Nonprofit	18%	18%	18%	18%	17%	16%	16%	13%	13%
	Private: For-Profit	4%	8%	10%	12%	15%	24%	27%	35%	34%

Part-time

Age Group	*Institutional Control*	*1995*	*1997*	*1999*	*2001*	*2003*	*2005*	*2007*	*2009*	*2011*
18–19	Public Institutions	206,363	215,865	240,516	253,314	264,001	276,894	293,956	330,839	363,067
	Private: Nonprofit	8,833	9,214	8,648	9,382	11,236	10,008	9,936	11,568	14,000
	Private: For-Profit	2,167	2,188	2,351	2,775	3,441	4,461	6,015	8,898	8,499
20–21	Public Institutions	264,846	272,328	287,809	316,161	333,196	340,775	350,445	383,076	433,795
	Private: Nonprofit	17,423	16,421	15,826	15,925	16,347	16,498	16,928	17,086	19,407
	Private: For-Profit	3,968	2,983	3,912	4,584	6,185	8,925	11,050	17,682	19,139
22–24	Public Institutions	374,012	358,493	365,976	401,011	443,976	453,542	463,220	498,692	526,139
	Private: Nonprofit	37,555	34,351	32,250	32,227	34,517	35,596	36,341	36,980	39,447
	Private: For-Profit	5,921	4,547	5,881	6,608	10,062	13,996	18,038	30,752	34,730

(*continued*)

Table 1 (continued)

Part-time

Age Group	*Institutional Control*	*1995*	*1997*	*1999*	*2001*	*2003*	*2005*	*2007*	*2009*	*2011*
Percent of 18–24 year olds	Public Institutions	92%	92%	93%	93%	93%	92%	92%	91%	91%
	Private: Nonprofit	7%	7%	6%	6%	6%	5%	5%	5%	5%
	Private: For-Profit	1%	1%	1%	1%	2%	2%	3%	4%	4%
25–29	Public Institutions	434,119	426,562	401,244	413,693	446,982	460,845	481,148	531,245	533,625
	Private: Nonprofit	52,215	49,183	43,345	41,072	43,944	45,942	47,132	49,252	51,376
	Private: For-Profit	8,184	6,453	7,856	8,208	13,659	20,146	28,600	50,802	56,205
30–34	Public Institutions	351,108	315,449	290,146	313,934	327,055	309,737	304,077	337,483	350,591
	Private: Nonprofit	46,836	42,550	36,024	34,738	36,206	35,900	35,327	38,275	41,268
	Private: For-Profit	6,386	4,649	5,298	5,882	9,576	14,529	20,121	38,725	46,082
35–39	Public Institutions	311,005	289,916	274,320	268,640	265,213	254,660	252,325	260,348	247,570
	Private: Nonprofit	44,053	41,774	35,026	31,861	31,637	31,738	31,583	33,533	32,736
	Private: For-Profit	5,290	3,550	4,229	4,451	7,094	10,934	15,690	30,072	34,075

Part-time

Age Group	*Institutional Control*	*1995*	*1997*	*1999*	*2001*	*2003*	*2005*	*2007*	*2009*	*2011*
40–49	Public Institutions	408,258	407,942	395,935	417,850	426,068	401,131	378,518	384,412	369,137
	Private: Nonprofit	62,834	63,591	55,462	51,679	52,879	51,709	48,994	52,144	53,301
	Private: For-Profit	6,138	4,060	4,959	5,419	8,834	13,444	19,486	38,931	47,958
50–64	Public Institutions	133,846	151,122	161,811	188,136	190,739	194,744	203,434	213,781	205,211
	Private: Nonprofit	16,822	19,276	18,196	17,799	19,557	21,130	22,284	26,564	27,985
	Private: For-Profit	1,451	1,032	1,256	1,393	2,422	4,298	7,075	16,812	23,521
Percent of 25–64 year olds	Public Institutions	61%	58%	56%	57%	51%	45%	44%	41%	41%
	Private: Nonprofit	38%	39%	39%	41%	40%	37%	39%	41%	42%
	Private: For-Profit	1%	3%	5%	2%	9%	17%	18%	18%	17%

Table 2 Graduate enrollment at for-profits by age

Age group	*Institutional control*	*1995*	*1997*	*1999*	*2001*	*2003*	*2005*	*2007*	*2009*	*2011*
18–19	Public Institutions	132	46	104	43	60	73	135	537	254
	Private: Nonprofit	45	58	26	93	122	101	221	592	710
	Private: For-Profit	248		1	2	1	9	10	15	70
20–21	Public Institutions	3,152	3,129	3,614	3,829	4,616	4,825	5,639	9,167	9,313
	Private: Nonprofit	2,044	2,748	2,038	2,680	3,073	3,180	3,438	7,898	7,886
	Private: For-Profit	640	172	61	24	139	132	135	258	407
22–24	Public Institutions	62,576	65,146	68,628	74,827	91,746	94,958	102,033	147,395	153,073
	Private: Nonprofit	33,654	36,530	39,236	41,776	53,833	60,116	67,880	116,213	123,968
	Private: For-Profit	873	1,209	1,336	644	2,117	4,967	5,363	8,508	7,910
Percent of 18–24 year olds	Public Institutions	64%	63%	63%	64%	62%	59%	58%	54%	54%
	Private: Nonprofit	35%	36%	36%	36%	37%	38%	39%	43%	44%
	Private: For-Profit	2%	1%	1%	1%	1%	3%	3%	3%	3%

Age group	*Institutional control*	*1995*	*1997*	*1999*	*2001*	*2003*	*2005*	*2007*	*2009*	*2011*
25–29	Public Institutions	72,683	80,492	81,759	81,155	97,646	101,736	106,761	144,154	149,328
	Private: Nonprofit	45,289	52,369	55,143	56,050	71,709	78,585	86,867	132,956	140,062
	Private: For-Profit	1,042	2,359	4,227	1,955	4,461	18,819	20,217	26,406	24,119
30–34	Public Institutions	31,295	31,912	33,559	35,371	40,855	40,785	41,893	49,373	51,773
	Private: Nonprofit	18,190	20,168	22,112	23,959	30,238	31,772	33,993	44,890	48,227
	Private: For-Profit	791	1,875	3,030	1,493	8,527	15,716	16,159	21,587	21,011
35–39	Public Institutions	19,286	18,828	18,278	17,062	19,062	19,731	20,725	22,702	22,890
	Private: Nonprofit	11,260	12,289	12,512	12,623	16,001	17,497	19,595	23,616	24,158
	Private: For-Profit	670	2,479	2,657	1,045	6,129	12,650	14,148	19,232	17,449
40–49	Public Institutions	26,891	25,651	24,334	22,545	24,540	22,902	21,968	23,307	23,712
	Private: Nonprofit	16,671	18,114	18,227	18,120	22,296	22,964	24,537	28,167	30,163
	Private: For-Profit	748	1,729	3,730	1,667	10,441	18,746	19,389	26,250	27,364

(*continued*)

Table 2 (continued)

Age group	*Institutional control*	*1995*	*1997*	*1999*	*2001*	*2003*	*2005*	*2007*	*2009*	*2011*
50–64	Public Institutions	5,559	6,709	7,576	7,761	9,672	10,101	10,091	10,987	10,461
	Private: Nonprofit	4,765	6,170	7,188	7,456	10,044	11,130	12,603	15,186	16,062
	Private: For-Profit	331	432	1,164	800	4,705	9,259	10,535	15,286	16,212
Percent of 25–64 year olds	Public Institutions	65%	65%	64%	64%	62%	59%	56%	53%	50%
	Private: Nonprofit	35%	35%	35%	35%	36%	38%	38%	39%	39%
	Private: For-Profit	0%	0%	1%	1%	2%	4%	6%	8%	12%

Part Time

Age group	*Institutional control*	*1995*	*1997*	*1999*	*2001*	*2003*	*2005*	*2007*	*2009*	*2011*
Ages 18–19	Public Institutions	138	48	30	27	31	29	32	42	39
	Private: Nonprofit	47	86	16	98	89	64	283	74	59
	Private: For-Profit					1	8	2	6	16

Part Time

Age group	*Institutional control*	*1995*	*1997*	*1999*	*2001*	*2003*	*2005*	*2007*	*2009*	*2011*
Ages 20–21	Public Institutions	1,000	780	824	788	1,123	1,070	974	1,242	1,723
	Private: Nonprofit	626	1,136	498	918	1,044	861	1,019	977	871
	Private: For-Profit	5	4	5	15	31	59	45	90	104
Ages 22–24	Public Institutions	34,743	32,004	33,935	35,744	43,287	43,036	43,470	46,341	44,053
	Private: Nonprofit	19,538	18,993	20,083	22,131	27,410	29,717	32,132	33,678	32,899
	Private: For-Profit	88	149	248	343	621	1,353	1,795	3,246	3,110
Percent of 18–24 year olds	Public Institutions	64%	62%	63%	61%	60%	58%	56%	56%	55%
	Private: Nonprofit	36%	38%	37%	39%	39%	40%	42%	41%	41%
	Private: For-Profit	0%	0%	0%	1%	1%	2%	2%	4%	4%
Ages 25–29	Public Institutions	96,391	103,043	104,585	98,941	111,806	112,032	116,221	122,399	115,180
	Private: Nonprofit	55,671	56,850	57,730	56,313	66,882	73,680	79,956	88,086	87,310
	Private: For-Profit	370	593	1,133	1,693	2,711	5,276	8,504	13,602	15,967

(*continued*)

Table 2 (continued)

Part Time										
Age group	*Institutional control*	*1995*	*1997*	*1999*	*2001*	*2003*	*2005*	*2007*	*2009*	*2011*
Ages 30–34	Public Institutions	62,360	61,277	64,471	68,227	74,964	72,362	71,793	75,520	74,216
	Private: Nonprofit	35,114	34,540	36,404	37,853	42,432	45,343	47,381	52,388	55,130
	Private: For-Profit	323	563	911	1,675	2,782	5,127	7,824	12,105	16,994
Ages 35–39	Public Institutions	53,334	50,101	48,789	45,511	49,824	51,068	53,157	53,978	49,314
	Private: Nonprofit	28,789	26,919	26,475	25,914	29,830	33,286	36,512	38,199	37,532
	Private: For-Profit	241	399	903	1,242	2,062	4,227	6,972	10,887	14,403
Ages 40–49	Public Institutions	104,410	100,130	96,496	87,027	89,952	83,108	77,756	77,078	72,332
	Private: Nonprofit	49,985	49,036	48,977	45,329	51,241	53,500	55,932	58,441	58,597
	Private: For-Profit	395	520	1,507	2,082	3,288	6,487	9,673	15,010	22,428
Ages 50–64	Public Institutions	29,424	34,048	39,613	42,599	49,451	50,321	49,263	49,054	44,399
	Private: Nonprofit	15,479	17,655	20,586	21,233	27,089	30,540	33,849	37,389	38,188
	Private: For-Profit	90	171	766	972	1,534	3,287	5,711	8,562	13,789

50 times among students at ages 50–64. (See Table 2 for comprehensive data on graduate enrollment at for-profits and non-profits by age groups.)

Enrollment at for-profit institutions by race and gender is presented in Table 3. With the exception of black and Hispanic women, in general fewer undergraduate women were enrolled full-time at for-profit institutions in 1995 than men. However by 2011, the number of undergraduate women enrolled full-time at for-profit institutions exceeded the number of undergraduate men enrolled full-time at for-profit institutions for all groups. Twice as many black women and nearly twice as many Native American women were enrolled as full-time undergraduate students at for-profit institutions as their male counterparts. This trend holds true for part-time undergraduate enrollment at for-profit institutions. Of course, it must be noted that the enrollment of women at *all* colleges and universities now exceeds that of men.

Since 1995, blacks and Hispanics have exceeded 15 percent of the full-time undergraduate student population at for-profit institutions. In 1995, blacks were 17 percent, Hispanics were 16 percent, and whites were 63 percent of the full-time undergraduate student population at for-profit institutions. By 2011 blacks were 27 percent, Hispanics were 22 percent and whites were 47 percent of the full-time undergraduate population at for-profit institutions.

Asians comprise a smaller percentage of the full-time undergraduate student population at for-profit institutions in 2011 than they did in 1995, 3.5 percent in 2011 compared to 4.1 percent in 1995. Among non-whites and Hispanics enrolled as full-time undergraduate students, the percentage enrolled full-time at for-profit institutions doubled between 1995 and 2011. For blacks and Native Americans, this percentage increased six fold between 1995 and 2011.

The trends in part-time undergraduate enrollment at for-profit institutions are similar to the full-time enrollment trends at for-profit institutions. In 1995, blacks and whites comprised nearly 90 percent of part-time undergraduate population at for-profit institutions, 17 percent and 73 percent respectively. By 2011, blacks were 31 percent, Hispanics were 14 percent and whites were 50 percent of the part-time undergraduate population at for-profit institutions. Asians comprised a larger percentage of the part-time undergraduate population at for-profit institutions in 2011, 5 percent, than they did in 1995, 3.1 percent. Of the part-time undergraduate students, the percentage enrolled part-time at for-profit institutions for all groups at least doubled between 1995 and 2011.

Table 3 Undergraduate enrollment at for-profit institutions: 1995–2011

Full-time students	*1995*	*1996*	*1997*	*1998*	*1999*	*2000*	*2001*	*2002*	*2003*
Native American	1,116	2,071	2,365	2,817	3,286	3,259	4,021	3,335	4,411
Female	552	1,165	1,241	1,544	1,831	1,593	2,026	1,785	2,532
Male	564	906	1,124	1,273	1,455	1,666	1,995	1,550	1,879
Race share of for-profit enrollment	0.7%	0.9%	0.9%	1.0%	1.1%	1.1%	1.2%	1.0%	1.0%
Share of race total enrollment	2%	3%	3%	4%	4%	4%	5%	4%	5%
Asian	6,441	11,256	13,758	15,929	18,692	20,171	21,207	19,826	21,526
Female	2,668	5,145	6,117	6,927	8,036	8,214	9,141	8,434	10,245
Male	3,773	6,111	7,641	9,002	10,656	11,957	12,066	11,392	11,281
Race share of for-profit enrollment	4.1%	4.7%	5.2%	5.9%	6.0%	6.7%	6.2%	5.9%	5.1%
Share of race total enrollment	2%	3%	3%	3%	4%	4%	4%	4%	4%
Black	25,824	38,134	42,946	44,576	51,000	53,191	64,823	69,624	90,630
Female	14,351	22,000	24,711	25,093	29,148	29,987	37,282	41,101	56,049
Male	11,473	16,134	18,235	19,483	21,852	23,204	27,541	28,523	34,581
Race share of for-profit enrollment	16.6%	15.9%	16.3%	16.4%	16.4%	17.7%	18.8%	20.7%	21.3%

Full-time students	*1995*	*1996*	*1997*	*1998*	*1999*	*2000*	*2001*	*2002*	*2003*
Share of race total enrollment	3%	5%	5%	5%	6%	6%	7%	7%	9%
Hispanic	24,471	38,675	41,453	45,509	52,701	52,139	58,742	60,631	79,221
Female	12,684	20,867	21,942	23,881	27,291	26,557	30,002	31,525	42,285
Male	11,787	17,808	19,511	21,628	25,410	25,582	28,740	29,106	36,936
Ethnicity share of for-profit enrollment	15.7%	16.1%	15.8%	16.7%	17.0%	17.4%	17.1%	18.0%	18.7%
Share of ethnicity total enrollment	4%	6%	6%	7%	7%	7%	7%	7%	9%
White	97,523	149,904	162,503	163,109	184,531	171,387	195,681	183,647	228,841
Female	47,217	79,672	82,269	79,666	87,704	77,999	91,117	88,301	117,147
Male	50,306	70,232	80,234	83,443	96,827	93,388	104,564	95,346	111,694
Race share of for-profit enrollment	62.8%	62.4%	61.8%	60.0%	59.5%	57.1%	56.8%	54.5%	53.9%
Share of race total enrollment	2%	3%	3%	3%	3%	3%	4%	3%	4%

(*continued*)

Table 3 (continued)

Full-time students	*1995*	*1996*	*1997*	*1998*	*1999*	*2000*	*2001*	*2002*	*2003*
Full-time for-profit enrollment subtotal	155,375	240,040	263,025	271,940	310,210	300,147	344,474	337,063	424,629
For-profit share of full-time enrollment	2%	3%	4%	4%	4%	4%	4%	4%	5%

Full-time students	*2004*	*2005*	*2006*	*2007*	*2008*	*2009*	*2010*	*2011*	*Grand total*
Native American	5,540	6,922	6,750	7,411	9,054	11,225	11,156	11,418	96,157
Female	3,316	4,262	4,040	4,744	5,819	7,030	7,110	7,477	58,067
Male	2,224	2,660	2,710	2,667	3,235	4,195	4,046	3,941	38,090
Race share of for-profit enrollment	1.2%	1.2%	1.2%	1.2%	1.2%	1.2%	1.1%	1.1%	1.1%
Share of race total enrollment	6%	8%	7%	8%	9%	10%	11%	12%	7%
Asian	21,722	24,781	23,645	25,207	30,336	32,770	33,236	35,637	376,140
Female	10,461	12,761	12,374	13,452	17,128	18,806	18,727	20,256	188,892
Male	11,261	12,020	11,271	11,755	13,208	13,964	14,509	15,381	187,248

Full-time students	2004	2005	2006	2007	2008	2009	2010	2011	*Grand total*
Race share of for-profit enrollment	4.5%	4.3%	4.3%	4.0%	4.0%	3.5%	3.3%	3.5%	4.4%
Share of race total enrollment	4%	4%	4%	4%	5%	5%	5%	5%	4%
Black	105,127	129,975	129,688	153,122	196,336	259,980	273,553	277,007	2,005,536
Female	67,298	87,139	87,560	104,556	136,148	178,009	184,534	189,058	1,314,024
Male	37,829	42,836	42,128	48,566	60,188	81,971	89,019	87,949	691,512
Race share of for-profit enrollment	21.9%	22.7%	23.7%	24.6%	25.7%	27.4%	27.0%	27.1%	23.3%
Share of race total enrollment	10%	11%	11%	13%	15%	18%	18%	18%	11%
Hispanic	88,090	99,784	99,329	108,707	130,064	169,027	203,955	223,130	1,575,628
Female	48,137	56,896	57,142	63,599	78,233	102,093	123,138	136,578	902,850
Male	39,953	42,888	42,187	45,108	51,831	66,934	80,817	86,552	672,778
Ethnicity share of for-profit enrollment	18.3%	17.4%	18.1%	17.4%	17.0%	17.8%	20.1%	21.8%	18.3%
Share of ethnicity total enrollment	9%	10%	10%	10%	11%	13%	14%	14%	10%

(*continued*)

Table 3 (continued)

Full-time students	*2004*	*2005*	*2006*	*2007*	*2008*	*2009*	*2010*	*2011*	*Grand total*
White	260,326	310,582	288,873	328,777	397,777	476,188	491,849	476,629	4,568,127
Female	136,127	172,212	161,851	192,076	240,767	292,623	302,345	297,583	2,546,676
Male	124,199	138,370	127,022	136,701	157,010	183,565	189,504	179,046	2,021,451
Race share of for-profit enrollment	54.1%	54.3%	52.7%	52.8%	52.1%	50.2%	48.5%	46.6%	53.0%
Share of race total enrollment	4%	5%	5%	5%	6%	7%	7%	7%	5%
Full-time for-profit enrollment subtotal	480,805	572,044	548,285	623,224	763,567	949,190	1,013,749	1,023,821	8,621,588
For-profit share of Full-time Enrollment	6%	6%	6%	7%	8%	9%	10%	10%	6%

Part-time students	*1995*	*1996*	*1997*	*1998*	*1999*	*2000*	*2001*	*2002*	*2003*
Native American	351	405	296	344	408	687	505	684	700
Female	115	148	138	175	208	297	275	354	387
Male	236	257	158	169	200	390	230	330	313

Part-time students	*1995*	*1996*	*1997*	*1998*	*1999*	*2000*	*2001*	*2002*	*2003*
Race share of for-profit enrollment	0.4%	0.7%	0.5%	0.6%	0.6%	1.0%	0.7%	0.8%	0.8%
Share of race total enrollment	0%	0%	0%	0%	0%	1%	0%	1%	1%
Asian	2,484	2,135	2,472	2,932	3,486	4,304	4,056	4,528	4,439
Female	1,122	906	1,199	1,290	1,579	1,892	1,742	1,992	1,915
Male	1,362	1,229	1,273	1,642	1,907	2,412	2,314	2,536	2,524
Race share of for-profit enrollment	3.1%	3.8%	4.4%	5.0%	5.2%	6.1%	5.7%	5.5%	4.9%
Share of race total enrollment	0%	0%	0%	1%	1%	1%	1%	1%	1%
Black	13,251	9,084	10,519	11,721	13,696	15,307	17,655	20,087	24,545
Female	7,799	5,409	6,415	7,217	8,226	9,175	10,560	12,204	15,355
Male	5,452	3,675	4,104	4,504	5,470	6,132	7,095	7,883	9,190
Race share of for-profit enrollment	16.5%	16.1%	18.7%	20.1%	20.6%	21.6%	24.7%	24.6%	27.2%
Share of race total enrollment	1%	1%	1%	1%	1%	1%	1%	1%	1%
Hispanic	5,661	5,732	5,748	7,201	8,780	10,803	10,116	11,738	13,963

(*continued*)

Table 3 (continued)

Part-time students	*1995*	*1996*	*1997*	*1998*	*1999*	*2000*	*2001*	*2002*	*2003*
Female	2,843	2,960	3,104	3,970	4,606	5,608	5,142	5,893	7,181
Male	2,818	2,772	2,644	3,231	4,174	5,195	4,974	5,845	6,782
Ethnicity share of for-profit enrollment	7.1%	10.2%	10.2%	12.3%	13.2%	15.2%	14.2%	14.4%	15.5%
Share of ethnicity Total enrollment	1%	0%	0%	1%	1%	1%	1%	1%	1%
White	58,521	39,100	37,142	36,248	40,069	39,852	39,146	44,638	46,709
Female	30,212	20,241	20,839	19,921	21,175	20,053	20,926	23,403	25,711
Male	28,309	18,859	16,303	16,327	18,894	19,799	18,220	21,235	20,998
Race share of for-profit enrollment	72.9%	69.3%	66.1%	62.0%	60.3%	56.2%	54.8%	54.7%	51.7%
Share of race total enrollment	1%	1%	0%	1%	1%	1%	1%	1%	1%
Part-time enrollment subtotal	80,268	56,456	56,177	58,446	66,439	70,953	71,478	81,675	90,356
Percent of for-profit enrollment	2%	1%	1%	1%	1%	1%	1%	2%	2%

Part-time students	*1995*	*1996*	*1997*	*1998*	*1999*	*2000*	*2001*	*2002*	*2003*
For-profit grand total	235,643	296,496	319,202	330,386	376,649	371,100	415,952	418,738	514,985

Part-time students	*2004*	*2005*	*2006*	*2007*	*2008*	*2009*	*2010*	*2011*	*Grand total*
Native American	906	943	1,152	1,214	1,869	1,936	2,871	3,549	18,820
Female	478	546	703	748	1,146	1,189	1,875	2,266	11,048
Male	428	397	449	466	723	747	996	1,283	7,772
Race share of for-profit enrollment	0.8%	0.8%	0.9%	0.8%	0.9%	0.8%	0.9%	1.0%	0.8%
Share of race Total enrollment	1%	1%	1%	1%	1%	1%	2%	2%	1%
Asian	4,616	4,567	4,632	5,391	7,259	8,410	9,209	17,077	91,997
Female	2,134	2,261	2,384	2,772	3,828	4,511	5,029	10,118	46,674
Male	2,482	2,306	2,248	2,619	3,431	3,899	4,180	6,959	45,323
Race share of for-profit enrollment	4.3%	4.1%	3.6%	3.7%	3.6%	3.5%	2.9%	4.9%	4.1%
Share of race total enrollment	1%	1%	1%	1%	1%	1%	1%	2%	1%

(*continued*)

Table 3 (continued)

Part-time students	*2004*	*2005*	*2006*	*2007*	*2008*	*2009*	*2010*	*2011*	*Grand total*
Black	29,915	30,720	36,777	42,653	61,004	75,910	106,545	107,297	626,686
Female	18,722	20,224	25,016	28,798	41,726	52,091	73,906	74,156	416,999
Male	11,193	10,496	11,761	13,855	19,278	23,819	32,639	33,141	209,687
Race share of for-profit enrollment	27.8%	27.4%	29.0%	29.3%	30.3%	31.8%	33.0%	30.9%	28.1%
Share of race total enrollment	1%	1%	1%	2%	2%	2%	3%	3%	2%
Hispanic	16,512	16,695	17,810	19,868	25,853	31,398	43,120	47,164	298,162
Female	8,369	9,042	9,880	10,905	14,373	17,324	23,892	27,174	162,266
Male	8,143	7,653	7,930	8,963	11,480	14,074	19,228	19,990	135,896
Ethnicity share of for-profit enrollment	15.4%	14.9%	14.0%	13.7%	12.8%	13.2%	13.4%	13.6%	13.3%
Share of ethnicity total enrollment	1%	1%	1%	1%	1%	1%	2%	2%	1%
White	55,574	59,050	66,656	76,218	105,427	120,988	160,767	172,293	1,198,398
Female	31,000	35,045	40,493	44,214	61,365	70,832	97,352	104,969	687,751
Male	24,574	24,005	26,163	32,004	44,062	50,156	63,415	67,324	510,647
Race share of for-profit enrollment	51.7%	52.7%	52.5%	52.4%	52.3%	50.7%	49.8%	49.6%	53.6%

Part-time students	2004	2005	2006	2007	2008	2009	2010	2011	*Grand total*
Share of race total enrollment	1%	1%	1%	1%	1%	2%	2%	2%	16%
Part-time enrollment subtotal	107,523	111,975	127,027	145,344	201,412	238,642	322,512	347,380	2,234,063
Percent of for-profit enrollment	1%	1%	1%	2%	2%	2%	3%	3%	2%
For-profit grand total	588,328	684,019	675,312	768,568	964,979	1,187,832	1,336,261	1,371,201	10,855,651

Between 1995 and 2001, the growth in full-time undergraduate enrollment at for-profit institutions was 559 percent or 6.5 times the 1995 enrollment level. For the same time period, the growth in part-time undergraduate enrollment at for-profit institutions was 333 percent or 4 times the 1995 enrollment level. The percentage of full-time undergraduate students enrolled at for-profit institutions increase from 2 percent in 1995 to 10 percent in 2011. The part-time undergraduate enrollment at for-profit institutions increased by only 1 percentage point going from 2 percent in 1995 to 3 percent in 2011. The for-profit share of all undergraduate enrollments increased from 2 percent in 1995 to 8 percent in 2011.

Next, considergraduate enrollment at for-profit institutions by race and gender. With the exception of Hispanics women, fewer graduate women were enrolled full-time at for-profit institutions in 1995 than men (See Table 4). However by 1996, all female groups analyzed exceeded the number of males enrolled, full-time at for-profit institutions at the graduate level. By 2007, with the exception of Asian women, the number of women pursuing and enrolled full-time at for-profit institutions was at least twice that of the men in their racial groups. The number of Asian women at for-profit institutions exceeded the number of Asian men, but the gender gap is much smaller, 1 male for every 1.4 females.

In 1995, blacks were 10 percent, Hispanics were 11 percent, and whites were 72 percent of the full-time graduate population at for-profit institutions. By 2011, blacks were 35 percent, Hispanics were 9 percent and whites were 50 percent of the full-time graduate population at for-profit institutions. The percentage of Asians enrolled as full-time graduate students at for-profit institutions was less in 2011, 5 percent, than the percentage in 1995, 6 percent.

In 1995, less than 5 percent of any race/ethnic group enrolled as a graduate student attended a for-profit institution. By 2011, 38 percent of blacks enrolled as full-time graduate students attended a for-profit institution compared to 15 percent of Native Americans, 6 percent of Asian, 10 percent of Hispanics, and 7 percent of whites. Between 1995 and 2001, the growth in full-time graduate enrollment at for-profit institutions was 955 percent or 10.5 times the 1995 enrollment level.

The race-gender composition for part-time graduate students enrolled at for-profit institutions shows fewer women enrolled in 1995, but women exceeded the male enrollment by 2011. The gender gap is largest for blacks, Hispanics and whites, with black women having enrollments that

Table 4 Graduate enrollment at for-profit institutions: 1995–2011

Full-time students	*1995*	*1996*	*1997*	*1998*	*2000*	*2001*	*2002*	*2003*
Native American	83	110	193	246	215	310	225	488
Female	35	49	108	127	122	181	149	302
Male	48	61	85	119	93	129	76	186
Race share of for-profit enrollment	0.7%	0.6%	1.0%	1.1%	0.9%	1.0%	0.8%	0.9%
Share of race full-time enrollment	2%	3%	4%	6%	5%	7%	5%	9%
Asian	700	1,177	1,161	1,766	2,293	2,309	1,849	3,021
Female	288	563	593	906	1,088	1,229	1,013	1,663
Male	412	614	568	860	1,205	1,080	836	1,358
Race share of for-profit enrollment	6%	6%	6%	8%	10%	8%	7%	6%
Share of race full-time enrollment	2%	3%	3%	4%	5%	5%	4%	6%
Black	1,163	1,877	2,307	2,953	3,816	5,397	5,830	11,278
Female	558	1,044	1,424	1,636	2,387	3,627	4,006	8,036
Male	605	833	883	1,317	1,429	1,770	1,824	3,242
Race share of for-profit enrollment	10%	10%	12%	13%	16%	18%	21%	22%
Share of race full-time enrollment	3%	4%	4%	6%	7%	9%	9%	15%
Hispanic	1,319	2,198	2,797	3,153	2,154	2,877	2,302	4,335
Female	736	1,197	1,608	1,793	1,115	1,541	1,311	2,596
Male	583	1,001	1,189	1,360	1,039	1,336	991	1,739
Ethnicity share of for-profit enrollment	11%	12%	14%	13%	9%	10%	8%	8%
Share of ethnicity full-time enrollment	4%	6%	7%	8%	5%	6%	5%	8%
White	8,881	12,747	12,999	15,296	15,255	18,710	16,987	32,268
Female	4,083	6,455	6,588	7,732	7,668	10,317	10,078	19,948
Male	4,798	6,292	6,411	7,564	7,587	8,393	6,909	12,320
Race share of for-profit enrollment	73%	70%	67%	65%	64%	63%	62%	63%
Share of race full-time enrollment	2%	3%	3%	3%	3%	4%	4%	6%
Full-time for-profit enrollment subtotal	12,146	18,109	19,457	23,414	23,733	29,603	27,193	51,390
For-profit share of full-time enrollment	2%	3%	3%	4%	4%	5%	4%	7%

(continued)

Table 4 (continued)

Full-time students	*2004*	*2005*	*2006*	*2007*	*2008*	*2009*	*2010*	*2011*	*Grand Total*
Native American	671	808	810	863	1,154	1,218	1,145	1,183	9,720
Female	424	557	538	614	812	854	798	839	6,508
Male	247	251	272	249	342	364	347	344	3,212
Race share of for-profit enrollment	0.9%	0.9%	0.9%	0.9%	1.0%	0.9%	0.9%	0.9%	0.9%
Share of race full-time enrollment	12%	14%	13%	14%	16%	13%	14%	15%	11%
Asian	4,040	4,810	4,822	5,140	6,817	7,355	6,669	6,806	60,693
Female	2,263	2,772	2,868	2,936	3,874	4,311	4,068	4,045	34,460
Male	1,777	2,038	1,954	2,204	2,943	3,044	2,601	2,761	26,233
Race share of for-profit enrollment	5.6%	5.6%	5.3%	5.6%	5.9%	5.7%	5.2%	5.3%	5.8%
Share of race full-time enrollment	8%	9%	9%	9%	9%	7%	6%	6%	6%
Black	16,909	22,182	25,420	27,781	37,144	41,614	43,137	44,334	293,130
Female	12,401	16,403	19,079	20,963	27,948	31,506	32,236	33,238	216,485
Male	4,508	5,779	6,341	6,818	9,196	10,108	10,901	11,096	76,645
Race share of for-profit enrollment	23.6%	25.7%	28.0%	30.2%	32.1%	32.3%	33.7%	34.6%	28.0%
Share of race full-time enrollment	32%	41%	45%	48%	51%	38%	38%	38%	31%

Table 4 (continued)

Full-time students	*2004*	*2005*	*2006*	*2007*	*2008*	*2009*	*2010*	*2011*	*Grand Total*
Hispanic	6,013	7,794	7,696	7,802	9,651	10,642	10,895	11,696	93,283
Female	3,696	4,929	4,954	5,074	6,335	7,023	7,155	7,602	58,643
Male	2,317	2,865	2,742	2,728	3,316	3,619	3,740	4,094	34,640
Ethnicity share of for-profit enrollment	8.4%	9.0%	8.5%	8.5%	8.3%	8.3%	8.5%	9.1%	8.9%
Share of ethnicity full-time enrollment	10%	12%	12%	12%	12%	10%	10%	10%	9%
White	44,103	50,584	52,189	50,264	61,051	67,951	65,977	64,149	589,146
Female	27,797	32,824	34,891	34,038	41,033	45,274	43,878	42,521	375,000
Male	16,306	17,760	17,298	16,226	20,018	22,677	22,099	21,628	214,146
Race share of for-profit enrollment	61.5%	58.7%	57.4%	54.7%	52.7%	52.8%	51.6%	50.1%	56.3%
Share of race full-time enrollment	8%	9%	9%	9%	9%	8%	8%	7%	7%
Full-time for-profit enrollment subtotal	71,736	86,178	90,937	91,850	115,817	128,780	127,823	128,168	1,045,972
For-profit share of full-time enrollment	10%	11%	12%	12%	13%	11%	10%	10%	8%

(*continued*)

Table 4 (continued)

Part-time students	*1995*	*1996*	*1997*	*1998*	*2000*	*2001*	*2002*	*2003*
Native American	12	35	28	40	50	57	72	98
Female	5	17	18	26	28	30	35	67
Male	7	18	10	14	22	27	37	31
Race share of for-profit enrollment	0.2%	0.6%	0.5%	0.6%	0.4%	0.5%	0.6%	0.6%
Share of race part-time enrollment	0%	1%	1%	1%	1%	1%	1%	2%
Asian	345	245	471	427	1,064	702	816	1,094
Female	91	116	151	187	503	359	396	528
Male	254	129	320	240	561	343	420	566
Race share of for-profit enrollment	6.4%	4.2%	8.4%	6.9%	8.1%	6.1%	6.4%	6.5%
Share of race part-time enrollment	1%	1%	1%	1%	3%	2%	2%	2%
Black	445	686	599	812	2,147	2,463	2,956	4,365
Female	252	453	358	526	1,448	1,698	2,042	3,055
Male	193	233	241	286	699	765	914	1,310
Race share of for-profit enrollment	8.2%	11.6%	10.6%	13.2%	16.3%	21.3%	23.0%	26.0%
Share of race part-time enrollment	1%	1%	1%	1%	2%	3%	3%	4%
Hispanic	165	187	360	291	660	674	774	1,047
Female	62	92	132	176	375	365	403	582
Male	103	95	228	115	285	309	371	465
Ethnicity share of for-profit enrollment	3.0%	3.2%	6.4%	4.7%	5.0%	5.8%	6.0%	6.2%
Share of ethnicity part-time enrollment	0%	0%	1%	1%	1%	1%	1%	1%
White	4,452	4,746	4,181	4,591	9,281	7,645	8,210	10,212
Female	1,588	2,273	2,053	2,281	5,135	4,171	4,299	5,475
Male	2,864	2,473	2,128	2,310	4,146	3,474	3,911	4,737
Race share of for-profit enrollment	82.2%	80.5%	74.1%	74.5%	70.3%	66.2%	64.0%	60.7%
Share of race part-time enrollment	1%	1%	1%	1%	1%	1%	1%	1%
Part-time for-profit enrollment subtotal	5,419	5,899	5,639	6,161	13,202	11,541	12,828	16,816
For-profit share of total enrollment	1%	1%	1%	1%	1%	1%	1%	2%
For-profit grand total	17,565	24,008	25,096	29,575	36,935	41,144	40,021	68,206

Part-time students	1995	1996	1997	1998	2000	2001	2002	2003
For-profit share of total enrollment	1%	2%	2%	2%	2%	3%	3%	4%

Part-time students	*2004*	*2005*	*2006*	*2007*	*2008*	*2009*	*2010*	*2011*	*Grand total*
Native American	167	233	249	359	430	584	697	851	3,957
Female	99	151	172	237	279	361	456	554	2,532
Male	68	82	77	122	151	223	241	297	1,425
Race share of for-profit enrollment	0.8%	0.9%	0.8%	0.8%	0.8%	0.9%	0.8%	0.8%	0.8%
Share of race part-time enrollment	3%	4%	4%	5%	6%	8%	10%	12%	4%
Asian	1,459	1,646	1,529	1,954	2,806	3,099	3,595	4,816	26,022
Female	643	820	796	1,076	1,439	1,627	1,925	2,680	13,313
Male	816	826	733	878	1,367	1,472	1,670	2,136	12,709
Race share of for-profit enrollment	6.7%	6.0%	4.7%	4.5%	5.4%	4.5%	4.1%	4.8%	5.1%
Share of race part-time enrollment	2%	2%	2%	2%	2%	2%	2%	3%	2%
Black	6,171	8,398	11,180	15,975	19,568	26,594	35,514	39,884	177,732
Female	4,375	6,180	8,508	12,134	14,841	19,973	26,859	30,148	132,842
Male	1,796	2,218	2,672	3,841	4,727	6,621	8,655	9,736	44,890
Race share of for-profit enrollment	28.3%	30.7%	34.3%	36.6%	37.4%	39.0%	40.5%	39.7%	34.8%
Share of race part-time enrollment	5%	7%	9%	12%	14%	17%	21%	23%	10%
Hispanic	1,404	1,750	1,935	2,526	3,235	4,602	6,189	7,342	33,094
Female	754	1,082	1,162	1,541	1,929	2,735	3,772	4,565	19,706
Male	650	668	773	985	1,306	1,867	2,417	2,777	13,388
Ethnicity share of for-profit Enrollment	6.4%	6.4%	5.9%	5.8%	6.2%	6.7%	7.1%	7.3%	6.5%

(*continued*)

Table 4 (continued)

Part-time students	*2004*	*2005*	*2006*	*2007*	*2008*	*2009*	*2010*	*2011*	*Grand total*
share of ethnicity	2%	2%	3%	3%	4%	5%	7%	8%	3%
Part-time enrollment									
White	12,582	15,309	17,669	22,837	26,231	33,337	41,727	47,595	270,380
Female	6,566	8,898	10,940	13,822	15,805	19,939	25,218	29,410	157,793
Male	6,016	6,411	6,729	9,015	10,426	13,398	16,509	18,185	112,587
Race share of for-profit enrollment	57.8%	56.0%	54.3%	52.3%	50.2%	48.9%	47.6%	47.4%	52.9%
Share of race part-time enrollment	2%	2%	2%	3%	4%	4%	6%	6%	2%
Part-time for-profit enrollment subtotal	21,783	27,336	32,562	43,651	52,270	68,216	87,722	100,488	511,185
For-profit share of total enrollment	2%	3%	3%	4%	5%	6%	8%	9%	3%
For-profit grand total	93,519	113,514	123,499	135,501	168,087	196,996	215,545	228,656	1,557,157

are 3 times greater than black men and white and Hispanic women having enrollments that are just over 1.5 times that of their male counterparts. By 2011, blacks and whites were 87 percent of the part-time enrollment at for-profit institutions. Of the blacks and Native Americans enrolled part-time as graduate students in 2011, 12 percent of the Native Americans and 23 percent of the blacks were enrolled at for-profit institutions. The corresponding percentage for Asians, Hispanics and whites is less than 10 percent. Between 1995 and 2001, the growth in part-time graduate enrollment at for-profit institutions was 1755 percent or 17.5 times the 1995 enrollment level. However, the for-profit share of graduate enrollment was 10 percent in 2011 up from 1 percent in 1995.

Conclusion

Our findings show that enrollment at for-profit institutions has grown significantly. However, the majority of traditional college age students are not enrolled at for-profit institutions. By 2011, for-profits enrolled less than 10 percent of the full-time undergraduate or graduate students, 3 percent of the part-time undergraduate students, and 9 percent of part-time graduate students.

Women across race, ethnicity, enrollment levels and status seem to have a greater preference, relative to men, for enrolling at for-profit institutions. More women may enroll at for-profit institutions because of the availability of on-line courses, which offer greater flexibility to manage work—the first shift, household responsibilities—the second shift, and education—the third shift (Kramarae 2001). This may also explain why older adults comprise a larger percentage of students enrolled at for-profit institutions. The higher percentage of black, native American and Hispanic students enrolled at for-profit institutions also may be explained by compatively low graduation rates from not-for-profit institutions.

Studies suggest that low income students and students from groups subject to discrimination students drop out/stop of school primarily for financial reasons. Therefore, the flexibility of for-profit institutions make them a feasible alternative for degree completion since for-profits require little if any time away from work. However, those without employment or who hold low wage jobs while enrolled still may have to depend heavily on government loans and can experience growing debt burdens. The capacity to meet those burdens, in turn, depends upon degree completion and the type of employment obtained post-degree.

Also like the "pragmatic" women in Kramarae's 2001 study, blacks, native Americans, and Hispanics may utilize for-profits to complete degrees for career advancement. Finally, we must note that attending college—whether for-profit or non-profit—is not the same thing as finishing college. This is especially true for black, native American, and Hispanic students.

References

Bennett, D. L., Lucchesi, A. R., & Vedder, R. K. (2010). *For-profit higher education: Growth, innovation and regulation.* Center for Collge Affordability and Productivity (CCAP). Washington, DC: CCAP.

Boardman, W. (2012 йил 14-Aug). *For-profit colleges: Socrates could have died rich.* Retrieved 2012 йил 26-Nov from Independent Voter Network: http://ivn.us/2012/08/14/for-profit-colleges-socrates-could-have-died-rich/

Breneman, D. W., Pusser, B., & Turner, S. E. (2006). *Earnings from learing: The rise of for-profit universities.* Albany: State Uniersity of New York Press.

Carey, K. (2010 йил 25-Jul). *Why do you think they're called for-profit colleges?* Retrieved 2012 йил 27-Nov from The Chronicle of Higher Education: http://chronicle.com/article/Why-Do-You-Think-Theyre/123660/

Cellini, S. R. (2010). Financial aid and for-profit colleges: Does aid enourage entry? *Journal of Policy Analysis and Management, 29*(3), 526–552.

Cellini, S. R. (2012). For-profit higher education: An assessment of the costs and benefits. *National Tax Journal, 65*(1), 153–180.

Coleman, J., & Vedder, C. (2008). *For-profit education in the United States: A primer.* Washington, DC: Center for College Affordability and Productivity (CCAP).

Coulson, A. J. (1999). *Market education.* New Brunswick: Transaction.

Goldin, C., & Katz, L. F. (1999 йил Winter). The shaping of higher education: The formative years in the United States, 1890 to 1940. *The Journal of Economic Perspectives, 13*(1), 37–62.

Heckman, J. J. (2000 йил Mar). Policies to foster human capital. *Research in Economics, 54*(1), 3–56.

Kamenetz, A. (2005 йил 16-Nov). *The profit chase: For-profit college have lots of champions – And lots of problems.* Retrieved 2012 йил 27-Nov from Slate: http://www.slate.com/articles/news_and_politics/college_week/2005/11/the_profit_chase.single.html

Kinser, K., & Levy, D. C. (2005 йил Feb). The for-profit sector: U.S. patterns and international echoes in higher education. *PROPHE working paper series,* WP No. 5.

Kramarae, C. (2001). *The third shift: Women learning online.* Washington, DC: American Association of University Women Educational Foundation.

Levine, A. (1997 йил Fall). How the academic profession is changing. *Daedalus, 126*(4), 1–20.

National Center for Education Statistics. (2011). *Students attending for-profit postsecondary institutions: Demographics, enrollment characterisics, and 6-year ouctomes.* Washington, DC: U.S. Department of Education.

Staff, N. N. (2012 йил 25-Jul). *For-profit college still seeing declines in enrollment.* Retrieved 2012 йил 30-Nov from NBCnews.com: http://usnews.nbcnews.com/_news/2012/07/25/12949437-for-profit-colleges-still-seeing-declines-in-enrollment

Turner, S. E. (2006). For-profit colleges in the context of the market for higher education. In D. W. Breneman, B. Pusser, & S. E. Turner (Eds.), *Earnings from learning: The rise of for-profit universities* (pp. 51–68). Albany: State University of New York Press.

Enrollment and Degree Completion at For-Profit Colleges versus Traditional Institutions

D. Diego Torres, Jane Rochmes, and David J. Harding

Introduction

On September 30, 2010, the Senate Committee on Health, Education, Labor, and Pensions (HELP), under the leadership of Chairman Tom Harkin and Ranking Member Michael B. Enzi, convened the third in a series of hearings examining the efficacy of federal investment in for-profit education (*The Federal Investment in For-Profit Education: Are Students Succeeding* 2010). While the specific aim of this gathering was to answer the question of whether students at for-profit postsecondary institutions are succeeding, much of the testimony centered on the well-publicized

---

Funding for this research was provided by the Spencer Foundation.

D.D. Torres (✉)
Houston Education Research Consortium, Rice University, Houston, TX, USA
e-mail: ddtorres@rice.edu

J. Rochmes
Center for Education Policy Analysis, Stanford University, Stanford, CA, USA
e-mail: jrochmes@stanford.edu

D.J. Harding
Department of Sociology, University of California at Berkeley, Berkeley, CA, USA
e-mail: dharding@berkeley.edu

T. McMillan Cottom, W.A. Darity, Jr. (eds.), *For-Profit Universities*,
DOI 10.1007/978-3-319-47187-7_8

faults associated with the for-profit education industry. After much back-and-forth and no small amount of contentious debate, Senator Richard Burr attempted to get to the heart of the matter by directly questioning the panelists about which was more important, the graduation rate of a particular institution type or whether the institution is for-profit or not-for-profit. With some hesitation and a couple of attempts to put forward caveats and qualifications, each of the witnesses answered that graduation rates were more important than institutional sector. This seemed the answer that Burr had anticipated as the senator went on to highlight graduation rates at two- and four-year institutions in his home state of North Carolina.

According to the data Senator Burr cited, of North Carolina's 26 two-year institutions that had a graduation rate exceeding 50 percent after three years, 20 were for-profit while the remaining 6 were community colleges. Of the 94 two-year institutions in North Carolina that had a three-year graduation rate below 50 percent, 88 were community colleges and 6 were for-profit schools. Citing statistics for North Carolina's four-year institutions, only 9 of the state's 58 four-year colleges and universities had a graduation rate greater than 50 percent after four years. After six years this number had improved slightly to 19 institutions, but still over half of North Carolina's four-year postsecondary institutions failed to graduate more than 50 percent of their students after eight years.

Senator Burr's primary point seemed to be that, regardless of sector, a large percentage of students fail to complete their degree programs. In absolute terms, then, it can be argued that graduation rates in all sectors of postsecondary education are suboptimal. In relative terms, however, the two-year for-profit schools appear to be outperforming their nonprofit counterparts, and not only in the state of North Carolina. Nationwide, the three-year graduation rate of first-time college students seeking a certificate or associate's degree at two-year institutions is 3 times greater in the for-profit sector than in the public nonprofit sector (60.3 percent compared to 20.4 percent) and 1.2 times greater than in the private nonprofit sector (60.3 percent compared to 51 percent; Snyder and Dillow 2012). The six-year graduation rate of first-time college students seeking an associate's degree was 19.5 percent at two-year for-profit schools and 14.4 percent at community colleges (Radford et al. 2010).

Regarding comparisons of graduation rates of students attending four-year institutions, for-profits still do better relative to both public and private colleges with respect to conferring associate's degrees after six years

(15 percent compared to about 4 percent). When it comes to graduation rates that focus on the traditional undergraduate terminal degree of four-year schools, however, only 15.7 percent of for-profit students earned a bachelor's degree after six years compared to 60 percent of public university students and 65 percent of private nonprofit university students (Radford et al. 2010).

While these numbers seem, *prima facie*, to offer substantive evidence that the for-profit sector is the more likely route to a degree, it is important to highlight that they do not take into account the characteristics of students that could be driving the differences seen between the various postsecondary sectors. Not adjusting for the individual-level factors that are also linked to educational attainment, for instance, can lead to misstatements about the impact of the for-profit sector. Moreover, to understand differences in graduation rates, we must understand the factors that lead some, and not others, to enroll in for-profit colleges and universities. It is additionally necessary to appreciate the fact that the college attendance patterns of individuals are more complex than many published statistics suggest. This is due primarily to the fact that many studies of for-profit colleges measure graduation rates based upon only the first college sector attended; they do not capture changes in attendance from one college sector type to another.

The goals of this chapter are twofold. First, we examine who attends the for-profit sector. Understanding differences in student characteristics between sectors is crucial for understanding differential graduation rates between sectors. We describe overall attendance in the various sectors, differences in sector attendance by respondents' sex, race/ethnicity, and parental education, and the extent of cross-enrollment at more than one sector. Our ability to measure this overlap in sector attendance is uniquely valuable, as for-profit students commonly attend other college types at some point in their college careers. We also use statistical models to identify the student characteristics that most strongly predict for-profit college attendance.

Second, accounting for the extent to which those who choose to attend the for-profit sector also choose to attend other sectors, we address how well for-profit institutions are doing at graduating their students compared to more traditional institutions. By measuring the cumulative time spent enrolled in each sector and comparing the likelihood that students attain either an associate's or a bachelor's degree, we examine whether for-profit institutions are more or less likely than other types of colleges to advance their students to a degree.

For-Profit Graduation Rates and the Attainment Gap

Whether for-profit institutions are succeeding at graduating their students is important, not least because these schools serve a considerably larger share of students who would either not attend college in the first place or who, even when they do, have the greatest risk of noncompletion (Adelman 1999, 2006; Horn et al. 2001). For example, 40 percent of students attending for-profit two-year schools are racial minorities compared to only 25 to 34 percent at community colleges (Cellini 2005; Cominole et al. 2007). Holding constant choice of major and transfer to a four-year institution, the same difference in proportions of for-profit attendance relative to attendance in other sectors holds with respect to economic disadvantage (Cellini and Conger 2010). Compared to community colleges, specifically, for-profits have nearly triple the proportion of students who qualify for Pell Grants (72 percent compared to 26 percent), a measure of low income status. The proportion of for-profit two-year students who are the first in their families to attend college is 55 percent; the corresponding number for community colleges is 42 percent. And 50 percent of for-profit students are both low-income and first generation compared to 26 percent of community college students (Cominole et al. 2007).

Four-year for-profit schools also attract traditionally underserved communities. According to Cominole et al. (2007), 50 percent of for-profit students attending four-year schools are black or Hispanic compared to about one-third in the public and private sectors. Fifty-three percent are first generation compared to 18 and 22 percent in the private and public sectors. Forty-four percent are both low-income and first generation. Only 11 percent of private university students and 12 percent of public university students are both low-income and first generation (Cominole et al. 2007).

Regarding the social factors that are risk factors for non-completion of a degree, the DoE lists seven that appear to have the greatest effect: they are (1) delayed enrollment in college after high school, (2) not having a high school diploma, (3) enrolling part-time rather than full-time in college, (4) being financially independent, (5) having dependent children, (6) being a single parent, and (7) working a full-time job while enrolled in college (Cominole et al. 2007). Among four-year postsecondary schools, for-profits have a larger percentage of students who have at least one of these risk factors, 78 percent versus 24 percent in the public sector and 21 percent in the private sector. Fifty-two percent of for-profit students had at least three risk factors compared to 6 percent of public students and 9 percent of private students.

A number of hypotheses have been offered to explain why the for-profit sector might be attractive to more disadvantaged students. First, for-profits invest a lot of time and effort into student services and they make it easier for students to schedule courses around their busy lives (Berg 2005; Rosenbaum et al. 2006; Ruch 2001). Because of this, for-profit schools may do a much better job than public and nonprofit schools of retaining students until degree completion. Also, whereas traditional institutions often include coursework in the liberal arts, for-profits focus on providing students with the skills needed in the labor market, which may be particularly appealing to students from disadvantaged backgrounds (Ruch 2001; Berg 2005). Frequent start dates and help navigating financial aid may also be attractive draws.

All of this, and the exponential growth rate of for-profit attendance among underrepresented communities, raises the question of whether the rise of the for-profit sector has the potential to reverse what has been a widening gap in degree attainment gap by race and income over the past four decades (Engle and Lynch 2009). More specifically, to the degree that these institutions disproportionately enroll low-income, minority, and first generation students, higher graduation rates may indicate that for-profit education is as viable a route, if not a better one, to closing the degree attainment gap as community colleges were perceived to be in an earlier period (Breneman and Nelson 1981). This last point is particularly salient given the different assumptions on which for-profit and traditional public two-year institutions are built. Whereas the best for-profit schools do not assume that the populations they serve come to the table with the attributes necessary for long-term success, community colleges operate on the belief that they do (Stephan et al. 2009). The result is a difference in the degree of assistance students receive in acquiring the information, skills, and motivation they need to achieve the degree they seek.

Prior Research

Previous studies examining the effectiveness of two-year private institutions have found that their students are more likely to graduate than students of traditional two-year public institutions, or community colleges. Person and Rosenbaum (2006) used data from the Beginning Postsecondary Students Longitudinal Study (BPS), a longitudinal sample of first-time beginning college students, to compare degree completion rates at two-year public and what they term "private colleges," which, due to small sample sizes, include for-profit and traditional private nonprofit schools. They found that, among degree-seekers who began college at a two-year institution for the first time in the 1995–1996 academic year, 42 percent of private college students completed their associate's degree within 150 percent of normal time to degree; only 8 percent of community college students did so. This unadjusted rate favoring private colleges was mirrored in logistic regression analyses controlling for a host of student characteristics, including sex, race/ethnicity, age, high school GPA, parent education, enrollment status in college (whether full-time or part-time), occupational major (as reported in the fall of 1995), and whether the institution offered job placement services. A private college student was 6.18 times more likely than his community college peers to obtain an associate's degree within three years of starting college. However, a serious drawback to the Person and Rosenbaum (2006) sample seems to be the fact that nearly 60 percent of students lacked data on high school achievement, a potentially important control variable.

In another empirical study examining degree outcomes, Stephan et al. (2009) used propensity score matching methods on National Educational Longitudinal Study (NELS) data to understand the chances of degree attainment a private college student (again, a combined category of for-profit and traditional private nonprofit students due to small sample sizes) would have had if he had enrolled in a community college. They found that, with respect to attaining an associate's degree or higher, the typical private college and community college student benefited from attending private schools. Students whose first college enrollment was a private school could expect to attain a degree at a rate 24 percent greater than similar students whose first college enrollment was in a community college. The estimated impact of attending a private school for a student who actually first enrolled in a community college was a 20 percent greater likelihood of degree attainment. However, it is difficult to draw conclusions about the for-profit sector from this study since the authors' sample of private college students was also comprised of those attending private nonprofit two-year schools; the for-profit sample was barely 3 percent of the overall sample. Another important limitation of Stephan et al.'s (2009) study is that it only accounts for the institutional sector of the first college a student attended and ignores the fact that both for-profit and community college students tend to switch frequently among sector types.

Not having accounted for this "swirling," as it's called in the literature (see Goldrick-Rab 2006; McCormick 2003; Sturtz 2006), likely means considerable measurement error is present in the authors' results. In particular, as we show below, a large proportion of for-profit students have also attended community colleges.

Providing evidence specific to the for-profit sector, Deming et al. (2012) use a later wave of BPS data to examine mean differences in associate's and bachelor's degree receipt between public and for-profit postsecondary institutions. The authors estimated unadjusted gaps and then analyzed how the gaps changed when they adjusted for a variety of student characteristics, including, but not limited to, sex, race/ethnicity, citizenship, whether born in the United States, whether English was the native language, household size, marital status, single parenthood, parental education, degree expectations, and individual adjusted gross income. While the unadjusted mean for associate's degree receipt was greatest at for-profit two-year institutions by six percentage points, this gap shrank to 4 percentage points when controlling for student characteristics in an ordinary least squares regression (OLS), and further to only 2 percentage points when propensity score matching was employed. The unadjusted 40 percentage point mean difference in bachelor's degree receipt favoring public over for-profit four-year schools was reduced to between 11.5 (propensity score matching) and 19 (OLS) percentage points. The results suggest that associate's degree attainment rates may be overstating the potential benefits of attending a for-profit, and bachelor's degree attainment rates may be understating the potential drawback of for-profits. Again, one should be cautious given the limitations of the data. Not only is the Deming et al. (2012) data restricted to examining the first sector type a student attended, it also is limited to first-time college students; as a result, many who are returning students are excluded from their analyses.

In sum, based on prior research, it appears that at the two-year level, those students actually attending true for-profit colleges may earn associate's degrees at a moderately better rate than their community college peers, but the difference between the two sectors is statistically insignificant. Public four-year students, on the other hand, may attain bachelor's degrees at a rate far surpassing their for-profit counterparts. Even this, however, is unclear given limitations of the data, particularly the exclusion of returning students and the failure to take into account student mobility across sectors.

The Current Study

The question of whether for-profit students are succeeding is of vital importance given the continued widening of the degree attainment gap between minorities (primarily blacks and Hispanics) and whites, and between the economically disadvantaged and the economically advantaged (Engles and Lynch 2009). Where the traditional public and private two- and four-year schools do not presently attract and graduate in large numbers those who would most benefit from achieving a college education (Brand and Xie 2010), the for-profit sector could ostensibly serve as a viable alternative, creating a new path out of poverty and into the middle class. And given the slow growth of the public and nonprofit sectors compared to the for-profit sector (Fischer and Hout 2006), the for-profit sector has the potential to more deftly meet the growing U.S. demand for higher education. If for-profit students are succeeding, and if they are outpacing their public and private counterparts with regard to likelihood of degree attainment, whether at two-year or four-year schools, or both, the combination of completers in all sectors may go a long way in allowing the United States to meet the needs of a highly skilled and knowledge-based economy.

Answering the question with certainty, however, has been difficult. There are three primary reasons for this. First, there is a dearth of high quality peer-reviewed research on for-profit institutions and their students (Breneman et al. 2006; Kinser 2006). Much of the research available has been conducted by those within the for-profit industry (e.g., Ruch 2001; Berg 2005). Second, to the degree that individual-level data on for-profit students exists, either the samples are too small (e.g., National Educational Longitudinal Studies) or students are not followed over time (e.g., National Postsecondary Student Aid Study), which makes it difficult to adequately assess the effects of for-profit attendance. Third, when students are followed over time (e.g., Beginning Postsecondary Study), only the first institution attended is analyzed. Students most likely to attend for-profit colleges often also attend college in other sectors or choose for-profits after struggling in other sectors. As a result, they are likely underrepresented in these studies. What is needed is a more complete understanding of the factors that both select individuals into particular sectors or degree programs and that assist or hinder them in earning the degree sought.

This chapter contributes to the literature on educational attainment at for-profits using data that allows us to address several of the limitations just highlighted. Utilizing a nationally representative cohort of individuals for whom there is information on all of their college enrollments, we track respondents monthly from the time they are eligible to begin postsecondary education through nearly ten years of young adulthood. We account for simultaneous enrollment at multiple colleges as well as whether a student is registered as part-time or full-time and the type of degree they report pursuing. Having monthly enrollment data on multiple schools allows us to accurately capture enrollment despite student "swirl" (Goldrick-Rab 2006; McCormick 2003; Sturtz 2006). That is, rather than having our analyses limited to the effect of the sector of the first institution type attended, we can analyze the time to degree more accurately even when a student shifts from sector to sector over time. Monthly enrollment data also allow us to better capture enrollment in for-profit institutions, which are less likely to adhere to a conventional semester or trimester calendar. Additionally, data on a nationally representative birth cohort allow us to include students who leave and then return to school; we are not only analyzing first-time attenders. Also, other data often exclude current non-attenders who eventually enroll in college. We include these individuals as an important comparison group to for-profit students since one of the claims is that for-profit institutions serve those not typically served by other institutions. Our research objectives are twofold. We first aim to answer the question of who attends for-profits. Understanding that, we will then examine how cumulative enrollment within the for-profit sector affects degree attainment compared to cumulative enrollment in other sectors. In other words, we plan to compare how efficiently enrollment in various sectors leads to degree completion, taking into account full-time and part-time status.

Data and Methods

Sample

We use data from the National Longitudinal Survey of Youth 1997 Cohort (NLSY97), which interviewed a nationally representative sample of 8,984 youth who were age 12 to 16 in 1997, including oversamples of black and Hispanic youth. Although respondents have been followed annually up to the present day, we draw on data up to and including the 2008 wave only. In addition to the public-use data, which allow us to track monthly enrollment in multiple colleges for each respondent in the NLSY97, we also utilize restricted-use data obtained under contract with the Bureau of Labor Statistics that allow us to identify the sector of each postsecondary school attended. Distinct advantages of these data over other longitudinal datasets are the presence of more than 600 individuals who attended the for-profit sector at some point during their college careers and the ability to follow individuals over time through monthly enrollments in multiple schools in multiple sectors. Finally, the NLSY97 includes detailed information on the backgrounds of respondents and their parents, as well as degree outcomes and timing.[1]

Of the total 8,984 respondents in the NLSY97 at study inception, there were 1,364 who never report receiving a high school diploma or general equivalency diploma (GED). These individuals were removed from our analytic sample if they never reported any postsecondary attendance, as they are arguably not reasonable comparisons for those enrolling in college.

Analytic Methods

Our analysis proceeds in two parts. The goal of the first part is to examine student enrollment in the for-profit sector as compared to students who enroll in other sectors as well as individuals who have a high school diploma or GED but who have never enrolled in college. Our focus is on how the characteristics of students vary across sectors, taking into account attendance in multiple sectors. It is important to verify that patterns of selection into for-profit colleges that others have documented are also present in the NLSY97 data and to understand these patterns in order to take them into account when examining differences across sectors in degree completion in the second part of our analysis. For this analysis we set our analytic data with the unit of analysis as individuals and model whether they have ever enrolled in different sectors. We estimate four binary logit regression models in which the outcome is one for any individual who has every enrolled in a for-profit college for an associate's or bachelor's degree, whether or not they have enrolled in another sector as well. In the first model, the outcome is zero for individuals who have ever enrolled in a community college but not in a for-profit college. In the second model, it is zero for individuals who have ever enrolled in a public four-year college but have not enrolled in a for-profit college. In the third model, the outcome is zero for individuals who have ever enrolled in a private nonprofit two-year or four-year college but not in a for-profit college. In the fourth model, the outcome is zero for individuals who have never enrolled in college but who have a GED or high school degree. We use as predictors in these models all baseline characteristics discussed below.

The goal of the second part of our analysis is to examine differences in degree attainment across sectors. Because some respondents have yet to graduate from college at the final data collection point in the 2008 wave, we employ discrete-time hazard models (Singer and Willett 2003) to estimate the time to completion separately for associate's and bachelor's degree receipt. For this analysis, we structure our analytic data such that respondents are only considered "at-risk" of attending college—and hence, receiving a degree—if they have received a high school diploma or GED. Past the point when "risk" begins, what we will refer to as our baseline, all individuals contribute a row for every month they remain in the study until graduation from college, attrition from the NLSY97, or the end of the observation period.[2] The model is formally specified as

$$logit\left(Y_t\right) = \beta_0 + \beta_1^C X_t^C + \beta_2^C X_t^{2C} + \beta_2 B \tag{1}$$

where Y_t is the estimated probability of degree completion in month t. Our primary interest is in student enrollment in a specific college sector in pursuit of a specific degree (AA or BA), represented by X_t^C and X_t^{2C}, indicating respectively, cumulative months enrolled and cumulative months enrolled-squared at degree sought-college type combination c at time t. B is a set of baseline covariates . Positive values of β_1^C suggest that additional months enrolled in a specific college type seeking a specific degree increases the probability of degree completion, while values of β_2^C (the coefficient on the squared term) denote the acceleration or deceleration over time in the probability of degree completion. To account for multiple observations per respondent over time, we use person-clustered standard errors.

Missing values of the independent variables were imputed using the predictive mean matching method (PMM; Little 1988) in Stata's –mi impute- command.[3] We do not need to impute values for college enrollment as enrollment information is collected retrospectively for all students, regardless of whether they were interviewed in a specific NLSY survey wave.

Variables

The dependent variables in this study are (1) receipt of associate's degree and (2) receipt of bachelor's degree. These dummy variables reflect, in continuous month format, when the associate's and bachelor's degrees were received, where 1 denotes that the relevant degree was earned in the present month and 0 that it was not. The date of receipt for each degree is recorded for all respondents regardless of whether or not they were interviewed in a given wave. If a respondent acquired more than one degree of the same level, only the earliest valid date of degree receipt is used. For all respondents, then, the pattern of the dependent variables is one in which all the months from high school graduation or GED receipt up to and excluding the month of attainment of a specific degree level is coded 0; the month of degree receipt is coded 1.

Our key independent variables are the cumulative months spent pursuing a particular degree type (associate's or bachelor's) at a particular institution type (public four-year, public two-year, private nonprofit, for-profit, or international/other university). Thus, it is the combination of the degree type sought *and* where it was sought that defines our independent variables. Including those who have never attended college in a given month, there are ten sector categories: (1) non-attender, (2) pursuing an associate's degree at a public four-year school, (3) pursuing a bachelor's degree at a public four-year school, (4) pursuing an associate's degree at a community college, (5) pursuing a bachelor's degree at a community college, (6) pursuing an associate's degree at a private two- or four-year school, (7) pursuing a bachelor's degree at a private two- or four-year school, (8) pursuing an associate's degree at a for-profit two- or four-year school, (9) pursuing a bachelor's degree at a for-profit two- or four-year school, and (10) pursuing any degree type at a non-U.S. or unidentifiable university.

We also include a number of baseline covariates. These measures include race/ethnicity, sex, secondary school type (whether public or other, where other is predominantly parochial/private), high school GPA, a variable denoting whether a respondent received a GED, parental educational attainment (categorized as "less than high school," "high school," "some college," and "bachelor's degree or higher"), family type (whether headed by both biological parents, coded 0, or some other type, coded 1), whether a respondent ever took the Scholastic Aptitude Test (SAT) or the American Collegiate Test (ACT), the natural log of gross family income, household size, urbanicity (urban versus rural), and census region of residence. We also control for Armed Services Vocational Aptitude Battery (ASVAB) percentile score, available for most NLSY97 respondents as an age-adjusted measure of cognitive ability and job trainability based on four subtests designed to assess mathematical knowledge, arithmetic reasoning, word knowledge, and paragraph comprehension. Finally, we adjust for the age at which respondents become at-risk for college attendance, whether they were married at this point (coded 1 if yes, 0 if no), number of own or adopted children in the household, the number of hours they worked in the month prior to the baseline month, and the natural log of their hourly pay in that month.

Results

Descriptive Statistics and Patterns of College Sector Attendance

Table 1 shows weighted descriptive statistics of the baseline covariates for all survey participants at-risk of attending college. The majority of the 7,620 respondents were white, as we would expect in a nationally representative sample. While the weighted means for blacks and Hispanics reflect their respective proportions in the larger population, they suggest that our specification of the analytic sample did not disproportionately exclude members of these subgroups from the analysis. About a third of respondents came from families where the highest degree of at least one parent was a bachelor's or higher—33.6 percent compared to 9.2, 30, and 27.2 percent, respectively, for families where the highest level of education of any parent was less than high school, high school, or some college. More respondents came from homes headed by both biological parents as opposed to some other family structure (55.6 percent compared to 44.4 percent). In the full NLSY sample of 8,984 respondents, greater than 10 percent of NLSY97 parents had less than a high school education, while the remaining 90 percent were divided fairly evenly among high school completers, college attenders (including those with less than a bachelor's degree), and college attenders with a bachelor's degree or higher. Family structure was more evenly divided between two-parent and other family structure types in the full sample.

The vast majority of respondents attended public high schools rather than a parochial, private, or other secondary school type. Just fewer than five in ten respondents had ever taken one of the two major college entrance exams. The mean age of the respondents at the point they became at-risk of college attendance was just above 18 years. The means for high school GPA and the ASVAB percentile score were at about the national average. The ratio of urban to rural respondents in our sample was about 2 to 1, with the majority of respondents coming from the South, followed in succession by the Midwest, West, and Northeastern regions of the United States. Only a handful of individuals were married

Table 1 Weighted characteristics of NLSY97 respondents at baseline (n = 7,620)

	Mean	*SD*	*Min*	*Max*	*# Missing & Imputed*
Race					
White	0.682	0.466	0	1	0
Black	0.146	0.353	0	1	0
Hispanic	0.119	0.324	0	1	0
Other race	0.053	0.223	0	1	0
Sex					
Female	0.495	0.500	0	1	0
Male	0.505	0.500	0	1	0
Parent's education					
Less than high school	0.092	0.290	0	1	268
High school	0.300	0.458	0	1	268
Some college	0.272	0.445	0	1	268
Bachelor's degree or higher	0.336	0.472	0	1	268
Family structure					
Both biological parents	0.556	0.497	0	1	22
Other family structure	0.444	0.497	0	1	22
Gross family income (natural log of 1997 dollars)	10.504	1.370	0	12.415	1987
Household size	4.429	1.414	1	16	0
Type of high school attended					
Public school	0.901	0.299	0	1	15
Parochial/Private/Other	0.099	0.299	0	1	15
Took ACT or SAT	0.454	0.498	0	1	
High school GPA	2.916	0.587	0.15	4.17	2131
ASVAB percentile	53.572	27.956	0	100	1427
Residence area					
Urban	0.690	0.462	0	1	0
Rural	0.310	0.462	0	1	0
Region					
Northeast	0.187	0.390	0	1	0
Midwest	0.270	0.444	0	1	0
South	0.333	0.471	0	1	0
West	0.209	0.407	0	1	0
Age (in years)	18.406	0.675	15.083	25	19
Married	0.009	0.099	0	1	22
Number of children	0.042	0.241	0	4	706
Monthly hours worked	84.49	77.472	0	360	146
Hourly pay (natural log)	1.33	0.969	−3.51	7.78	95

or had children at baseline. Monthly work hours and hourly wages were relatively low but showed considerable variation, which is to be expected in such a young sample.

Figure 1 presents two graphical representations that are analogous to a 4 × 2 sector attendance-by-degree sought table. It shows two ways of looking at the data. The upper graph corresponds to column proportions

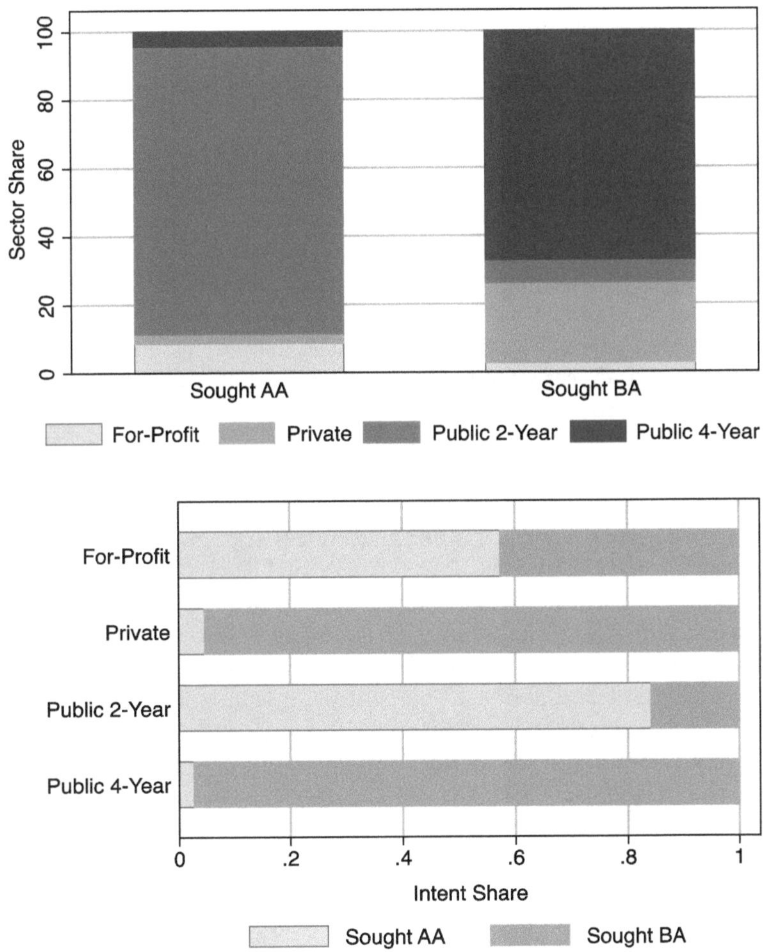

Fig. 1 Sector share-by-intent and intent share-by-sector (person-months)

of the total number of person-months in pursuit of either the associate's or bachelor's degree accumulated by students within each of the four U.S. postsecondary sectors. The lower graph corresponds to the row proportions of the total number of person-months that students within each sector spent pursing either an associate's or bachelor's degree. The upper graph reveals that the majority of time spent pursuing an associate's degree, which was almost 85 percent of the more than 55,000 total person-months, was accumulated by those who attended the public two-year sector while the majority of time spent pursing the latter degree, approximately 67 percent of the 132,000 total person-months, was accumulated by those who attended the public four-year sector. Focusing on the for-profit share of accumulated person-months, specifically, the graph shows that it was three times greater among those who sought an associate's (8.72 percent) rather than a bachelor's degree (2.72 percent). Those in the for-profit sector accumulated more person-months seeking an associate's degree than those in either the private or public four-year sector. Contrastingly, the accumulation of person-months of attendance was the smallest among for-profit attenders than among students who attended any of the other three sectors.

Turning to the lower graph of Fig. 1, the share of accumulated person-months toward an associate's degree was nearly 85 percent compared to only about 15 percent among public two-year attenders. The share of accumulated person months toward a bachelor's degree was approximately 97 percent compared to about 3 percent among public four-year attenders. The proportion of person-months having sought a bachelor's versus an associate's degree was similar among attenders at public four-year and private institutions. Finally, the lower graph of Fig. 1 reveals a more even split in the proportion of for-profit person-months accumulated between the two intent categories, "Sought AA" and "Sought BA." About 57 percent of for-profit person-months were accumulated having sought an associate's degree and about 43 percent were accumulated having sought a bachelor's degree.

Next we examined the patterns of attendance and graduation rates across the various sectors of postsecondary education. Figure 2 shows the proportions of respondents who ever attended each of four types of institutions: community colleges, traditional public four-year colleges and universities, private schools, and for-profits. Attendance at any institution type was not exclusive, so respondents are often represented in multiple categories in the data. The most common type of institution attended was community colleges and public four-year schools, the more traditional

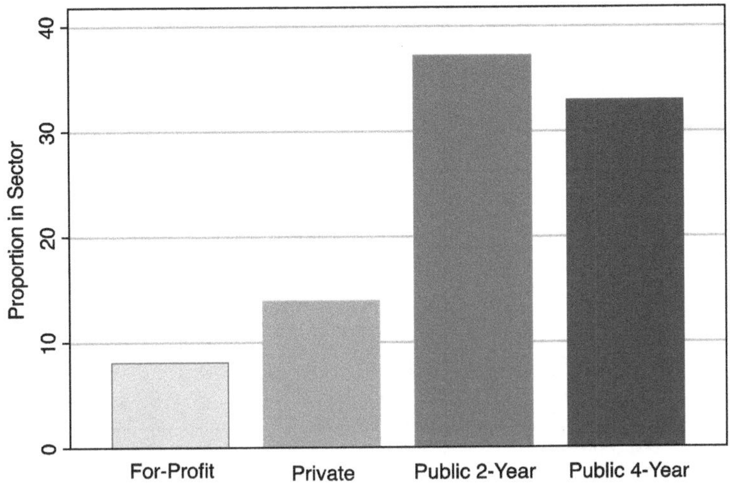

Fig. 2 Proportion of NLSY97 respondents ever attending each sector

sectors of the education industry. Much smaller proportions of students spent time in private and for-profit schools.

When sector attendance was broken down by sex (Fig. 3), two things became apparent. First, there were larger proportions of females than males in all sectors. Second, the biggest difference in sector attendance between the sexes occurred at public two- and four-year schools. The gender gap in attendance did shrink somewhat in the private sector, but only in the for-profit sector did males appear to come close to being represented in the same proportion as females.

Racial differences in sector attendance were much greater than sex differences, particularly between whites and blacks, whites and Hispanics, other race individuals and blacks, and other race individuals and Hispanics (Fig. 4). While whites and other race individuals were more likely than either blacks or Hispanics to attend public four-year or private institutions, they were less likely than members of these groups to attend the for-profit sector. Both blacks and whites, however, attended the community college sector less often than their Hispanic and other race peers. This indicates that for-profits do indeed disproportionately serve underrepresented racial/ethnic groups like blacks and Hispanics, but so do community colleges.

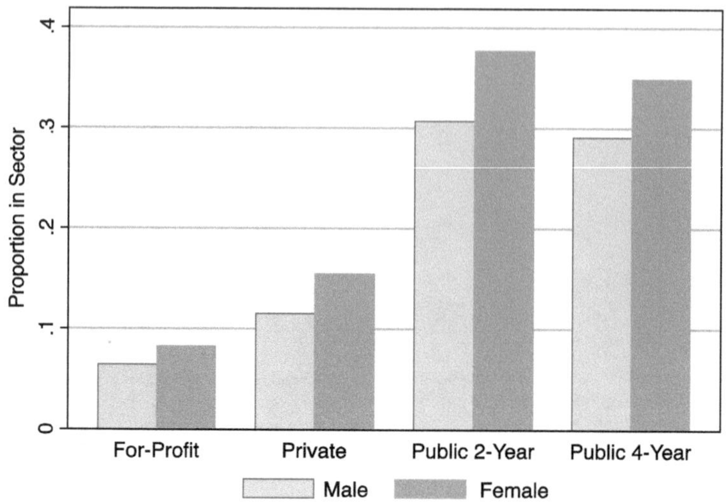

Fig. 3 Proportion of NLSY97 respondents ever attending each sector by sex

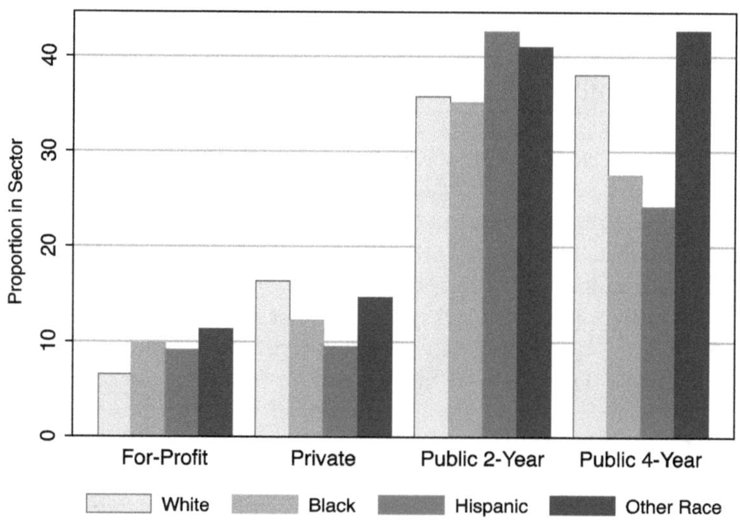

Fig. 4 Proportion of NLSY97 respondents ever attending each sector by race/ethnicity

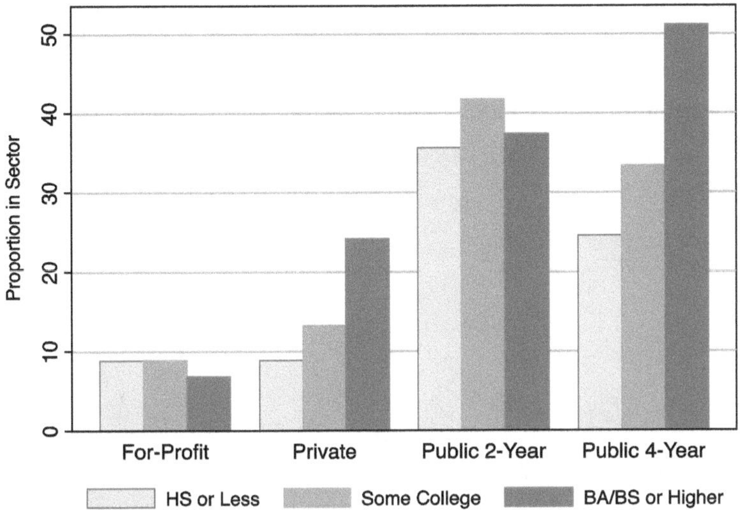

Fig. 5 Proportion of NLSY97 respondents ever attending each sector by parental educational attainment

An examination of Fig. 5 reveals, similarly, that those from low education households were more likely than their peers from homes with more educated parents to attend for-profit schools. They were at least as likely to attend community college as their counterparts from more educated households, but much less likely to attend the private sector. Conversely, respondents from highly educated homes attended public four-year and private schools in higher proportions than degree-seekers from homes where the highest level of education was reported as some college or high school or less.

Table 2 presents the extent of attendance overlap among postsecondary sectors. The percentages in each cell beneath the second through fifth columns represent the proportion of students who reported ever attending a row sector (as shown in the leftmost column) who also reported attending the sector to which the column refers. We note the small number of students who reported ever attending a for-profit college relative to those who reported ever attending other school types. But striking was the large percentage of for-profit students who reported also attending another sector (see the row denoting for-profit attendance). That greater than half of all those who reported ever attending a for-profit also reported at some point attend-

Table 2 Percent of overlap between two postsecondary sectors

	Percent who also attended:			
Sectors ever attended:	*Public 4-year*	*Public 2-year*	*Private*	*For-profit*
Public 4-year (n = 2,508) 32.91%	—	37.53	11.28	4.00
Public 2-year (n = 2,832) 37.17%	35.96	—	12.44	10.56
Private (n = 1,061) 13.92%	31.05	26.97	—	13.89
For-profit (n = 616) 8.08%	18.78	51.79	27.29	—

Note: The percent of overlap refers to the proportion of students who attended a sector in the leftmost column who also attended a different sector among the last four columns. Percentages in the leftmost column represent the proportion of students in the overall sample who ever attended the respective sector.

ing a public two-year school could, in some ways, be an indication of the degree of similarity among students who attend these two sectors. No other sector overlap proportion came close to mirroring this 50 percent. Nearly a fifth and more than a quarter of for-profit students also reported enrollment in the public four-year and private two- or four-year sectors, respectively. Although it is significant that more than 10 percent of community college students and about 14 percent of private students also spent time at a for-profit college, this represented a much smaller degree of overlap between all other sectors and the for-profit sector (see the column denoting for-profit attendance). It seems likely that this pattern is due to the smaller size of the for-profit sector relative to the other institutional sectors. However, that there was some degree of non-overlap is consistent with the idea that there is something about the model of the for-profit postsecondary sector that is attractive to a nontraditional student.

Patterns of Selecting into For-Profit Colleges

Understanding differences in degree completion across sectors first requires understanding differences in student characteristics across sectors. What are the characteristics of students who select into for-profit postsecondary institutions? We ran logistic regression analyses to test the importance of a variety of individual characteristics in predicting the likelihood of attending a for-profit college relative to ever attending each of the other sectors and to never attending college. The results are shown in Table 3. Each of the four columns of results represents a separate logistic regression in which individuals who had ever attended a for-profit college were coded 1 and individuals in the comparison group who had not attended a for-profit college were coded 0. For the purposes of these models, an individual who had ever attended both a for-profit college and the other type of institution in the binary comparison was coded as having attended a for-profit.

Considering race/ethnic differences in the odds of attending a for-profit school versus attending some other institution type net of the other baseline covariates in the model, we found that, relative to whites, blacks were 1.47 times ($e^{0.385}$) more likely to attend a for-profit than a community college. There was no statistically significant difference in the odds of attending a for-profit compared to a community college between whites and Hispanics; both groups were equally likely to attend either sector. Those classified as "other race," though, were 1.70 times ($e^{0.529}$) more likely than whites to go to a for-profit college than to a community college. All nonwhite racial/ethnic groups had greater odds of attending a for-profit college than not attending postsecondary school. Blacks, Hispanics, and other race individuals were, respectively, 2.44 times ($e^{0.892}$), about 1.49 times ($e^{0.396}$), and 3.05 times ($e^{1.115}$) more likely than whites to attend a for-profit than to never attend college at all. Relative to whites, other race individuals were more likely, and blacks and Hispanics were less likely, to attend a for-profit college compared to either a public four-year or private two- or four-year college, though these differences were not statistically significant. While there was no difference between for-profit and community college students with regard to high school GPA or ASVAB score, those with higher GPAs and ASVAB scores were less likely to attend for-profits than public four-years and private colleges but more likely to attend for-profits than to not attend college at all. Possessors of GEDs or those without a high school diploma were less likely than their diploma-holding counterparts to attend college at all, but when they did, they had greater odds of attending a for-profit than either a public four-year or private two- or four-year institution. There was no difference in the odds of attending a for-profit versus a community college for these individuals. The same trend was at work with respect to the baseline covariate denoting number of children in the home. Those from two-parent families were more

Table 3 Predictors of attending a for-profit college relative to ever attending other sectors and never attending college (logit coefficients)

	Compared to public 2-year	*Compared to public 4-year*	*Compared to private 2- or 4-year*	*Compared to never attending*
	(n = 2492)	*(n = 2511)*	*(n = 1237)*	*(n = 2710)*
Race (Ref = White)				
Black	0.385*	−0.189	−0.425	0.892***
	(0.156)	(0.175)	(0.221)	(0.162)
Hispanic	0.055	−0.003	−0.107	0.396*
	(0.167)	(0.180)	(0.224)	(0.178)
Other race	0.529*	0.255	0.402	1.115***
	(0.243)	(0.245)	(0.301)	(0.304)
Male	−0.007	−0.065	0.006	−0.512***
	(0.119)	(0.126)	(0.149)	(0.126)
Attended public school	−0.354	−0.209	0.012	−0.111
	(0.183)	(0.196)	(0.213)	(0.193)
Took ACT or SAT	0.025	−0.291*	−0.395**	0.519***
	(0.113)	(0.121)	(0.147)	(0.119)
High school GPA	−0.106	−0.808***	−0.647***	0.480***
	(0.124)	(0.139)	(0.165)	(0.126)
ASVAB percentile	0.002	−0.011***	−0.010**	0.016***
	(0.003)	(0.003)	(0.004)	(0.003)
GED or no diploma	0.212	1.554***	1.196**	−0.603**
	(0.216)	(0.334)	(0.398)	(0.208)
Parent's education (Ref = less than high school)				
High school	−0.290	−0.046	0.130	0.054
	(0.200)	(0.221)	(0.288)	(0.200)
Some college	−0.252	−0.052	0.039	0.460*
	(0.207)	(0.224)	(0.292)	(0.203)
Bachelor's degree or higher	−0.439*	−0.616**	−0.615*	0.866***
	(0.220)	(0.235)	(0.306)	(0.220)
Family structure	0.071	0.198	0.195	−0.132
	(0.119)	(0.129)	(0.163)	(0.133)
Gross family income (log of 1997 dollars)	0.026	0.009	−0.085	0.136**

(*continued*)

Table 3 (continued)

	Compared to public 2-year	*Compared to public 4-year*	*Compared to private 2- or 4-year*	*Compared to never attending*
	(n = 2492)	*(n = 2511)*	*(n = 1237)*	*(n = 2710)*
	(0.037)	(0.041)	(0.074)	(0.052)
Household size	−0.066	−0.041	−0.070	−0.090
	(0.042)	(0.044)	(0.050)	(0.046)
Rural (vs. urban)	−0.024	−0.079	−0.155	−0.296*
	(0.139)	(0.147)	(0.175)	(0.139)
Region (Ref = Northeast)				
Midwest	−0.300	−0.165	0.128	−0.302
	(0.177)	(0.187)	(0.209)	(0.188)
South	−0.456**	0.026	0.744***	−0.433*
	(0.171)	(0.182)	(0.200)	(0.175)
West	−0.357*	0.213	1.011***	−0.138
	(0.180)	(0.189)	(0.221)	(0.196)
Age relative to 18th birthday	−0.016	−0.022	0.011	−0.034**
	(0.011)	(0.012)	(0.030)	(0.011)
Age-squared	−0.000	−0.000	0.001	−0.000
	(0.000)	(0.000)	(0.001)	(0.000)
Currently married	0.363	−0.453		0.133
	(0.576)	(0.758)		(0.470)
Number of children	−0.214	0.954**	0.833	−0.297
	(0.273)	(0.332)	(0.472)	(0.238)
Number of children squared	0.402*	0.058	−0.186	0.242
	(0.180)	(0.205)	(0.298)	(0.124)
Monthly hours worked	−0.001	0.001	0.002	−0.004**
	(0.001)	(0.002)	(0.002)	(0.001)
Monthly hours worked squared	0.000*	0.000	0.000	0.000
	(0.000)	(0.000)	(0.000)	(0.000)
Log of hourly pay	0.100	−0.000	0.040	0.295**
	(0.094)	(0.109)	(0.133)	(0.100)
Log of hourly pay squared	−0.098	0.015	−0.035	−0.226***
	(0.054)	(0.074)	(0.065)	(0.065)

(*continued*)

Table 3 (continued)

	Compared to public 2-year	*Compared to public 4-year*	*Compared to private 2- or 4-year*	*Compared to never attending*
	(n = 2492)	*(n = 2511)*	*(n = 1237)*	*(n = 2710)*
Constant	−1.031** (0.362)	−0.768 (0.432)	−0.115 (0.632)	−2.139*** (0.341)

Notes: Standard errors in parentheses. *$p < 0.05$, **$p < 0.01$, ***$p < 0.001$. Each column represents a separate model of a binary comparison in which individuals who ever attended a for-profit college were coded 1 and students who only fell into the comparison category were coded 0

likely to attend public four-year and private institutions than for-profits, but family structure was unrelated to attendance at a for-profit compared to a community college or compared to not attending college at all. There was no effect of a respondent's household size or gross family income at baseline on the probability of for-profit attendance once the other covariates in the model were controlled. Rural students were no more or less likely than urban students to attend a for-profit relative to a community college, public four-year, or private institution, but rural students were less likely than urban students to attend a for-profit relative to not attending college at all. Relative to students from the Northeast, students from the Midwest region were less likely to attend a for-profit than to not attend college at all. Students from the South were less likely than students from the Northeast to attend a for-profit than a community college, but were more likely to attend a private school than a for-profit and less likely to attend a for-profit than to not attend college at all. Relative to students from the Northeast, students from the West were more likely to attend a private college than a for-profit college. These geographic associations may reflect the differential availability of for-profit schools in various parts of the country.

Descriptive Statistics on Degree Attainment by Sector

Table 4 shows unadjusted degree attainment rates of NLSY97 respondents after 4, 6, and 8 years from baseline (receipt of high school diploma or GED). In the first panel, we show that, relative to the other sectors, a greater percentage of those who had ever attended a for-profit institution

Table 4 Degree attainment rates after 4, 6, and 8 years by sector ever attended by degree type (associate's or bachelor's)

	Percent receiving associate's degree			*Percent receiving bachelor's degree*		
Ever attended sector	*After 4 years*	*After 6 years*	*After 8 years*	*After 4 years*	*After 6 years*	*After 8 years*
Any college type	7.8	10.8	12.3	16.7	35.0	38.7
For-profit	13.8	20.4	23.9	9.7	17.8	20.7
Public 2-year	11.8	16.8	19.0	5.6	16.8	20.1
Public 4-year	7.3	10.0	11.1	19.7	50.1	56.3
Private	5.9	8.4	9.5	36.4	56.2	60.7

Note: Rates are measured from study baseline (see text for definition)

received an associate's degree by each time point. The second panel shows the corresponding unadjusted bachelor's degree attainment rates. Here, clearly it is the public four-year and private schools that had higher rates of graduation while the rates for for-profits and community colleges were roughly similar to one another. Much of the information shown in Table 4 comports with the unadjusted graduation rates reviewed in the introduction. For-profits appear to do a better job relative to other sectors at producing associate's degree holders, yet they fail to keep up with traditional public four-year and private colleges and universities at producing bachelor's degree holders. The difference with our data, however, is that individuals who ever attended one sector might also be counted as having ever attended another sector; hence, degree attainment rates are an effect of both attendance in the one sector and the tendency of those in that sector to move among sectors, or to "swirl."

We finally present graphs showing the cumulative probability of both associate's degree and bachelor's degree receipt by cumulative months enrolled in each sector. Differences across sectors in the average length of a college term—and thus variability in term end points when a degree could plausibly be earned—likely contribute to the cumulative probability lines for the for-profit and private sectors being less smooth than the line for community colleges. However, most important in interpreting these graphs is the relative positioning of the sectors over time, and we focus on the cumulative probability of degree receipt at comparison points relative to "normal" degree completion time. Not accounting for characteristics that vary among individuals, Figure 6 reveals that, beyond about the thirteenth month of cumulative enrollment, for-profit students had a higher probability of receiving an associate's degree than their community college or private school peers. This probability rose rather dramatically for for-profit students relative to students in the other two sectors so that by the end of the eighteenth cumulative month of enrollment, or the equivalent of two academic years of schooling, it exceeded 30 percent. The corresponding rate in the community college and private school sector was closer to 10 percent. At 27 months of cumulative enrollment, or the equivalent of 150 percent of the time it should take to attain an associate's degree, the difference in the cumulative probability of degree receipt favored for-profit over community college students by 45 percentage points (about 70 percent compared to 25 percent).

Figure 7 shows the cumulative probability of bachelor's degree receipt by institutional sector. Here, as we saw in Fig. 6, for-profit students appeared to have an increasing advantage relative to students in the public four-year and private sectors when it comes to the likelihood of attaining a degree. In the 36 months of cumulative enrollment that it should take to complete a bach-

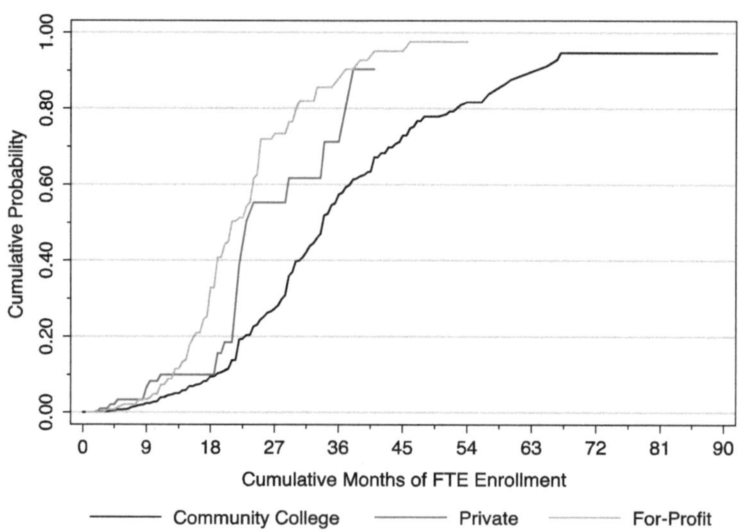

Fig. 6 Cumulative probability of associate's degree receipt by institutional sector type (unadjusted Kaplan-Meier failure estimate)

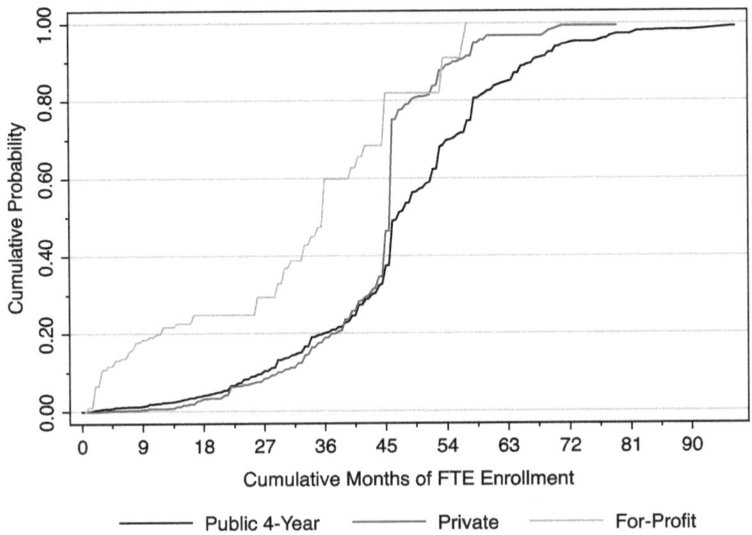

Fig. 7 Cumulative probability of bachelor's degree receipt by institutional sector (unadjusted Kaplan-Meier failure estimate)

elor's degree, for-profit students had a cumulative probability of attaining the degree that was about twice that for individuals in the other two sectors (about 40 percent compared to about 20 percent). At 150 percent of normal time to bachelor's degree completion, i.e., 54 months, for-profit students still had a higher cumulative probability of degree receipt over public four-year students, but their advantage over private sector students had disappeared. The difference between these results and those from Table 4 (which indicated a considerable disadvantage among for-profit students in bachelor's degree receipt) is that additional months of enrollment in Fig. 7 capture students who had continued to attend college for a bachelor's degree, suggesting that probability of continuation in enrollment may be a key difference between for-profits and other institutions when it comes to bachelor's degrees, a point relevant for future research that we return to in the conclusion of this chapter.

We advise a degree of caution when interpreting the lines in Figs 5 and 6. Since neither graph adjusts for differences in student characteristics or specific characteristics of sector types that make them different, the trends for any of the lines could be over- or understating sector differences in students' likelihood of degree receipt. Regarding student-level characteristics, in particular, none of the lines accounts for differences in demographic realities such as the timing of family formation, extent of participation in the labor force, financial liabilities arising from the emancipation and complete independence from parents, or other factors that might interrupt normal time to degree completion.

Discrete-Time Hazard Models of Degree Attainment by Sector

For each of the two outcomes, associate's degree receipt and bachelor's degree receipt, five logistic discrete-time hazard models were run. First, we used only the linear and quadratic functional forms of cumulative months of attendance in any of five postsecondary school types (public four-year, public two-year, private two- or four-year, for-profit two- or four-year, and international/other school) to predict degree receipt, conditional on degree sought. These models show essentially descriptive results of how months of enrollment in each sector are related to degree attainment controlling only for enrollment in other sectors. A second model added baseline covariates to adjust for differences in who attends each sector and pursues each degree. For ease of interpretation, the coefficients for the controls were excluded from the tables showing this second set of models. For those interested in full results, we provide full tables in Appendix A. Finally, in order to examine differences by race, gender, and parental education in the effects of sector on degree receipt, we also estimated models that included, in turn, the interactions between (1) race and cumulative months within each sector, (2) sex and cumulative months within each sector, and (3) parental educational attainment and cumulative months within each sector. These interaction models are provided in Appendix B.

Associate's Degree Attainment

Models 1 and 2 for associate's degree receipt are shown in Table 5. The first column of Model 1 shows that each additional month spent pursuing an associate's degree at a public two-year, private nonprofit, or for-profit college is associated with a greater likelihood of receiving an associate's degree. The coefficient was greatest in the for-profit sector relative to the other postsecondary institution types, though for each of the three sectors, the trend appeared to be one of declining returns the longer one spent in school. That is, the likelihood of associate's degree receipt for each additional month of schooling was strongest in the earlier months of an individual's college career, while the odds of finishing college over

Table 5 Logistic regression coefficients for likelihood of attaining an associate's degree by cumulative months within sector by degree being sought. (n = 7,610; 594,772 person-months)

	Model 1		*Model 2*	
Cumulative months within sector	*Pursuing associate's degree*	*Pursuing bachelor's degree*	*Pursuing associate's degree*	*Pursuing bachelor's degree*
Public 4-year	0.061	0.007	0.128*	−0.004
	(0.052)	(0.017)	(0.052)	(0.017)
Squared	0.0016	−0.0003	0.0005	0.0002
	(0.001)	(0.000)	(0.002)	(0.000)
Public 2-year	0.223***	0.057*	0.243***	0.061*
	(0.013)	(0.024)	(0.014)	(0.024)
Squared	−0.002***	−0.0003	−0.002***	0.0004
	(0.000)	(0.001)	(0.000)	(0.001)
Private	0.358***	−0.076	0.325***	−0.067
	(0.045)	(0.050)	(0.050)	(0.056)
Squared	−0.005***	0.0006	−0.003*	0.0005
	(0.001)	(0.001)	(0.002)	(0.002)
For-profit	0.346***	−0.174*	0.394***	−0.104
	(0.024)	(0.081)	(0.025)	(0.069)
Squared	−0.005***	0.004**	−0.005***	0.004**
	(0.001)	(0.002)	(0.001)	(0.001)

Notes: Models 1 and 2 each include the college sector variables listed as well as an international/other school type variable, which is rarely attended and omitted from the table for simplicity. Model 2 controls for race/ethnicity, sex, type of high school attended, whether respondent took the ACT or SAT, high school GPA, ASVAB percentile, GED receipt, parental educational attainment, family structure, natural log of gross family income, household size, region, whether respondent was married at baseline, respondent's number of own or adopted children, respondent's monthly hours worked, and the natural log of respondent's hourly pay rate. Both the baseline and time-varying value of age and age-squared are also entered. Models are weighted by sampling weights and by inverse probability of attrition over time. Person-clustered standard errors are in parentheses

*$p < 0.05$, **$p < 0.01$, ***$p < 0.001$

the longer run were somewhat diminished. A test of the equality of coefficients in Model 1 revealed that, between for-profit and community college students, for-profit students had significantly greater odds of completing an associate's degree for every month of schooling ($\chi^2 = 24.73$, $p < 0.001$). The coefficient for cumulative months in private two- and four-year schools was nearly identical to that for cumulative months in for-profit schools, and there was no statistically significant difference between students in the two sectors with respect to their likelihood of degree attainment ($\chi^2 = 0.06$, $p = 0.807$). We note, however, that the standard error was much larger for cumulative months in a private school than for cumulative months in a for-profit school, most likely due to the small sample size of students pursuing associate's degrees at private nonprofit colleges, which is quite small compared to the sample size of students pursuing associate's degrees at for-profit colleges.

The second column of Model 1 shows the likelihood of associate's degree completion when the degree sought is actually the baccalaureate. While the coefficient for each additional month of schooling was still statistically significant for for-profits, the sign is reversed. As we would expect, the more months students pursuing bachelor's degrees spend in college, the less likely they are to receive an associate's degree. The coefficient for cumulative months in a private college or university suggested the same thing. Because many community colleges in the United States often have matriculation agreements with traditional public four-year institutions, many of their finishing students transfer with an associate's degree in hand. We would therefore expect to see a positive effect of additional time pursuing a bachelor's degree at a public two-year college on associate's degree attainment, which is what we see in the second column of Model 1 of Table 5.

Model 2 of Table 5 adjusted for student characteristics. For all sectors, including public four-year colleges and universities, there was a strong, positive impact of cumulative months spent pursuing an associate's degree on associate's degree receipt. For every month a student spends in a for-profit school, he multiplies his odds of earning an associate's degree by nearly 1.5 times ($e^{0.394}$). This effect is not only statistically significant within Model 2, but it is also statistically significantly higher than the odds shown in Model 1, net of the differences in student characteristics ($\chi^2 = 14.93$, $p < 0.001$). The squared term for for-profits, however, suggested that this increased odds of associate's degree attainment declines over time. The effect of additional months in school on associate's degree attainment still favored for-profit students over community college students, and it was statistically significant ($\chi^2 = 42.92$, $p < 0.001$). Consistent with the results shown under Model 1 of Table 5, which suggested no significant difference in the likelihood of associate's degree attainment between for-profit and private school students pursuing associate's degrees, Model 2 of Table 5 revealed the same thing; the likelihood of associate's degree attainment did not differ between students in the two sectors ($\chi^2 = 1.64$, $p = 0.199$). Interestingly, the coefficient for cumulative months spent pursuing an associate's degree in a public four-year postsecondary institution, statistically insignificant in

Model 1, was now not only statistically significant but slightly larger than double the size.

When we included interactions between both the linear and quadratic functional forms of cumulative months within each sector and race/ethnicity, sex, and parental educational attainment, we found few statistically significant differences between the different groups on associate's degree attainment. While we do not discuss those models, we do present the tables in Appendix B for those interested in seeing the results.

Bachelor's Degree Attainment

Model 1 of Table 6 shows the logistic regression coefficients for the likelihood of attaining a bachelor's degree by cumulative months within sector, separately for those pursuing an associate's and for those pursuing a bachelor's. Controls were excluded from the model. Immediately obvious is the lack of any statistically significant impact on the likelihood of earning the baccalaureate among for-profit students, regardless of the degree being sought. This contrasts rather glaringly with the increased odds of bachelor's degree attainment for additional months spent in school by community college students pursing associate's degrees. This may reflect the fact that a core mission of most community colleges remains preparing students for transfer to a four-year institution.

Among those pursuing a bachelor's degree, the likelihood of bachelor's degree attainment was greatest for those at traditional public four-year and private two- and four year postsecondary institutions. For each month an individual remained in the former, he multiplied his odds of earning a bachelor's degree by about 1.17 times ($e^{0.153}$). Students at private colleges multiplied their odds by 1.15 times ($e^{0.136}$). Only the coefficient for cumulative months in a public four-year school was significantly different from the coefficient for cumulative months in a for-profit school ($\chi^2 = 4.25$, $p < 0.05$).

Model 2 of Table 6 included student background controls. Additional months spent pursing an associate's degree did not lead to a higher likelihood of bachelor's degree attainment among for-profit students, or among public four-year and private two- and four-year students. Only among community college students pursuing associate's degrees was the likelihood of bachelor's degree receipt higher as a function of time spent in school. This mirrors the results under Model 1, though the positive change in the coefficient from 0.074 to 0.111 represented a statistically significant difference in the odds between the two models ($\chi^2 = 10.61$, $p < 0.01$). Granting a decline over time

Table 6 Logistic regression coefficients for likelihood of attaining a bachelor's degree by cumulative months within sector by degree being sought. (n = 7,617; 625,167 person-months)

	Model 1		*Model 2*	
Cumulative months within sector	*Pursuing associate's degree*	*Pursuing bachelor's degree*	*Pursuing associate's degree*	*Pursuing bachelor's degree*
Public 4-year	0.048	0.153***	0.094*	0.126***
	(0.051)	(0.009)	(0.045)	(0.008)
Squared	−0.001	−0.0001***	−0.002	−0.0004***
	(0.003)	(0.000)	(0.002)	(0.000)
Public 2-year	0.0740***	−0.007	0.111***	−0.0127
	(0.020)	(0.032)	(0.018)	(0.023)
Squared	−0.001	0.0002	−0.001**	0.002
	(0.001)	(0.002)	(0.001)	(0.001)
Private	−0.170	0.136***	−0.0308	0.123***
	(0.141)	(0.012)	(0.085)	(0.012)
Squared	0.007	−0.0002	0.003	−0.00007
	(0.004)	(0.000)	(0.003)	(0.000)
For-Profit	−0.180	0.048	−0.097	0.052
	(0.167)	(0.050)	(0.093)	(0.045)
Squared	0.005	0.001	0.003	0.002
	(0.003)	(0.001)	(0.002)	(0.001)

Notes: Models 1 and 2 each include the college sector variables listed as well as an international/other school type variable, which is rarely attended and omitted from the table for simplicity. Model 2 controls for race/ethnicity, sex, type of high school attended, whether respondent took the ACT or SAT, high school GPA, ASVAB percentile, GED receipt, parental educational attainment, family structure, natural log of gross family income, household size, region, whether respondent was married at baseline, respondent's number of own or adopted children, respondent's monthly hours worked, and the natural log of respondent's hourly pay rate. Both the baseline and time-varying value of age and age-squared are also entered. Models are weighted by sampling weights and by inverse probability of attrition over time. Person-clustered standard errors are in parentheses

*$p < 0.05$, **$p < 0.01$, ***$p < 0.001$

in the positive odds of bachelor's degree attainment suggested by the squared term for cumulative months in a public two-year, the community college student still had a 1.12 times ($e^{0.108}$) greater odds of earning a bachelor's degree for each month spent pursuing an associate's degree.

While the coefficient for cumulative months in a for-profit under the second column of Model 2 was now positive given the added controls, it nonetheless remained small and statistically insignificant. Again, it was only those students at traditional public baccalaureate and private institutions who increased their likelihood of degree completion with each additional month of schooling pursuing bachelor's degrees. Each month of additional schooling was associated with 1.13 ($e^{0.126}$) and 1.13 ($e^{0.123}$) greater odds of bachelor's degree attainment, respectively, for public four-year and private two- and four-year baccalaureate students.

When we modeled demographic differences in bachelor's degree attainment rates by including interactions between cumulative months within each sector/degree sought combination and (1) race/ethnicity, (2) gender, and (3) parental educational attainment, we found few statistically significant interaction effects worth exploring at length for students pursuing a bachelor's degree. One notable result from these models, however, was that, relative to whites and "other race" individuals attending a for-profit college, black students attained a bachelor's degree from a for-profit college at a significantly faster rate, controlling for baseline covariates (see Table B2 for all interaction models).

Discussion

The aim of this chapter was to answer two questions. First, who attends for-profit postsecondary institutions, taking into account attendance in other sectors? Second, for those who attend for-profit postsecondary institutions, how does their enrollment in that sector translate into degree attainment? In response to the first question, it is evident that for-profit colleges and universities are attractive to students who might not otherwise pursue a degree. As our results examining predictors of attendance at the various sectors revealed, the students who have the highest odds of attending for-profits relative to the other school types are racial minorities, those with a GED instead of a high school diploma, those from a family not headed by both biological parents, and those with a higher number of children. Blacks and those classified as "other race" are more likely than their white counterparts to attend a for-profit school compared to a community college, but all racial minorities have a greater likelihood than whites of attending a for-profit college compared to never attending a postsecondary institution at all. We also presented overlap statistics revealing that large percentages of those who reported ever attending a for-profit also reported attending each of the other three sector types. While very few of those who ever reported attending the more traditional public and private sector schools also reported attending a for-profit school, they did report attending another of the traditional sector schools in large numbers. And descriptive graphs demonstrated that, while individuals whose parents' highest education level was high school or less were *as* likely to attend community college as their peers from higher educated homes, they were ***moderately more likely*** to attend the for-profit sector than these same individuals.

In response to the second question, our discrete-time hazard models revealed that, controlling for attendance in other sectors, attendance in the for-profit sector is associated with an increased likelihood of associate's degree receipt over time for those actually seeking an associate's degree. This holds net of the effect of individual student characteristics such as race, sex, parental educational attainment, high school GPA, and family income, among other things. The difference in the odds of associate's degree attainment among those pursuing an associate's degree at community colleges and for-profits is statistically significant and favors for-profits in the absence of controls. Adding controls, the statistically significant difference favors for-profits over all other sectors: public four-year schools, community colleges, and private two- and four-year schools. However, the for-profit student seeking a bachelor's degree is less likely to attain an associate's degree, whereas a comparable community college student actually has an increased likelihood of attaining an associate's degree even when pursuing a bachelor's.

Although attendance in other sectors—notably public four-year and private nonprofit colleges—significantly increases the odds of attaining a bachelor's degree, there is no evidence that attendance in the for-profit sector is beneficial to the likelihood of achieving a bachelor's degree, regardless of the degree sought. This pattern is net of attendance in other sectors and of individual-level characteristics.

Prior research indicates that those least likely to attend college benefit the most from it (Brand and Xie 2010). To the degree that for-profits are effective at both attracting and graduating even a fraction of those who are least likely to attend college, they may be a viable alternative to the traditional model of postsecondary education for addressing the attainment gap. For-profit education is but one route, but it is one that appears to be doing a decent job at increasing minority degree attainment. This is not to discount the past and present failings of the for-profit sector, which have been addressed elsewhere, but, given the general failure of the traditional sectors to close the attainment gap or to graduate large percentages of their students (particularly more disadvantaged students), the for-profit sector appears to be charting a path to success for some of the more vulnerable segments of the United States population, at least with regard to associate's degrees. Indeed, an important puzzle for future research is why students at for-profits appear to be more successful at attaining associate's degrees than community college students but less successful at attaining bachelor's degrees than students at private nonprofit and public four-year colleges and universities.

We note a few limitations of the present study that should prompt caution in interpreting the results. First, some of the degree sought-sector type combinations, as well as some subgroups of respondents, have small sample sizes. One should thus be concerned about the reliability of subgroup comparisons and aware of the possibility that a true effect exists where none was found, or, alternatively, that no true effect exists where one was found. However, we reiterate that our data contains one of the largest samples of for-profit students that we have encountered in existing longitudinal research, and that we believe these data more accurately capture enrollment in for-profit colleges than data used in other studies, which only capture the sector of first enrollment.

Second, we unfortunately cannot measure within-sector variation. Not accounting for those factors that make schools within the same sector different—e.g., selectivity, location, resources, academic counseling services, etc.—means that we may miss differences that make some schools unreasonable comparisons for the for-profit sector, or may not be able to distinguish more successful for-profit institutions from less successful ones. In other words, we do not incorporate data on the mechanisms behind the associations we find.

Third, our data represent a particular historical moment in the evolution of the for-profit sector and a particular cohort of young people transitioning to adulthood. Much of the enrollment and degree completion captured in our data occurred in the early- and mid-2000s, before the financial crisis and the great recession, and before the most recent wave of public scrutiny of for-profit colleges. Although only time will tell, it seems that there are important shifts in the for-profit sector underway. For example, Corinthian Colleges, one of the largest for-profit college corporations appears to be shutting down after financial and regulatory problems (Perez-Pena 2014).

Fourth, we may lack important data on the factors that affect students' choice of college sector. Although we control for many student characteristics, it is possible that there is unobserved selection in who attends each college sector. That is, perhaps some variable we fail to account for, such as student motivation, is related to both sector choice and degree receipt; if this is so, that omitted variable could drive our results, rather than sector. Finally, we do not take into account that characteristics of individuals change over time during the course of college enrollment. Many students, particularly those in the nontraditional for-profit sector, are working, forming families, raising children, or engaging in a host of other activities that could affect their time to degree. Simply controlling for these factors as they change over time can lead to biased estimates (Robins et al. 2000). However, properly accounting for such time-varying confounding in the context of multiple outcomes and ten treatment categories is a complex and difficult undertaking that is beyond the scope of the current chapter. For that reason, we chose to restrict our predictor set to factors measured either at NLSY97 inception or when a respondent became at-risk of college entrance.

In conclusion, for-profit students do appear to be succeeding when success is defined as associate's degree attainment. For-profit institutions do a better job than institutions in other sectors of graduating their students with associate's degrees, even when models are adjusted for compositional differences in the type of students that attend each sector. The impact that such a trend has in people's lives cannot be discounted given what we know are the economic returns to increased education (Park 2011). Importantly, though, the literature is mixed on the market value of the degrees being offered, particularly with respect to the differential economic returns to associate's degree attainment by sector and the different costs of attendance by sector born by the student. Research by Lang and Weinstein (2012), for instance, shows that the premium of increased education favors, by a statistically significant margin, degree attainment in the not-for-profit versus the for-profit sector. Controlling for a host of characteristics, this premium amounted to a $3,000 higher income in 2009 for associate's degree holders from the nonprofit sector. However, using somewhat different methods, and accounting for major, Lang and Weinstein (2013) found no statistically significant difference in the economic returns to receiving an associate's degree between the for-profit and nonprofit sectors. In fact, when looking just at degrees in business, registered nursing, and the health-assisting field, for-profit associate's degree recipients fared better than their community college counterparts. Given both the limitations of their data (the authors used the BPS in both studies), already addressed with respect to previous research, and the two foregoing conflicting studies, future research will need to continue to attempt to understand whether there are indeed differences in the quality of degrees among the postsecondary sectors and whether any disparity leads to different outcomes regarding incomes. Relatedly, it will be necessary in future research to track individuals' enrollments in all sectors and not merely only in the first. Issues of persistence within a sector (with respect to students) and retention (with respect to schools) are also important dynamics to be understood in future research on the time that it takes one to earn a degree.

Notes

1. We have compared the demographic characteristics of for-profit students in the 2004 wave of the NLSY97 to benchmark data from the 2004 NPSAS, finding roughly comparable distributions on descriptive statistics such as race, gender, and family background. Detailed results are available from the authors upon request.
2. In models of associate's degree receipt, receipt of either an associate's or bachelor's degree concludes the risk period. By attrition we mean the failure to be interviewed in the most recent survey round or in the most recent two or more survey rounds uninterrupted. For instance, if an individual was not interviewed in the 2000 survey round or any round thereafter, that individual has been deemed to have dropped out of the survey. The same person would not be a leaver if that person were interviewed in the latest round that comprises our data. Finally, for the small proportion of NLSY97 respondents who enrolled in college at 17, we begin their data then rather than at age 18. It is typical in longitudinal surveys such as the NLSY97 for some subjects to drop out prior to either the outcome event occurring or before the study ends. This censoring due to attrition, when it is correlated with covariates and degree completion, can lead to biased estimates. We therefore construct censoring weights to adjust for attrition owing to time-varying factors (Robins et al. 1995, 2000; Robins 1999). The censoring weight is quantified as

$$cw_t = \prod_1^t \frac{\Pr\left(C_t = 0 | B, X_{t-1}\right)}{\Pr\left(C_t = 0 | B, X_{t-1}, V_{t-1}\right)}, \quad (2)$$

where the numerator is the predicted probability of remaining uncensored up to month *t*, given baseline covariates, treatment status in the previous month, and the one-month lag of the time-varying variables. The denominator represents the probability of remaining uncensored up to month t, given baseline covariates, treatment status in the previous month, time-varying covariates (age, work hours, wages, marital status, and number of dependents), and the one-month lag of these time-varying variables. This procedure allows us to observe the associations that would have been seen had no respondents left the study, assuming that any attrition related to our outcome (degree receipt) is accounted for by the above time-varying covariates. (Attrition due to baseline covariates is handled by the baseline covariates entered directly into the regression model.) The intuition is that these censoring weights give greater weight to months for which the probability of remaining uncensored is low for a given respondent and a smaller weight to months for which a person has a high probability of remaining uncensored. Normally, the numerator of the inverse probability of being censored would be 1. However, the above formula produces a lower variance in the resulting weight. The product of the wave 1 sampling weight and the censoring weight are included in our logit models.

3. A combination of nonparametric and parametric techniques, PMM is preferable to linear regression for imputing missing values of a continuous variable because it produces values that are within the range of the observed data (Schenker and Taylor 1996). Not only are the predicted values more appropriate if there is concern that the assumption of normality is violated (Horton and Lipsitz 2001), they are also robust to deviations from linearity (Schenker and Taylor 1996). While some have argued that no more than three to five imputed datasets are needed for efficient estimates (Rubin 1987; Schafer and Olsen 1998), others advocate for a great deal more, perhaps twenty or more datasets (Graham et al. 2007). Meeting halfway between these two stances, the analyses here are based on ten imputed datasets.

Appendix A

Table A1 Full model results for Table 5: Logistic regression coefficients for likelihood of attaining an associate's degree by cumulative months within sector by degree being sought. (n = 7,610; 594,772 person-months)

	Model 1		*Model 2*	
Time-varying variables				
Age (relative to 18th birthday)			−0.016	(0.006)**
Age-squared (relative to 18th birthday)			−0.000	(0.000)
Cumulative months pursuing an associate's degree at				
Public 4-year	0.061	(0.052)	0.128	(0.052)*
Public 4-year-squared	0.002	(0.001)	0.001	(0.002)
Public 2-year	0.223	(0.013)***	0.243	(0.014)***
Public 2-year-squared	−0.002	(0.000)***	−0.002	(0.000)***
Private	0.358	(0.045)***	0.325	(0.050)***
Private-squared	−0.005	(0.001)***	−0.003	(0.002)*
For-profit	0.346	(0.024)***	0.394	(0.025)***
For-profit-squared	−0.005	(0.001)***	−0.005	(0.001)***
Cumulative months pursuing a bachelor's degree at				
Public 4-year	0.008	(0.017)	−0.004	(0.017)
Public 4-year-squared	−0.000	(0.000)	0.000	(0.000)
Public 2-year	0.057	(0.024)*	0.061	(0.024)*
Public 2-year-squared	−0.000	(0.001)	0.000	(0.001)
Private	−0.076	(0.050)	−0.067	(0.056)
Private-squared	0.001	(0.001)	0.000	(0.002)
For-profit	−0.174	(0.081)*	−0.104	(0.069)
For-profit-squared	0.005	(0.002)**	0.004	(0.001)**
Cumulative months pursuing a degree at				
International institution	0.399	(0.127)**	0.443	(0.120)***
International institution-squared	−0.015	(0.005)**	−0.017	(0.005)**
Time-invariant baseline variables				
Race (Ref = white)				
Black			−0.386	(0.207)
Hispanic			−0.283	(0.199)
Other race			0.015	(0.255)
Male			−0.089	(0.132)
Attended public school			−0.112	(0.221)
Took ACT or SAT			0.096	(0.132)
High school GPA			0.519	(0.163)**
ASVAB percentile			0.002	(0.003)
GED or no diploma			−0.560	(0.359)
Parent's education (Ref = less than high school)				

(*continued*)

Table A1 (continued)

	Model 1		*Model 2*	
High school			0.462	(0.274)
Some college			0.287	(0.277)
Bachelor's degree or higher			0.590	(0.281)*
Family structure			0.009	(0.136)
Gross family income (log of 1997 dollars)			−0.020	(0.046)
Household size			0.056	(0.049)
Rural (vs. urban)			0.411	(0.142)**
Region (Ref = Northeast)				
Midwest			−0.003	(0.211)
South			0.044	(0.203)
West			0.212	(0.214)
Age			0.013	(0.015)
Age-squared			−0.000	(0.000)
Currently married			−0.132	(0.675)
Number of children			0.064	(0.326)
Number of children-squared			0.083	(0.186)
Monthly hours worked			−0.002	(0.002)
Monthly hours worked-squared			0.000	(0.000)
Log of hourly pay			0.214	(0.104)*
Log of hourly pay-squared			−0.076	(0.067)
Constant	−8.842	(0.124)***	−8.762	(0.498)***

Notes: Both models are weighted by the product of the sampling weights and by inverse probability of attrition over time. Person-clustered standard errors are in parentheses

$^{*}p < 0.05$, $^{**}p < 0.01$, $^{***}p < 0.001$

Table A2 Full model results for Table 6: Logistic regression coefficients for likelihood of attaining a bachelor's degree by cumulative months within sector by degree being sought. (n = 7,610; 594,772 person-months)

	Model 1		*Model 2*	
Time-varying variables				
Age (relative to 18th birthday)			0.060	(0.008)***
Age-squared (relative to 18th birthday)			−0.001	(0.000)***
Cumulative months pursuing an associate's degree at				
Public 4-year	0.048	(0.051)	0.094	(0.045)*
Public 4-year-squared	−0.001	(0.003)	−0.002	(0.002)
Public 2-year	0.074	(0.020)***	0.111	(0.018)***
Public 2-year-squared	−0.001	(0.001)	−0.002	(0.001)**
Private	−0.170	(0.141)	−0.031	(0.085)

(*continued*)

Table A2 (continued)

	Model 1		*Model 2*	
Private-squared	0.007	(0.004)	0.003	(0.003)
For-profit	−0.180	(0.167)	−0.097	(0.093)
For-profit-squared	0.005	(0.003)	0.003	(0.002)
Cumulative months pursuing a bachelor's degree at				
Public 4-year	0.153	(0.009)***	0.126	(0.008)***
Public 4-year-squared	−0.001	(0.000)***	−0.000	(0.000)***
Public 2-year	−0.007	(0.032)	−0.013	(0.023)
Public 2-year-squared	0.000	(0.002)	0.002	(0.001)
Private	0.136	(0.012)***	0.123	(0.012)***
Private-squared	−0.000	(0.000)	−0.000	(0.000)
For-profit	0.048	(0.050)	0.052	(0.045)
For-profit-squared	0.001	(0.001)	0.002	(0.001)
Cumulative months pursuing a degree at				
International institution	0.109	(0.025)***	0.089	(0.028)**
International institution-squared	−0.000	(0.000)	0.000	(0.000)
Time-invariant baseline variables				
Race (Ref = white)				
Black			−0.427	(0.145)**
Hispanic			−0.366	(0.144)*
Other race			0.045	(0.162)
Male			−0.164	(0.074)*
Attended public school			−0.017	(0.112)
Took ACT or SAT			0.072	(0.077)
High school GPA			0.365	(0.090)***
ASVAB percentile			0.007	(0.002)***
GED or no diploma			−0.707	(0.600)
Parent's education (Ref = less than high school)				
High school			0.123	(0.232)
Some college			0.265	(0.228)
Bachelor's degree or higher			0.212	(0.229)
Family structure			−0.063	(0.090)
Gross family income (log of 1997 dollars)			0.049	(0.040)
Household size			0.026	(0.033)
Rural (vs. urban)			−0.066	(0.085)
Region (Ref = Northeast)				
Midwest			−0.229	(0.107)*
South			−0.148	(0.114)
West			−0.152	(0.123)
Age			−0.043	(0.041)
Age-squared			−0.001	(0.001)
Currently married			−0.188	(0.764)
Number of children			−0.288	(0.318)
Number of children-squared			0.262	(0.130)*

(*continued*)

Table A2 (continued)

	Model 1		*Model 2*	
Monthly hours worked			0.000	(0.001)
Monthly hours worked-squared			0.000	(0.000)
Log of hourly pay			0.012	(0.059)
Log of hourly pay-squared			−0.021	(0.031)
Constant	−8.818	(0.164)***	−10.088	(0.672)***

Notes: Both models are weighted by the product of the sampling weights and by inverse probability of attrition over time. Person-clustered standard errors are in parentheses

*$p < 0.05$, **$p < 0.01$, ***$p < 0.001$

Appendix B

Table B1 Logistic regression coefficients for likelihood of attaining an associate's degree by cumulative months within sector by degree being sought by race/ethnicity, gender, and parent's education. (n = 7,610; 594,772 person-months)

	Cumulative months × Race/Ethnicity		*Cumulative months × Gender*		*Cumulative months × Parent's education*	
Time-invariant baseline variables						
Race (Ref = white)						
Black			−0.482	(0.208)*	−0.483	(0.214)*
Hispanic			−0.374	(0.208)	−0.258	(0.205)
Other race			−0.090	(0.259)	0.042	(0.255)
Male	−0.056	(0.135)			−0.069	(0.139)
Attended public school	−0.047	(0.229)	−0.187	(0.221)	−0.142	(0.223)
Took ACT or SAT	0.058	(0.135)	0.058	(0.136)	0.070	(0.134)
High school GPA	0.576	(0.166)***	0.500	(0.163)**	0.553	(0.165)***
ASVAB percentile	0.003	(0.003)	0.002	(0.003)	0.001	(0.003)
GED or no diploma	−0.697	(0.388)	−0.703	(0.381)	−0.851	(0.441)
Parent's education (Ref = less than high school)						
High school	0.269	(0.253)	0.375	(0.263)		
Some college	0.064	(0.256)	0.182	(0.271)		
Bachelor's degree or higher	0.452	(0.265)	0.513	(0.277)		
Family structure	0.004	(0.136)	0.011	(0.134)	0.051	(0.137)
Gross family income (log of 1997 dollars)	−0.033	(0.041)	−0.037	(0.044)	−0.014	(0.040)
Household size	0.073	(0.049)	0.071	(0.049)	0.047	(0.049)
Rural (vs. urban)	0.413	(0.142)**	0.406	(0.143)**	0.390	(0.145)**
Region (Ref = Northeast)						
Midwest	0.034	(0.217)	−0.044	(0.213)	−0.044	(0.210)

(*continued*)

Table B1 (continued)

	Cumulative months × Race/Ethnicity		*Cumulative months × Gender*		*Cumulative months × Parent's education*	
South	0.119	(0.207)	0.026	(0.203)	0.023	(0.201)
West	0.268	(0.216)	0.163	(0.217)	0.157	(0.215)
Age	0.017	(0.013)	0.005	(0.019)	0.020	(0.014)
Age-squared	−0.000	(0.000)	−0.000	(0.000)	−0.000	(0.000)
Currently married	−0.134	(0.653)	0.016	(0.658)	−0.077	(0.664)
Number of children	0.165	(0.339)	0.023	(0.308)	0.049	(0.326)
Number of children squared	0.019	(0.204)	0.139	(0.155)	0.079	(0.177)
Monthly hours worked	−0.001	(0.002)	−0.002	(0.002)	−0.001	(0.002)
Monthly hours worked squared	0.000	(0.000)	0.000	(0.000)	0.000	(0.000)
Log of hourly pay	0.224	(0.106)*	0.214	(0.109)	0.201	(0.111)
Log of hourly pay squared	−0.054	(0.061)	−0.069	(0.067)	−0.085	(0.070)
Time-varying variables and interactions						
Age (relative to 18th birthday)	−0.016	(0.006)**	−0.016	(0.006)**	−0.019	(0.006)**
Age-squared (relative to 18th birthday)	−0.000	(0.000)	−0.000	(0.000)	−0.000	(0.000)
Cumulative months pursuing an associate's degree at						
Public 4-year	0.145	(0.062)*	0.145	(0.086)	0.125	(0.178)
Public 4-year-squared	0.000	(0.002)	0.001	(0.003)	−0.007	(0.009)
Public 2-year	0.256	(0.016)***	0.257	(0.017)***	0.254	(0.025)***
Public 2-year-squared	−0.002	(0.000)***	−0.003	(0.000)***	−0.003	(0.001)***
Private	0.325	(0.063)***	0.251	(0.086)**	−0.440	(0.237)
Private-squared	−0.002	(0.002)	−0.001	(0.003)	0.036	(0.010)***
For-profit	0.412	(0.032)***	0.403	(0.032)***	0.477	(0.093)***
For-profit-squared	−0.006	(0.001)***	−0.006	(0.001)***	−0.009	(0.004)*
By race (Ref = white)						
Public 4-year × black	−0.107	(0.136)				
Public 4-year-squared × black	0.009	(0.005)				
Public 2-year × black	−0.021	(0.022)				
Public 2-year-squared × black	0.000	(0.001)				

(*continued*)

Table B1 (continued)

	Cumulative months × Race/Ethnicity		*Cumulative months × Gender*		*Cumulative months × Parent's education*	
Private × black	0.006	(0.107)				
Private-squared × black	−0.002	(0.003)				
For-profit × black	−0.118	(0.097)				
For-profit-squared × black	0.004	(0.004)				
Public 4-year × Hispanic	0.091	(0.145)				
Public 4-year-squared × Hispanic	−0.008	(0.006)				
Public 2-year × Hispanic	−0.033	(0.022)				
Public 2-year-squared × Hispanic	0.000	(0.001)				
Private × Hispanic	−0.042	(0.210)				
Private-squared × Hispanic	0.001	(0.006)				
For-profit × Hispanic	−0.022	(0.055)				
For-profit-squared × Hispanic	0.001	(0.002)				
Public 4-year × male			−0.049	(0.108)		
Public 4-year-squared × male			−0.000	(0.003)		
Public 2-year × male			−0.022	(0.018)		
Public 2-year-squared × male			0.001	(0.000)		
Private × male			0.113	(0.105)		
Private-squared × male			−0.003	(0.003)		
For-profit × male			−0.052	(0.052)		
For-profit-squared × male			0.003	(0.002)		
By parent's education (Ref = less than high school)						
Public 4-year × high school					0.138	(0.189)

(*continued*)

Table B1 (continued)

	Cumulative months × Race/Ethnicity		*Cumulative months × Gender*		*Cumulative months × Parent's education*	
Public 4-year-squared × high school					0.004	(0.009)
Public 2-year × high school					0.003	(0.029)
Public 2-year-squared × high school					0.000	(0.001)
Private × high school					−1.023	(0.789)
Private-squared × high school					0.043	(0.035)
For-profit × high school					−0.046	(0.101)
For-profit-squared × high school					0.003	(0.004)
Public 4-year × some college					−0.277	(0.242)
Public 4-year-squared × some college					0.024	(0.012)*
Public 2-year × some college					−0.017	(0.026)
Public 2-year-squared × some college					0.001	(0.001)
Private × some college					0.796	(0.253)**
Private-squared × some college					−0.040	(0.011)***
For-profit × some college					−0.180	(0.106)
For-profit-squared × some college					0.008	(0.004)
Public 4-year × bachelor's degree or higher					0.008	(0.199)
Public 4-year-squared × bachelor's degree or higher					0.009	(0.009)
Public 2-year × bachelor's degree or higher					0.020	(0.028)

(*continued*)

Table B1 (continued)

	Cumulative months × Race/Ethnicity		*Cumulative months × Gender*		*Cumulative months × Parent's education*	
Public 2-year-squared × bachelor's degree or higher					−0.000	(0.001)
Private × bachelor's degree or higher					0.830	(0.256)**
Private-squared × bachelor's degree or higher					−0.041	(0.011)***
For-profit × bachelor's degree or higher					−0.084	(0.118)
For-profit-squared × bachelor's degree or higher					0.006	(0.005)
Cumulative months pursuing a bachelor's degree at						
Public 4-year	−0.007	(0.021)	0.007	(0.019)	0.020	(0.109)
Public 4-year-squared	0.000	(0.001)	0.000	(0.000)	−0.002	(0.004)
Public 2-year	−0.002	(0.032)	0.038	(0.033)	0.259	(0.083)**
Public 2-year-squared	0.003	(0.001)**	0.002	(0.001)	−0.007	(0.005)
Private	−0.011	(0.052)	−0.021	(0.085)	−0.119	(0.233)
Private-squared	−0.001	(0.002)	−0.002	(0.004)	−0.003	(0.013)
For-profit	−0.114	(0.088)	−0.137	(0.131)	−0.162	(0.359)
For-profit-squared	0.004	(0.002)*	0.003	(0.003)	0.006	(0.009)
By race (Ref = white)						
Public 4-year × black	−0.006	(0.038)				
Public 4-year-squared × black	0.000	(0.001)				
Public 2-year × black	0.095	(0.080)				
Public 2-year-squared × black	−0.002	(0.003)				
Private × black	−0.059	(0.092)				
Private-squared × black	0.003	(0.002)				

(*continued*)

Table B1 (continued)

	Cumulative months × Race/Ethnicity		*Cumulative months × Gender*		*Cumulative months × Parent's education*	
For-profit × black	0.615	(0.177)***				
For-profit-squared × black	−0.030	(0.010)**				
Public 4-year × Hispanic	0.070	(0.069)				
Public 4-year-squared × Hispanic	−0.002	(0.002)				
Public 2-year × Hispanic	0.197	(0.063)**				
Public 2-year-squared × Hispanic	−0.007	(0.002)**				
Private × Hispanic	0.020	(0.483)				
Private-squared × Hispanic	−0.017	(0.030)				
For-profit × Hispanic	−0.130	(0.245)				
For-profit-squared × Hispanic	0.002	(0.006)				
Public 4-year × male			−0.024	(0.042)		
Public 4-year-squared × male			−0.000	(0.002)		
Public 2-year × male			0.047	(0.048)		
Public 2-year-squared × male			−0.002	(0.001)		
Private × male			−0.043	(0.115)		
Private-squared × male			0.003	(0.004)		
For-profit × male			−0.075	(0.182)		
For-profit-squared × male			0.006	(0.004)		
By parent's education (Ref = less than high school)						
Public 4-year × high school					−0.013	(0.116)
Public 4-year-squared × high school					0.003	(0.004)

(*continued*)

Table B1 (continued)

	Cumulative months × Race/Ethnicity		*Cumulative months × Gender*		*Cumulative months × Parent's education*	
Public 2-year × high school					−0.308	(0.096)**
Public 2-year-squared × high school					0.011	(0.005)*
Private × high school					0.144	(0.247)
Private-squared × high school					0.003	(0.013)
For-profit × high school					0.267	(0.404)
For-profit-squared × high school					−0.012	(0.012)
Public 4-year × some college					−0.013	(0.113)
Public 4-year-squared × some college					0.002	(0.004)
Public 2-year × some college					−0.148	(0.095)
Public 2-year-squared × some college					0.008	(0.005)
Private × some college					0.060	(0.281)
Private-squared × some college					0.003	(0.014)
For-profit × some college					−0.180	(0.423)
For-profit-squared × some college					0.003	(0.010)
Public 4-year × bachelor's degree or higher					−0.033	(0.113)
Public 4-year-squared × bachelor's degree or higher					0.002	(0.004)
Public 2-year × bachelor's degree or higher					−0.184	(0.092)*
Public 2-year-squared × bachelor's degree or higher					0.006	(0.005)

(*continued*)

Table B1 (continued)

	Cumulative months × Race/Ethnicity		*Cumulative months × Gender*		*Cumulative months × Parent's education*	
Private × bachelor's degree or higher					0.103	(0.239)
Private-squared × bachelor's degree or higher					0.003	(0.013)
For-profit × bachelor's degree or higher					0.181	(0.378)
For-profit-squared × bachelor's degree or higher					−0.005	(0.009)
Cumulative months pursuing degree at						
International institution	0.397	(0.172)*	0.493	(0.135)***	−6.096	(3.434)
International institution-squared	−0.012	(0.006)*	−0.016	(0.005)**	0.061	(3.460)
By race (Ref = white)						
International institution × black	1.386	(0.431)**				
International institution-squared × black	−0.170	(0.039)***				
International institution × Hispanic	0.773	(0.349)*				
International institution-squared × Hispanic	−0.125	(0.040)**				
International institution × male			0.079	(0.393)		
International institution-squared × male			−0.028	(0.030)		
By parent's education (Ref = less than high school)						
International institution × high school					6.808	(3.919)
International institution-squared × high school					−0.102	(6.153)

(*continued*)

Table B1 (continued)

	Cumulative months × Race/Ethnicity		*Cumulative months × Gender*		*Cumulative months × Parent's education*	
International institution × some college					6.924	(3.652)
International institution-squared × some college					−0.136	(.)
International institution × bachelor's degree or higher					6.564	(3.976)
International institution-squared × bachelor's degree or higher					−0.075	(2.409)
Constant	−8.806	(0.475)***	−8.791	(0.515)***	−8.352	(0.437)***

Notes: The sample size for those classified as "other race" is too small to model interactions, so the main effects of college attendance can be considered to apply to both whites and other race individuals. All models are weighted by sampling weights and by inverse probability of attrition over time. Person-clustered standard errors are in parentheses. *$p < 0.05$, **$p < 0.01$, ***$p < 0.001$

Table B2 Logistic regression coefficients for likelihood of attaining a bachelor's degree by cumulative months within sector by degree being sought by race/ethnicity, gender, and parent's education. (n = 7,610; 594,772 person-months)

	Cumulative months × Race/Ethnicity		*Cumulative months × Gender*		*Cumulative months × Parent's ewducation*	
Time-invariant baseline variables						
Race (Ref = white)						
Black			−0.502	(0.145)***	−0.520	(0.148)***
Hispanic			−0.423	(0.146)**	−0.387	(0.145)**
Other race			0.023	(0.161)	0.052	(0.163)
Male	−0.161	(0.075)*			−0.141	(0.073)
Attended public school	−0.017	(0.114)	−0.007	(0.110)	0.000	(0.109)
Took ACT or SAT	0.069	(0.078)	0.071	(0.078)	0.082	(0.078)
High school GPA	0.385	(0.091)***	0.389	(0.091)***	0.376	(0.092)***

(*continued*)

Table B2 (continued)

	Cumulative months × Race/Ethnicity		*Cumulative months × Gender*		*Cumulative months × Parent's ewducation*	
ASVAB percentile	0.008	(0.002)***	0.007	(0.002)**	0.007	(0.002)**
GED or no diploma	−0.642	(0.594)	−1.299	(0.987)	−0.706	(0.623)
Parent's education (Ref = less than high school)						
High school	0.189	(0.231)	0.133	(0.229)		
Some college	0.329	(0.229)	0.256	(0.225)		
Bachelor's degree or higher	0.258	(0.230)	0.192	(0.226)		
Family structure	−0.081	(0.092)	−0.042	(0.090)	−0.035	(0.094)
Gross family income (log of 1997 dollars)	0.048	(0.040)	0.055	(0.041)	0.066	(0.045)
Household size	0.023	(0.033)	0.024	(0.033)	0.020	(0.033)
Rural (vs. urban)	−0.070	(0.084)	−0.067	(0.084)	−0.088	(0.085)
Region (Ref = Northeast)						
Midwest	−0.238	(0.110)*	−0.227	(0.108)*	−0.198	(0.109)
South	−0.164	(0.116)	−0.122	(0.115)	−0.090	(0.112)
West	−0.145	(0.124)	−0.168	(0.124)	−0.130	(0.125)
Age	−0.040	(0.043)	−0.047	(0.043)	−0.030	(0.041)
Age-squared	−0.001	(0.001)	−0.001	(0.001)	−0.001	(0.001)
Currently married	−0.139	(0.770)	0.223	(0.763)	−0.177	(0.717)
Number of children	−0.236	(0.310)	−0.697	(0.463)	−0.178	(0.325)
Number of children squared	0.230	(0.137)	0.395	(0.138)**	0.219	(0.134)
Monthly hours worked	0.000	(0.001)	0.000	(0.001)	0.000	(0.001)
Monthly hours worked squared	0.000	(0.000)	0.000	(0.000)	0.000	(0.000)
Log of hourly pay	0.007	(0.059)	0.008	(0.059)	0.009	(0.058)
Log of hourly pay squared	−0.019	(0.031)	−0.016	(0.029)	−0.021	(0.030)
Time-varying variables and interactions						
Age (relative to 18th birthday)	0.056	(0.008)***	0.056	(0.008)***	0.051	(0.008)***
Age-squared (relative to 18th birthday)	−0.001	(0.000)***	−0.001	(0.000)***	−0.001	(0.000)***

(*continued*)

Table B2 (continued)

	Cumulative months × Race/Ethnicity		*Cumulative months × Gender*		*Cumulative months × Parent's ewducation*	
Cumulative months pursuing an associate's degree at						
Public 4-year	0.095	(0.043)*	0.123	(0.065)	0.154	(0.162)
Public 4-year-squared	−0.002	(0.002)	−0.004	(0.003)	−0.005	(0.011)
Public 2-year	0.122	(0.021)***	0.111	(0.024)***	0.099	(0.024)***
Public 2-year-squared	−0.002	(0.001)**	−0.001	(0.001)*	−0.000	(0.000)
Private	−0.014	(0.110)	0.165	(0.109)	−0.173	(0.175)
Private-squared	0.003	(0.004)	−0.009	(0.007)	0.015	(0.008)
For-profit	−0.161	(0.171)	0.253	(0.118)*	−11.735	(2.062)***
For-profit-squared	0.004	(0.003)	−0.015	(0.009)	0.250	(0.013)***
By race (Ref = white)						
Public 4-year × black	0.070	(0.132)				
Public 4-year-squared × black	−0.007	(0.006)				
Public 2-year × black	−0.081	(0.037)*				
Public 2-year-squared × black	0.002	(0.001)*				
Private × black	0.080	(0.152)				
Private-squared × black	−0.004	(0.006)				
For-profit × black	0.370	(0.218)				
For-profit-squared × black	−0.014	(0.009)				
Public 4-year × Hispanic	−0.072	(0.083)				
Public 4-year-squared × Hispanic	0.003	(0.003)				
Public 2-year × Hispanic	0.004	(0.035)				

(*continued*)

Table B2 (continued)

	Cumulative months × Race/Ethnicity		*Cumulative months × Gender*		*Cumulative months × Parent's ewducation*	
Public 2-year-squared × Hispanic	0.000	(0.001)				
Private × Hispanic	0.049	(0.223)				
Private-squared × Hispanic	−0.006	(0.010)				
For-profit × Hispanic	0.469	(0.193)*				
For-profit-squared × Hispanic	−0.018	(0.007)**				
Public 4-year × male			−0.062	(0.082)		
Public 4-year-squared × male			0.003	(0.004)		
Public 2-year × male			0.024	(0.031)		
Public 2-year-squared × male			−0.001	(0.001)		
Private × male			−0.105	(0.122)		
Private-squared × male			0.010	(0.007)		
For-profit × male			−0.422	(0.186)*		
For-profit-squared × male			0.023	(0.009)*		
By parent's education (Ref = less than high school)						
Public 4-year × high school					−0.035	(0.172)
Public 4-year-squared × high school					0.002	(0.011)
Public 2-year × high school					0.011	(0.037)
Public 2-year-squared × high school					−0.001	(0.001)

(*continued*)

Table B2 (continued)

	Cumulative months × Race/Ethnicity		*Cumulative months × Gender*		*Cumulative months × Parent's ewducation*	
Private × high school					−1.065	(0.378)**
Private-squared × high school					0.046	(0.017)**
For-profit × high school					11.775	(2.065)***
For-profit-squared × high school					−0.250	(.)
Public 4-year × some college					−0.088	(0.192)
Public 4-year-squared × some college					0.003	(0.012)
Public 2-year × some college					0.051	(0.035)
Public 2-year-squared × some college					−0.002	(0.001)*
Private × some college					0.730	(0.209)***
Private-squared × some college					−0.044	(0.012)***
For-profit × some college					11.683	(2.064)***
For-profit-squared × some college					−0.246	(0.013)***
Public 4-year × bachelor's degree or higher					−0.085	(0.172)
Public 4-year-squared × bachelor's degree or higher					0.004	(0.011)

(*continued*)

Table B2 (continued)

	Cumulative months × Race/Ethnicity		*Cumulative months × Gender*		*Cumulative months × Parent's ewducation*	
Public 2-year × bachelor's degree or higher					0.011	(0.036)
Public 2-year-squared × bachelor's degree or higher					−0.001	(0.001)
Private × bachelor's degree or higher					0.292	(0.189)
Private-squared × bachelor's degree or higher					−0.016	(0.009)
For-profit × bachelor's degree or higher					12.184	(.)
For-profit-squared × bachelor's degree or higher					−0.282	(.)
Cumulative months pursuing a bachelor's degree at						
Public 4-year	0.133	(0.009)***	0.137	(0.010)***	0.134	(0.020)***
Public 4-year-squared	−0.000	(0.000)***	−0.001	(0.000)***	−0.001	(0.000)
Public 2-year	−0.010	(0.027)	−0.002	(0.031)	0.000	(0.166)
Public 2-year-squared	0.002	(0.001)	0.001	(0.001)	0.001	(0.012)
Private	0.123	(0.013)***	0.130	(0.014)***	0.024	(0.083)
Private-squared	0.000	(0.000)	−0.000	(0.000)	0.003	(0.002)
For-profit	0.039	(0.062)	0.160	(0.053)**	−0.012	(0.112)
For-profit-squared	0.002	(0.001)	−0.001	(0.001)	0.004	(0.003)

(*continued*)

Table B2 (continued)

	Cumulative months × Race/Ethnicity		*Cumulative months × Gender*	*Cumulative months × Parent's ewducation*
By race (Ref = white)				
Public 4-year × black	−0.022	(0.013)		
Public 4-year-squared × black	0.000	(0.000)		
Public 2-year × black	−0.015	(0.169)		
Public 2-year-squared × black	−0.004	(0.013)		
Private × black	−0.013	(0.028)		
Private-squared × black	0.000	(0.001)		
For-profit × black	0.126	(0.110)		
For-profit-squared × black	−0.002	(0.003)		
Public 4-year × Hispanic	−0.008	(0.013)		
Public 4-year-squared × Hispanic	−0.000	(0.000)		
Public 2-year × Hispanic	0.050	(0.059)		
Public 2-year-squared × Hispanic	−0.002	(0.002)		
Private × Hispanic	0.024	(0.024)		
Private-squared × Hispanic	−0.001	(0.000)		
For-profit × Hispanic	0.088	(0.090)		
For-profit-squared × Hispanic	−0.002	(0.002)		

(*continued*)

Table B2 (continued)

	Cumulative months × Race/Ethnicity		*Cumulative months × Gender*		*Cumulative months × Parent's ewducation*	
Public 4-year × male			−0.015	(0.008)*		
Public 4-year-squared × male			0.000	(0.000)		
Public 2-year × male			−0.008	(0.046)		
Public 2-year-squared × male			−0.000	(0.002)		
Private × male			−0.009	(0.017)		
Private-squared × male			0.000	(0.000)		
For-profit × male			−0.264	(0.100)**		
For-profit-squared × male			0.007	(0.002)**		
By parent's education (Ref = less than high school)						
Public 4-year × high school					−0.014	(0.022)
Public 4-year-squared × high school					0.000	(0.000)
Public 2-year × high school					0.033	(0.172)
Public 2-year-squared × high school					0.001	(0.012)
Private × high school					0.120	(0.084)
Private-squared × high school					−0.004	(0.002)
For-profit × high school					0.176	(0.129)
For-profit-squared × high school					−0.004	(0.003)

(*continued*)

Table B2 (continued)

	Cumulative months × Race/Ethnicity		*Cumulative months × Gender*		*Cumulative months × Parent's ewducation*	
Public 4-year × some college					0.011	(0.021)
Public 4-year-squared × some college					−0.000	(0.000)
Public 2-year × some college					−0.007	(0.172)
Public 2-year-squared × some college					0.001	(0.012)
Private × some college					0.108	(0.084)
Private-squared × some college					−0.003	(0.002)
For-profit × some college					0.111	(0.128)
For-profit-squared × some college					−0.003	(0.003)
Public 4-year × bachelor's degree or higher					0.004	(0.020)
Public 4-year-squared × bachelor's degree or higher					0.000	(0.000)
Public 2-year × bachelor's degree or higher					−0.023	(0.168)
Public 2-year-squared × bachelor's degree or higher					0.002	(0.012)
Private × bachelor's degree or higher					0.103	(0.083)

(*continued*)

Table B2 (continued)

	Cumulative months × Race/Ethnicity		*Cumulative months × Gender*		*Cumulative months × Parent's ewducation*	
Private-squared × bachelor's degree or higher					−0.003	(0.002)
For-profit × bachelor's degree or higher					0.136	(0.137)
For-profit-squared × bachelor's degree or higher					−0.004	(0.003)
Cumulative months pursuing degree at						
International institution	0.106	(0.030)***	0.073	(0.040)	0.233	(0.131)
International institution-squared	−0.000	(0.000)	0.001	(0.001)	−0.003	(0.004)
By race (Ref = white)						
International institution × black	1.262	(0.370)***				
International institution-squared × black	−0.535	(0.082)***				
International institution × Hispanic	−0.029	(0.069)				
International institution-squared × Hispanic	0.001	(0.001)				
International institution × male			0.025	(0.053)		
International institution-squared × male			−0.001	(0.001)		

(*continued*)

Table B2 (continued)

	Cumulative months × Race/Ethnicity		*Cumulative months × Gender*		*Cumulative months × Parent's ewducation*	
By parent's education (Ref = less than high school)						
International institution × high school					−0.142	(0.144)
International institution-squared × high school					0.004	(0.004)
International institution × some college					−0.118	(0.170)
International institution-squared × some college					0.003	(0.004)
International institution × bachelor's degree or higher					−0.163	(0.135)
International institution-squared × bachelor's degree or higher					0.004	(0.004)
Constant	−10.234	(0.679)***	−10.493	(0.717)***	−9.894	(0.636)***

Notes: The sample size for those classified as "other race" is too small to model interactions, so the main effects of college attendance can be considered to apply to both whites and other race individuals. All models are weighted by sampling weights and by inverse probability of attrition over time. Person-clustered standard errors are in parentheses. *$p < 0.05$, **$p < 0.01$, ***$p < 0.001$

References

Adelman, C. (1999). *Answers in the tool box: Academic intensity, attendance patterns, and bachelor's degree attainment.* Washington, DC: US Department of Education.

Adelman, C. (2006). *The toolbox revisited: Paths to degree completion from high school through college.* Washington, DC: US Department of Education.

Berg, G. A. (2005). *Lessons from the edge: For-profit and nontraditional higher education in America.* Westport: Praeger.

Brand, J. E., & Xie, Y. (2010). Who benefits most from college? Evidence for negative selection in heterogeneous economic returns to higher education. *American Sociological Review, 75*(2), 273–302.

Breneman, D. W., & Nelson, S. C. (1981). *Financing community colleges: An economic perspective.* Washington, DC: Brookings Institution Press.

Breneman, D. W., Pusser, B., & Turner, S. E. (2006). *Earnings from learning: The rise of for-profit universities.* Albany: State University of New York Press.

Cellini, S. R. (2005). *Community colleges and proprietary schools: A comparison of sub-baccalaureate institutions.* University of California at Los Angeles California Center for Population Research (CCPR) Working Paper 2005–012.

Cellini, S. R., & Conger, D. (2010). Disadvantaged students, expensive colleges: Who goes to a private two-year college? Manuscript, George Washington University. Retrieved June 30, 2013, from http://home.gwu.edu/~scellini.

Cominole, M., Wheeless, S., Dudley, K., Franklin, J., & Wine, J. (2007). 2004/06 Beginning Postsecondary Students Longitudinal Study (BPS: 04/06). Methodology Report. NCES 2008–184. National Center for Education Statistics.

Deming, D. J., Goldin, C., & Katz, L. F. (2012). The for-profit postsecondary school sector: Nimble critters or agile predators? *Journal of Economic Perspectives, 26*, 139–164.

Engle, J., & Lynch, M. (2009). *Charting a necessary path: The baseline report of public higher education systems in the access to success initiative.* The Education Trust. ERIC Document 507873. Retrieved July 19, 2013, from http://www.eric.ed.gov/PDFS/ED507873.pdf.

Fischer, C. S., & Hout, M. (2006). *Century of difference: How America changed in the last one hundred years.* New York: Russell Sage Foundation.

Goldrick-Rab, S. (2006). Following their every move: An investigation of social-class differences in college pathways. *Sociology of Education, 79*(1), 67–79.

Graham, J. W., Olchowski, A. E., & Gilreath, T. D. (2007). How many imputations are really needed? Some practical clarifications of multiple imputation theory. *Prevention Science, 8*(3), 206–213.

Horn, L., Kojaku, L., & Carroll, C. D. (2001). *High school academic curriculum and the persistence path through college, Report No. NCES 2001-163.* Washington, DC: U.S. Department of Education, Office of Educational Research and Improvement.

Horton, N. J., & Lipsitz, S. R. (2001). Multiple imputation in practice: Comparison of software packages for regression models with missing variables. *The American Statistician, 55*(3), 244–254.

Kinser, K. (2006). *From Main Street to Wall Street: The transformation of for-profit higher education.* New York: Jossey-Bass.

Lang, K., & Weinstein, R. (2012). *Evaluating student outcomes at for-profit colleges (No. w18201).* Cambridge, MA: National Bureau of Economic Research.

Lang, K., & Weinstein, R. (2013). *The wage effects of not-for-profit and for-profit certifications: Better data, somewhat different results (No. w19135).* Cambridge, MA: National Bureau of Economic Research.

Little, R. J. A. (1988). Missing-data adjustments in large surveys. *Journal of Business and Economic Statistics, 6*, 287–296.

McCormick, A. C. (2003). Swirling and double-dipping: New patterns of student attendance and their implications for higher education. *New Directions for Higher Education, 121*(Spring), 13–24.

Park, S. (2011). Returning to school for higher returns. *Economics of Education Review, 30*(6), 1215–1228.

Perez-Pena, R. (2014, July 5). College group run for profit looks to close or sell schools. *New York Times*, p. A10.

Person, A. E., & Rosenbaum, J. E. (2006). Educational outcomes of labor-market linking and job placement for students at public and private 2-year colleges. *Economics of Education Review, 25*(4), 412–429.

Radford, A. W., Berkner, L., Wheeless, S. C., & Shepherd, B. (2010). *Persistence and attainment of 2003-04 Beginning Postsecondary Students: After 6 years* (NCES 2011–151). U.S. Department of Education. Washington, DC: National Center for Education Statistics. Retrieved June 15, 2013, from http://nces.ed.gov/pubsearch.

Robins, J. A. (1999). Association, causation, and marginal structural models. *Synthese, 121*, 151–179.

Robins, J. A., Hernan, M. A., & Brumback, B. (2000). Marginal structural models and causal inference in epidemiology. *Epidemiology, 11*, 550–560.

Robins, J. M., Rotnitzky, A., & Zhao, L. P. (1995). Analysis of semiparametric regression models for repeated outcomes in the presence of missing data. *Journal of the American Statistical Association, 90*(429), 106–121.

Rosenbaum, J. E., Deil-Amen, R., & Person, A. E. (2006). *After admission: From college access to college success.* New York: Russell Sage Foundation.

Rubin, D. B. (1987). *Multiple imputation for nonresponse in surveys.* New York: John Wiley & Sons.

Ruch, R. S. (2001). *Higher ed, inc.: The rise of the for-profit university*. Baltimore: Johns Hopkins University Press.

Schafer, J. L., & Olsen, M. K. (1998). Multiple imputation for multivariate missing-data problems: A data analyst's perspective. *Multivariate Behavioral Research, 33*(4), 545–571.

Schenker, N., & Taylor, J. M. (1996). Partially parametric techniques for multiple imputation. *Computational Statistics & Data Analysis, 22*(4), 425–446.

Singer, J. D., & Willett, J. B. (2003). *Applied longitudinal data analysis: Modeling change and event occurrence*. Oxford: Oxford university press.

Snyder, T. D., & Dillow, S. A. (2012). *Digest of Education Statistics 2011* (NCES 2012-001). National Center for Education Statistics, Institute of Education Sciences, U.S. Department of Education. Washington, DC.

Stephan, J. L., Rosenbaum, J. E., & Person, A. E. (2009). Stratification in college entry and completion. *Social Science Research, 38*, 572–593.

Sturtz, A. J. (2006). The multiple dimensions of student swirl. *The Journal of Applied Research in the Community College, 13*(2), 151–158.

The Federal Investment in For-Profit Education: Are Students Succeeding. (2010). *Hearing before the Committee on Health, Education, Labor, and Pensions of the United States Senate*. 111th Cong. 1. Retrieved June 15, 2013, from http://www.gpo.gov/fdsys/.

Index[1]

[1] Note: Page numbers with "n" denote endnotes.

T. McMillan Cottom, W.A. Darity, Jr. (eds.), *For-Profit Universities*,
DOI 10.1007/978-3-319-47187-7

Kolibri 360 GmbH
Ferdinand-Jühlke-Straße 7
99095 Erfurt, Deutschland
produktsicherheit@kolibri360.de